WITHDRAWN

A SOCIAL HISTORY OF WESTERN EUROPE
1880–1980

Hartmut Kaelble

A SOCIAL HISTORY
OF WESTERN EUROPE
1880–1980

Translated by Daniel Bird

Gill and Macmillan

Barnes and Noble

PUBLISHED IN IRELAND BY
GILL AND MACMILLAN LTD
GOLDENBRIDGE
DUBLIN 8
with associated companies in
Auckland, Delhi, Gabarone, Hamburg, Harare,
Hong Kong, Johannesburg, Kuala Lumpur, Lagos, London,
Manzini, Melbourne, Mexico City, Nairobi,
New York, Singapore, Tokyo
First published in Federal Republic of Germany in 1987
by Verlag C. H. Beck, Munich as
Auf dem Weg zu einer Europäischen Gesellschaft:
eine Sozialgeschichte Westeuropas 1880–1980
© C. H. Beck'sche Verlagsbuchhandlung
(Oscar Beck), Munich 1987
© English translation Gill and Macmillan Ltd 1989
Translation and manufacture of this book
arranged by Martello Editions Ltd, Dublin
under licence from Gill and Macmillan
Translated by Daniel Bird/Pholiota Translations Ltd,
7 Caledonian Road, London N1 9DX
Typeset in 11/12 Baskerville
in the Republic of Ireland by Officina Typographica, Galway
Printed in Great Britain by
The Camelot Press, Southampton

BRITISH LIBRARY CATALOGUING IN PUBLICATION DATA
Kaelble, Hartmut
A social history of Western Europe, 1880–1980.
1. Western Europe. Social conditions, 1815–
I. Title II. Auf dem Weg zu einer Europäischen Gesellschaft, *English*
940.2'8

ISBN 0–7171–1724–3

PUBLISHED IN THE UNITED STATES 1990 BY
BARNES AND NOBLE LTD
8705 BOLLMAN PLACE
SAVAGE, MARYLAND 20763

ISBN 0–389–20898–1

Front cover illustration
Town Hall Square, Copenhagen

Contents

List of Tables and Figures

Preface

The basic idea behind this book underwent gradual development in discussions with many colleagues. Though by no means an exhaustive list, the following deserve mention. I learned a great deal from Willi P. Adams, Cathleen Conzen, Hannes Siegrist and Heinrich Volkmann during a number of comparative seminars. Wolfram Fischer also added his insights after reading the manuscript. The book received valuable moral support from Gerhard A. Ritter and Hans-Ulrich Wehler at crucial stages. Lectures gave an opportunity to reformulate the ideas contained in the book and discuss them with students. In 1982, during a stay at the Erasmus University in Rotterdam, I had time to examine the theme of the book and discuss it with my host, Henk van Dijk. I completed the manuscript in 1985, at the Maison des Sciences de l'Homme in Paris, then put it under the microscope in intensive seminar discussions with Patrick Fridenson. The Department of Economic and Social History at the Freie Universität, Berlin, provided a very helpful atmosphere in which to undertake comparative work of this nature. Heike Siesslack remained patient at all stages of the manuscript's development. Rüdiger Hohle made sense of the chaotic European statistics and Andrea Schmelz combed the notes for technical errors.

I

Introduction

Is the history of European integration merely a matter of high politics and economics? Are the advances, crises and shifts in European integration dependent upon the desire for unity and the integrationist tendencies of the various national economies? Is integration only advanced by forceful and far-sighted resolutions passed in the European Parliament, or when goods in the department stores of Paris, Düsseldorf, Milan, Amsterdam and London become increasingly similar? On examining research into the history and present state of European integration, this might appear to be the case. There are whole libraries containing a vast range of scholarly works, focusing for the most part on two themes: first, the origins and development of European political institutions and, second, integration into a common market. It is therefore primarily a history of political and economic integration, a history of state ceremonial and trade statistics. It is a history without a society.

The absence of research into the social integration of Europe has a number of regrettable consequences. First, it means that very little is known about the role played in political integration by the development of European communities. The dynamism of the European economy and the basic decisions made by Europe's founding fathers—Monnet, Schuman, Adenauer, de Gasperi and Spaak—have both been of fundamental importance. The European Community would never have come into existence without them. In addition, however, European integration has been accelerated by the growing similarity between European societies and their increasing interaction. A lasting European consciousness has emerged among electorates and elites. There has been an increasing exchange of social models, ideas, lifestyles and consumer trends between European countries. It would be overstating the case to suggest that the social integration of European societies has determined individual decisions on political or economic integration. However, it would not be unreasonable to suggest that the effects of social integration will be long-term.

The sheer longevity of the European Community—a novelty for supranational institutions in recent European history—must have advanced the social integration of Europe. Alternatively, it might be claimed that the recent crises within the European Community may have been precipitated because political integration has been pushed hardest and has advanced furthest in the very sector in which national differences between European societies remain most acute—in agriculture. Worse still, European Community crises might, in fact, be alarm signals. They could be signs that in the 1970s and 1980s, the days of the oil crisis and the long economic slump, European societies began to drift apart again. These are all vague and perhaps even incorrect speculations, the truth of which cannot be judged while so little is known of the history of social integration in Europe.

This neglect also means that we have squandered an opportunity to trace the history of European integration from below, through the eyes of ordinary Europeans. How have their interests been affected? What are their views? Has there been more to link them with Europeans in other countries since 1945 than there was before the war? The political integration of Europe may well have been—as is often claimed—the bloodless creation of a bunch of technocrats, to whom the interests or opinions of the average European meant little. "We are not combining states, we are uniting people," is a slogan which appears in Jean Monnet's memoirs. However, one hears only the voices of statesmen and government officials, with hardly a single ordinary European voice raised. Notwithstanding, has the process of integration been given a decisive transfusion from below, unplanned by the technocrats? Certainly, there are growing similarities between basic social problems in different European countries. Has it been sustained by a growing readiness amongst Europeans to learn from the political ideas and models of neighbouring countries and to dilute old hatreds and national rivalries? Has it been given an impetus through common European patterns of life and thought, perhaps also through a consciousness of a European identity rooted in everyday social life? Once again, little research has been carried out in this area.

Beyond this, the separate course, the peculiar pace and the particular contradictions and crises of social integration remain uncharted. The history of social integration is important for its own sake, but it also enables one to detect other trends towards integration, developing independently of the European Community and stretching beyond the boundaries of the member states. It leads to the discovery of a history of integration, which embraces the everyday life and broader interests of the average European, outside the narrow confines of Community politics. It has different priorities from those of the Community, priorities which are assessed differently by Europeans than by the Community. It suggests alternatives to present Community policies. Whether these other trends towards social integration really existed, and whether, with a change in Community institutions—a more powerful European Parliament for instance—they could provide a corrective to previous Community policies, will never be known unless more intensive research is undertaken.

Finally, a central theme of particular relevance to the history of Germany remains unclear. Did the integration of Europe really mark the end of Germany's separate path of political development (*des deutschen Sonderwegs*), that delayed process of democratization, which collapsed under the Nazi regime? Has society in West Germany really become more like other European societies than was the case before, not only in the Nazi era, but also under Weimar and the Empire? This question should not be taken too lightly, since very little is yet known about how deeply rooted the German political *Sonderweg* was in the peculiarities of the social and economic history of Germany. The history of white-collar workers, of further education and social policy, so far provide the only notable exceptions in the field of research, where this has been accurately traced and verified.[1] It is only by doing more intensive research into the social integration of Europe that we can expect to find new approaches and answers to the question of the social foundations of the German political *Sonderweg*.

Five aspects are central to the concept of social integration. Each will be briefly outlined here, without reference to historical examples or research findings, even though this might try the reader's patience somewhat.

A history of the social integration of Europe must first of all apply itself to the peculiarities within European societies, and thereby isolate those very structures and ways of life which set European societies as a whole apart from countries overseas and in Asia. In so doing, however, it makes sense only to compare societies at similar stages of development. It would be unrealistic to expect these European peculiarities to be equally in evidence in every country and in every region. If they were found in most European countries and in Europe as a whole, they would be considered an important aspect of a combined European social history, and a history of European integration. One sure test of what may be regarded as European peculiarities would be to see whether these were absent or dying out in the "new" modern societies originally founded by Europeans and, therefore, very similar in nature to Europe—countries such as the United States, Canada or Australia. Less interesting, but important none the less, would be the comparison with modern countries which are adapting themselves more closely to the European model but where, at the same time, strong anti-Western or anti-European currents have been at work—countries like Japan or the Soviet Union. These distinctive features are important because they may have been foci of common interests and ways of life and maybe even of national identity. This is not the place to study early modern Europe's pioneering role in fields like science, civil rights, parliamentary development, the autonomy of cities and the growth of state bureaucracies. Instead an attempt must be made to pinpoint distinctive features of European societies in the present century.[2]

Secondly, any history of European social integration must address divergent and convergent processes at work across European societies. It must judge whether social structures and ways of life in Europe have become more similar, above all in post-war times. It is impossible to treat this aspect of social integration satisfactorily from the study of post-war history in isolation. Such convergence as has occurred since 1945 can only be judged properly when compared with divergences observed before 1945 and, besides these, any conceivable processes of convergence in the same period. Only then can it be decided if since

1945 an unprecedented process of convergence has taken place that has also stimulated political and economic integration. The investigation should deal chiefly with regional disparities and similarities and not those of national proportions.

Thirdly, any history of social integration would need to examine changes in exchange relations between European countries, and question whether economic exchange of capital and goods, labour and technology has been paralleled in non-economic communication. This covers everything from the exchange of political thinking and concepts to scientific knowledge and culture, from contact through travel and study abroad to the sphere of personal and private relationships. Besides the growth in the range of such communication in European countries, it is essential to keep a close eye on its comparative scale. Have certain countries acted as centres while others were more marginal? Have roles evened out during the course of the twentieth century? Again, it is clear even at this juncture that post-war developments can only be properly seen from the deeper historical perspective and that the period up to 1914 must therefore also be scrutinised.

Fourthly, a history of European social integration must examine the foundations of political, social and economic organizations, formal and informal, beneath the level of actual European institutions. European and international congresses and federations, whether political or economic, have displayed important trends in their origins and development which could form the basis of integrated European institutions. But they could also have highlighted the weaknesses of these institutions and revealed alternative patterns of integration. The same is true of the growth and expansion of supranational European enterprises and economic clearing agencies, and links between European political parties, federations and trade unions as well as European movements in the narrower sense. Here, too, the long-term view must be borne in mind, because crucial modern developments have roots which go back way beyond 1945.

Fifthly and finally, attitudes to Europe not only among the elites but also among average citizens are essential to the history of European integration from below. Here again, the long-term view will be unavoidable. There are two conceivable approaches to this subject, though their possibilities and complications are unclear at the moment. On the one hand, while ignoring the history of thought which, in its narrower sense, made such a contribution to Europeans' historical view of their continent in the 1950s,[3] historians could attempt to extrapolate the results of post-war opinion polls further back into history using other methods and sources. Thus, they could examine the variable manner in which a European consciousness developed among elites and average citizens, as well as any variations in integrationist sentiment. Naturally, an over-rigid concept of what constitutes a desire for political integration is unhelpful. To illuminate this question, one has a mine of information at one's disposal in the journals of European travellers in those "new" developed societies overseas. The history and economic development of such societies followed the European course closely and made Europeans reflect on their own society without affecting attention to the conventional and unreal wisdom of the superiority of European civilizations over the "barbarians". Writings on the United States are the most prolific and level-headed. Even a cursory review reveals how deeply these Europeans thought about Europe as a whole, while expending far less mental effort on their own specific countries.[4] The other possible approach would be to investigate exceptional events in nineteenth- and twentieth-century history which attacked illegitimate forms of European interaction. Such events could be used to gauge prevailing attitudes to Europe. The carving up of the European market by nation states and the destruction of international scientific cooperation caused by World War I are both examples of an illegitimate process. The National Socialist domination of Europe is another and the defiant idea of Europe as a partnership fought for by the European resistance is an important and better-studied example of the application of this method, which takes action and reaction rather than reflection as its starting point.

Overall, the social integration of Europe as outlined here is a vast field of research, not a mere illusion. Much research data and material exists covering the two most essential aspects of social integration in Europe: the distinctive features of European societies, and their divergent and convergent trends. This book is therefore concerned with such material, the conclusion containing as a supplement a brief survey of the history of attitudes to Europe. While the book is in no sense definitive, it shows that a large amount of knowledge already exists concerning the history of European social integration, material that has hitherto been scattered and is in need of organization.[5]

It is appropriate here to correct some of the misunderstandings that might easily be caused by the brevity of this survey. Although the similarities and divergences within twentieth-century European societies are highlighted here, I do not maintain that European similarities have replaced or eliminated national and regional features in that time. It seems both unnecessary and artificial to fabricate a conflict between the identity of European society as a whole and the identities of individual societies and regions within Europe. Such a conflict may exist to some extent, because over the past decades the conflict between European nationhood and individual national identities has been a subject of frequent debate within European movements. The Germans, in particular, have attempted to substitute a European national consciousness for their discredited nationalism. Nevertheless, such conflicts have no place in a socio-historical context. Just as regional and national identities exist simultaneously, so there may be a coexisting European identity.

Using the identity of France as an example, Fernand Braudel's last book gave an impressive demonstration of the way in which varying identities may exist together in historical reality. He revels in that country's regional diversity, which he views as a component of a wider European identity. The length of this study is the chief reason for foregoing a similar account of the diversity of regional and national societies in Europe. Besides this, it is broadly true to say that European social history—which includes comparative research—has, in the past, been rather too preoccupied with distinctive national features and has also become too sensitive to national socio-historical characteristics. There is thus a danger of losing sight of the other aspect of socio-historical reality, namely the common features of European society. This book is an attempt at a balanced survey of this other aspect of European reality.

There are other questions. What acts as the foil to the identity of twentieth-century European society? Which societies provide the background against which the distinctive features of Europe become apparent? Comparisons with Third World countries—even comparisons with older civilizations such as India or China—cannot be expected to provide the answers.

The features which distinguish Europe from these countries are generally common to other industrial nations; they offer no help in identifying the distinct European course. Comparisons such as these have therefore been avoided almost entirely, although they may be relevant to other long-term studies, such as comparisons of eighteenth- or nineteenth-century Europe with conditions in the Third World today. Other industrialized countries are therefore taken as benchmarks for the comparisons below.

A range of possible comparisons can be made between industrialized countries. One might compare countries settled by Europeans which are relatively similar culturally to Europe—such as the United States, Canada, Australia or New Zealand—with Asiatic or semi-Asiatic countries like Japan or the USSR. It would also be possible to compare the superpowers with lower-ranking countries such as Japan, Australia and Canada, a group to which Europe has also belonged in the post-war age. For the purposes of this book, however, it has been decided to use a fixed point of reference, the United States. The reason is primarily a practical one. Because of the novelty of the approach taken here, there is little similarly directed comparative research to refer back to. Comparisons must therefore be constructed afresh in many cases. The United States was therefore chosen as being the country for which research has been most intensive. A second reason for choosing the United States is that its history and present-day social structure and culture resembles Europe more closely than Japan or the USSR. If there has been any clear European identity in the twentieth century, then the United States will be the toughest test of its individuality, the country where European-style features are the most expected. If an individual European course can still be isolated from the American way, then it is likely that it also existed separately—though in another form—from the Japanese or Soviet course. Thirdly, it was decided not to pursue comparisons with other countries such as Canada, Australia or New Zealand, because their populations are relatively small, even though they are frequently very similar to Western Europe. Comparisons between such countries and a whole civilization like that of Europe, with its population of one-third of a billion, are likely to result in distortions. In any case they have not been as well-researched as the United States. Other non-European industrialized countries besides the United States have certainly been included as examples from time to time, to the extent that my linguistic ability has permitted. The result is that Europe's identity is sometimes thrown into surprisingly sharp relief.

Besides this, the great societies of the United States and the Soviet Union provide the most important measure of the scale of convergence that may be expected between the countries of Western Europe. Where social variation in Europe has shrunk to the kind of level observed within the United States or the Soviet Union, then this should be regarded as very acute convergence. More rigid statistical yardsticks have also been used, but these can admittedly only put values on convergence, they have no subjective power of assessment or evaluation.

A further note of qualification. The book deals exclusively with Western Europe, not the whole continent by any definition. Admittedly, this is again largely for practical reasons. The comparative research and international data compilations on which this book is based generally limit their scope to Western Europe as it is understood today. Eastern European countries tend to be excluded. Knowledge of several Eastern European languages, as well as familiarity with the often complicated history of the region, would be necessary to do justice to the whole of Europe. There are, however, more than mere technical reasons for restricting the study to Western Europe, whose living and working population is nearly three-quarters of the whole population of the continent. Those features common to Western European countries are not necessarily common to the whole of Europe, east and west. Social structures and ways of life were not completely spared the effects of the division of Europe after World War II, which has in many respects made political boundaries into sociological ones. This is especially true in areas such as education, social insurance, social conflict and corporate structures, which are all heavily dependent on political considerations. It is therefore my intention to scrutinize very closely and identify those features common to all Western European societies which have survived the fragmentation of Europe, as well as the significant social changes that have occurred since World War II. In fact, there were major sociological differences between east and west even prior to World War II. Family structures, towns, villages, the middle classes and the intelligentsia differed considerably from East to West. There can be no doubt that, geographically, the dividing lines were by no means the same as the political boundaries drawn since World War II, which have criss-crossed the heart of industrialized Europe where socio-historical demarcations never existed. Even in the first half of the century, pan-European features frequently only extended as far as an Eastern European border. Precise study is thus necessary here too; research has so far only been piecemeal. A brief exploratory account such as this cannot hope to achieve it adequately.

Lastly, some brief comments on the structure of the book, particularly the long-term view taken, the many countries under scrutiny and the method employed. As has already been pointed out, long-term investigation of features common to the societies of Western Europe and the manner in which they resemble each other is a particular object of the study. It is necessary because developments in the post-1945 period are only really apparent when compared with the inter-war years and the period prior to World War I. The starting point will therefore be the decades of social upheaval before World War I. It would be desirable to start earlier, but this is difficult for technical reasons. Any attempt at pinpointing the differences between European countries would fail for lack of material.

Where geography is concerned, all those Western European countries whose populations exceed that of a large city—Austria, Belgium, Denmark, Ireland, West Germany, Finland, France, Great Britain, Greece, Italy, the Netherlands, Norway, Portugal, Spain, Sweden and Switzerland—will be included. In the case of the pre-1914 period and the inter-war years, no after-the-fact boundaries will be drawn for Eastern Europe. This broad approach is necessary because the processes of integration are not necessarily limited to European Community countries. I have not avoided making comparisons when information is only available for a very few countries: regrettably, it becomes clear time and again that research data is available for countries at the centre of Europe but not for those on the periphery. Comparisons between so many countries also entail a certain amount of omission. The indisputable features of individual countries, in themselves so characteristic of Europe, cannot be dealt with in full.[6]

Above all, it is the aim of this book to open up a new perspective and put a finger on something that up to now has been too little regarded. Besides regional and national social histories, there is also a European social history that is something other than the stringing together of regional and national histories. I hope to demonstrate to the reader that this history does not only make more sense than it did before, but can even be written to a great extent. This view is not such a novelty: it has gained currency in recent years, chiefly among economic historians. In social history, however, it remains unusual.

Distinctive Features of European Societies in the Twentieth Century

In their treatment of the peculiarities of European social history during the last few centuries, social scientists and historians have stressed Europe's achievements and pioneering role in the early modern history of human rights; the separation of powers and of church and state; the development of secularization and modern scientific thought; and the origin of modern, rational systems of state administration. This catalogue is based on nineteenth-century liberal thought. Doubtless these ideas were of great importance to those living in the last century and are still important for current historical research into the nineteenth century and modern times. However, they constitute a diversion from an enquiry into the distinctive features of European societies in the twentieth century because Europe no longer has a special role to play in most of these areas, with the notable exception of state administration.

It was countries outside Europe, and especially the United States, who in the first half of the twentieth century became the true world bastions of human rights and parliamentary government. It can rightly be asked whether European societies have shared any basic common features in the twentieth century. Equally, has the worldwide process of modernization and industrialization not ironed out or whittled away diversities between developed countries, both European and non-European? Certainly there will be no talk of a new pioneering world role for European societies. It seems that in the twentieth century, Europeans have had to find their own solutions to a number of problems in the long term; these problems may also have affected countries outside Europe, but within Europe they have been experienced differently.

Diverse but detailed empirical research undertaken within

the last ten years has provided important indications of distinctively European features in the history of the family, employment, large industrial concerns, mobility and education, social inequality and lines of social demarcation, of cities, social conflicts and social policies. What emerges from these individual empirical studies is a characteristic family structure, a particular type of industry-intensive employment, businesses of a rather traditional kind, somewhat reduced opportunities for social ascent, a particularly limited range of secondary and further education, less social inequality but sharply-defined lines of social demarcation, better quality of life in the cities, an advanced welfare state, and distinctive developments in trade unions and labour conflicts. All these results have been presented individually. There are probably close links between these specifically European features but they will only be mentioned briefly, so as not to overburden this short outline. Some reflections on this subject will be provided at the end of the chapter.

1. The European family
One of Europe's most basic distinctive features emerges from the history of the family. In recent years, this subject has been researched in great depth by John Hajnal, Peter Laslett, Michael Mitterauer and Richard Wall. They have supplied much detailed information, especially covering the centuries up to and including the nineteenth century. They have demonstrated that, contrary to a widely-held view, the extended family has been far less common in Europe than in Russia or Japan since the sixteenth century or even as early as the late Middle Ages. Thus the phenomenon of parents and children living in the same household with grandparents and other close relatives has been far less common in Europe than elsewhere. So the nuclear family, often and incorrectly regarded as recent and modern, had been dominant in Europe for a long time. Besides this characteristically European pattern of family life, Hajnal proves that the age of marriage in Europe has been higher than elsewhere for both men and women. In Europe, the average age on marrying for the first time was between 25 and 30, as against 20 to 25 years in Russia and the United States. A final distinctive feature of the European scene is the consider-

ably higher proportion of unmarried people. It has been particularly large among young adults but in Europe the incidence of people who never married was also higher than elsewhere. This large proportion of unmarried people existed in the late Middle Ages too. These three traits also occurred individually outside Europe but the combination of all three is a peculiarly European phenomenon.

The result in the European family has been a very distinctive family cycle. Childhood and adolescence would generally be spent in a household with only natural or remarried parents and not, as elsewhere, with other relatives living in the same household. A long period of pre-marital adulthood would follow. The eventual departure from the paternal home probably occurred in far more cases than in countries in which the age of marriage was lower. Marriage would nearly always signal the establishment of an *independent* household and not, as elsewhere, acceptance into the parental household, or that of the in-laws. The result was that heads of households were not mostly elderly patriarchs or matriarchs as was the case outside Europe, but were on average unusually young. The majority of older members of a family lived in their own separate households away from their adult offspring, and for the most part were neither heads of extended families nor living in their offspring's household, as was the case outside Europe.[1] What particularly concerns us here is this earlier and more radical severance from the parental household. Although it did not necessarily lead to a complete break in the ties between parents and adult offspring, it substantially reduced the power of the head of the household, since this power is much greater in extended families. It thus had significant socio-historical consequences for European societies, and these will be examined shortly.

However, this "European family" was not typical of the whole of Europe. Research has hitherto concentrated on the period between the sixteenth and nineteenth centuries, and at least in these centuries, there is only evidence of its existence in Northern Europe, i.e. in England, Scotland, Scandinavia, northern France, the Netherlands, Germany and Austria.[2] The nuclear family was predominant only in those countries where at the same time both men and women married late. In Mediterranean countries and Eastern Europe on the other hand, family units of three generations or other types of extended family were significantly more common and marriage took place much earlier. In spite of this it may be assumed that in the nineteenth century, the "European" family was predominant in what would today be considered as Western Europe. It is this region which concerns us here.

More importantly, in the twentieth century, the era with which we are dealing here, the distinctive features of the European family have endured and in certain cases even consolidated themselves. Thus the nuclear family has continued to be more widespread in Europe than elsewhere. Most recently, Wall has demonstrated that even around 1970 the nuclear household was slightly less common in Poland, Hungary and Yugoslavia than it was in Western Europe; in the Soviet Union and Japan, it was even less typical. At the same time, there was a decline in the number of differences that had existed between Mediterranean countries and those of northern and central Europe since the nineteenth century. In the Western Europe of today, the nuclear family is practically universal.[3]

Another of our main concerns is age at marriage, which has remained substantially higher in twentieth-century Western Europe than it has in the United States. Our evidence applies at least to four of the larger European countries—France, Great Britain, Italy and West Germany—as well as to a number of smaller countries, including Ireland, Norway, Finland and Austria (see Table 1). Less precise information also gives similar indications for Spain, Portugal, Greece as well as Belgium and Switzerland. Thus twentieth-century Western Europeans have married late in most cases. It ought to be stated, however, that disparities between figures for Europe and elsewhere are not vast, and that in post-war years there has even been a tendency towards convergence. In spite of this, ages in Europe remained an average of two to three years higher than, for instance, North America (see Table 1). Because Europeans married later, there were fewer marriages in Western Europe even immediately after World War II. In fact, Europe is bottom of the world league table of marriage figures.[4]

This feature of European family life has found clearer expression in modern household arrangements than it did in the nineteenth century. In post-war years, there have been substantially more single-person households in Europe than in North America. That is because young unmarried people

Table 1: Age at marriage in Europe, America and Australia
1880–1970

Women	1880	1900	1910	1920	1930	1940	1950	1960	1970
Germany	–	26	25	26	25	26	25	24	23
France	–	25	–	–	23	–	23	24	23
Great Britain	26	26	–	26	–	25	–	24	22
Italy	–	24	24	25	24	25	25	25	23
Finland	25	25	–	25	25	25	25	24	30
Norway	26	26	26	25	25	26	26	25	23
Netherlands	27	26	26	26	26	26	25	24	22
Austria	28	27	–	–	25	–	25	–	22
Ireland	–	–	–	29	–	–	28	27	25
USA	22	22	22	21	21	22	20	23	21
Australia	–	–	–	24	23	24	22	22	21

Men	1880	1900	1910	1920	1930	1940	1950	1960	1970
Germany	–	29	27	29	28	29	28	26	26
France	–	31	–	–	27	–	26	26	25
Great Britain	27	27	–	28	–	27	–	26	24
Italy	–	28	27	29	27	28	29	29	28
Finland	27	27	27	28	28	28	28	26	25
Norway	28	28	28	28	29	29	29	28	25
Netherlands	28	28	28	28	28	28	27	26	25
Austria	31	30	–	–	28	–	28	–	24
Ireland	–	–	–	35	–	–	33	31	28
USA	26	26	25	25	24	24	23	23	23
Australia	–	–	–	27	26	27	25	25	23

began setting up their own homes after leaving those of their parents. This is a striking feature when all single-person households are under consideration. These include not only young unmarried people but also the many who are divorced, separated or widowed. Even though the United States has a greater number of divorcees and also more widows than Europe (because of the great disparity between the life expectancy of men as against women in America), in Europe as a whole the proportion of single-person households is still high by comparison with the United States, Canada, and even Japan. Overall, although there are some European countries such as England and the Netherlands in which conditions are the same as in North America, Europe as a whole gives a different picture. If we narrow the field down and deal only with single-person households consisting of young unmarrieds, then the disparity becomes much clearer. Admittedly, data is available only for a handful of countries. However, in the case of France, Germany, the Netherlands and Switzerland it can be shown that in *c*.1970, the proportion of this type of household was two to three times greater than in the United States and Canada. The advanced age at marriage and the large number of young unmarried people in Europe are responsible. While marriage remained late, it also became more common to quit the parental household.[5] It is quite possible that a high age at marriage has had a bearing on the European way of life; on phenomena like the generation gap; or on European sophistication and leisure activities, such as nightlife and tourism. It might also have had a darker side, an impact on the higher incidence of suicide and accidental death among young adults. As yet, we have too little information on which to base international comparisons.

All in all, the distinctive European family structure holds its own even in the present century. The traditionally high numbers of lifelong bachelors and spinsters so frequently encountered in European societies in the nineteenth century have undoubtedly disappeared. In twentieth-century Europe, the nuclear family prevails more strongly than elsewhere. Age at marriage has remained higher than in non-European countries and this has probably been reflected in types of household, modes of life and probably also in the average European's relative sophistication.

There are two areas of family history that have recently

attracted the attention of historians. One concerns the way in which family life developed in this century, the other the existence of peculiarly European characteristics in relationships between parents and between parents and children. The most influential of these studies are those conducted by Philippe Ariès. He does not deliberately compare European societies as opposed to non-European ones, but claims to have proved that there are certain features common to the European family. He places the European eighteenth- and nineteenth-century family at the heart of the private sphere, a place to which to retreat from the outside world, in which members were bound by emotional ties rather than those of business or a job. In it, the relationship between marriage partners was governed by affection and not, as in traditional European societies, by calculating the amount of property it was likely to yield. Provision of a loving, selfless upbringing characterised the relationship between parents and their children who were no longer regarded primarily as workers in the family business.

Ariès contends that the private family sphere was sharply divided from the outside world of state, community, street, neighbourhood, workmates and other family relations. It was the result of a gradual process that had begun in the upper strata of society in the Middle Ages. Ariès regards it partly as a defence against the modern European state, partly as a product of the new introverted piety and morality of the sixteenth and seventeenth centuries, and partly as a result of increased literacy and communications skills thanks to "solitary" reading and writing. The family became the hub of life.[6] In his frequently sketchy suggestions about modern European societies, Ariès undoubtedly underestimates some of the forces at work within the European family: the intense role-playing pressure especially as exerted upon women; tensions and emotional conflicts; as well as the pressures on emotional ties and signs of their loosening in the private family sphere after World War II. Nevertheless, Ariès' studies of European family life remain of great importance.

Several areas still require closer investigation. Were relationships between members of families in Europe closer and more affectionate than outside Europe, despite more relentless role pressure? Was the family in Europe more sheltered from outsiders and did it place greater emphasis on the dividing line between the private and the public sphere? European émigrés and visitors to America have come away with strong impressions of the contrasts in their own and the Americans' home life. They have registered surprise at the business-like tone that prevailed in North American families, which they felt was responsible for a lack of the warm, emotional emphasis on European family contact. Above all, they disapproved of the attitudes of American women which were wholly inconsistent with the woman's role in the close-knit European family. The women were thus held to be lazy, cold-hearted and feckless.[7] In all probability, there is more to this than mere prejudice. Rather, it seems that here is a conflict between the rich intimacy and insularity of the European family and its female role, and other distinct forms of family life. Europeans became conscious of this insularity when they left Europe and observed it from a distance. The Irishman, Canon Hannay, is but one of many examples. In 1914, after a trip to America he gave a typically waspish description of the external aspect of this European private sphere:

> The first thing an Englishman does when he builds a house is to surround it with a high wall. This, indeed, is not an English peculiarity. It prevails all over Western Europe.... The suburbs of Dublin, to take an example, ought to be very beautiful. There are mountains to the south and hills to the west and north of the city, all of them lovely in outline and colouring. There is a wide and beautiful bay. But the casual wayfarer cannot see either the mountains or the bay. He must walk between high yellow walls, walls built round houses; but we can only know this by hearsay. For the walls hide the houses as well as the view. In Sorrento, which is even more exquisitely situated than Dublin, you walk for miles and miles between high walls, white in this case.... The absence of walls in America is simply another evidence of the wonderful sociability of the people. Walls outside houses are like doors inside. The European likes both because the desire of privacy is in his blood. The American likes neither.

In the 1950s, an English council house tenant living in Dagenham said of his neighbours, "I'm not bothered about them. I'm only interested in my own little family. My wife and my two children—they're the people that I care about. My life down here is my home."[8]

The latest research reviews a variety of reasons for the distinctive nature of the European family. Some historians have sought an explanation in the very early modernization of Western European agriculture. Some have argued that the introduction of intensive farming between the seventeenth and nineteenth centuries imposed new limits on the amount of labour that could be put to productive use in agricultural concerns. Extended families became an economic burden and were thus slimmed down. The nuclear household is much more suited to the labour requirements of intensive farming. Another argument claims that the extended family was split up by the capitalization of agriculture and the introduction of waged work in agricultural concerns, because some members of a family would have become property owners while others became hired labour. Other historians have proposed that the Reformation and Counter-Reformation brought drastic changes in outlook that led to later marriage and closer emotional ties within families. According to this interpretation, when the family focus turned inwards and all aspects of life were subject to careful planning, the raising of children became a central aim of the family. The way to achieve this aim was through very close bonds between parents and children; later marriage improved the stability of the marriage and the household. Other historians have questioned whether it is even possible to talk of the "disbanding" of the extended family and the "delaying" of marriage. The nuclear family and high age at marriage could represent the older model, with the extended family and lower marrying age only developing during the Middle Ages or the early modern age.[9] A more detailed examination of these hypotheses might reveal whether the twentieth-century European family structure and family life should be regarded as a fixed component of modern European societies, or whether it is a hardy throwback to earlier stages of society, but one that is none the less doomed to disappear.

The repercussions of the special nature of the European family on other aspects of European society are, by contrast, more obvious and require discussion here. Three such consequences are paramount. First, European family structure has dictated that at critical stages of life there is a greater requirement for social assistance from outside the family than there is in other parts of the world. Because marriage tends to come late in Europe, there are more young adults with fewer family ties than elsewhere. There are also more people who remain unmarried all their lives. Above all, thanks to the prevalence of the nuclear family, there are more old people with no relatives. In Europe therefore, illness, unemployment or poverty in retirement are crises in which all these groups can rely less on the help and support of a family than they can do anywhere else. Of course, the real achievements, even of the European family, should not be underestimated. They have been clearly demonstrated by Michael Anderson in a study of nineteenth-century Lancashire. In spite of the public assistance provided by churches, foundations, communities, trade associations and eventually—in the late nineteenth century—by governments, the family was under far greater pressure in Europe than anywhere else.[10] We shall return to this subject when we focus attention on the development of state systems of social security.

Secondly, the high age at marriage for both men and women in Europe, as well as the high proportion of people who never married which has continued right into the twentieth century, meant that there was a far larger reserve of mobile male and female labour available for training and relocation. In the nineteenth and early twentieth centuries, this mobile pool of labour was the means that enabled Europe to lead the world in rapid and labour-intensive growth in new trades and industries. This point will be discussed again when dealing with the development of employment structures in Europe.

Thirdly, the structure of the European family had important political repercussions. The large pool of young unattached people provided great potential for political mass movements. The same source was also available to supply the large numbers of young men required for Europe's worldwide commercial and military expansion. Well into the nineteenth century, political equality—to the extent that it existed—meant equality between heads of households. Thus in a Europe having more numerous and often younger heads of households, the advance towards wider political rights was greater than it would have been in a society dominated by extended families and patriarchs. These consequences of European family structure will also be reconsidered in greater depth at a later stage.

2. The structure of European employment
Labour history is a second area in which important common European features may be distinguished. However, while a similar pattern of family life existed from as early as the Middle Ages, in the case of labour history a pattern only emerges from the Industrial Revolution onwards. From the mid-nineteenth century and into the twentieth century, employment in Europe was unusually industry-intensive. To put it another way, Europe was pre-eminent in the number of people employed in industry. From the Industrial Revolution up until the very recent past, European societies were alone in having industrial sectors that remained larger than their service sectors. It is only in European societies that employment history has stuck strictly to the textbook course, with agrarian society giving way to a true period of industrial society, where industry was indeed the largest employer. As the service sector has gradually overtaken the industrial sector in Europe in recent years, so the latter has nevertheless remained larger than elsewhere (see Figure 1).[11]

This characteristic, though common to all, is not evident to the same extent in all European countries. Besides Great Britain, the prime example, it is particularly marked in Germany, Italy, Belgium, Austria and Switzerland—those countries that are home to almost half of all Western Europeans, as the term is understood today. In France, Spain, Portugal, Sweden and Finland, the industrial sector outweighed the service sector to a lesser extent, though for a very long time. Thus these countries have also left their mark on Europe's peculiar employment structure. Finally the European pattern of industry-intensive employment is also discernible in Eastern Central Europe. In Hungary, Czechoslovakia and Yugoslavia, the industrial sector employed more people than the service sector; the same has been true in Poland since the inter-war period and in Rumania in post-war years.

The Western European countries that deviate from this pattern are the Netherlands, Ireland, Norway, Denmark and Greece. In these countries, the service sector has always been larger than the industrial sector. Of course, it must not be forgotten that only a small proportion of the population of Western Europe lives in these countries. They are not even true exceptions, but part of an inner-European division of tasks

Figure 1: Employment structure of Western Europe, United States, Canada, Australia, Japan and USSR, 1880–1980

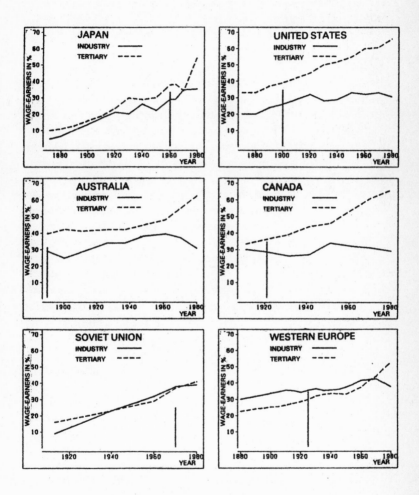

The vertical line marks the year of the first survey of trades and profession when agriculture ceased to be the largest employer. The length of the line indicates the proportion of employment in agriculture.

between agricultural, industrial and service regions. While the Danish and Irish economies were largely agricultural, the Norwegian and, to a greater extent, the Dutch economies provided services. This inner-European division altered nothing in the basic industry-intensiveness of Europe and was, in fact, an important precondition for it.

The situation is different in the Mediterranean. Within the general European economic framework, Mediterranean countries were less developed, marginal regions in which large numbers were employed in traditional service jobs. The marginal position of the Mediterranean is reflected clearly in the strength of the service sector, particularly in Greece, but also in Spain, Portugal and even France. However, between them the impact of these marginal regions was not great enough to alter the overall structure of European employment which remained unusually industry-intensive.

The European pattern is absent from all non-European countries at similar stages of economic development, including "new" societies set up by Europeans, like the United States, Canada and Australia, as well as Asian countries such as Japan (see Figure 1). Of course, one cannot simply lump all these countries together. What they have in common, however, is that, barring serious economic crises, industry never took precedence over the service sector. There never was a true period in these countries when the industrial sector was dominant. Instead, their societies switched directly from the industrial to the service pattern. Taking an overall view of these countries, the level of employment in the industrial sector, even in the most recent past, has lagged considerably behind the European level.[12] In the Soviet Union, where industrial employment in post-war years briefly exceeded service sector levels, this expansion was due to massive state intervention. It would thus be over-hasty to attempt to identify Europe's industry-intensive pattern with the position in the Soviet Union.

In conclusion, it seems that "Third World" countries are going down the road taken by other non-European countries, and that although the industry-intensive path served as an example, especially to communist countries, it was in effect a one-off in terms of world economic history and will remain thus.

What are the causes of this European pattern? Four conditions were crucial. First, there was Europe's unusually high population density, which was and remains several times higher than that in developed countries outside Europe. The only exception is Japan. This high population density saved labour in the service sector. Distances for transport and communication within Europe were significantly shorter and therefore fewer service sector employees were required. Even outside the chief centres of population in Europe, the density was still so high that a single doctor, teacher, administrative official, clergyman or salesperson could attend to a greater number of people than was possible anywhere else.

The extent of the service sector was undeniably conditioned by other factors as well as this demographic one. Quality of service, technical and organizational standards, the range of available service staff and political priorities all played their part, but population density was none the less of considerable importance.

Secondly, industry-intensive employment in Europe was linked to the pronounced export orientation of European industry. Neither American nor Russian/Soviet industry exported such a large proportion of industrial output, and for a long time the same was true of Japanese industry. This also applies when only those exports to markets outside Europe are taken into consideration.[13] This level of export orientation created the extra industrial employment in European societies which was absent from others. It also had the effect of reducing service sector employment because exports were largely handled by transport operators and traders outside Europe. Europeans mostly traded their industrial goods for raw materials and food, bulk commodities which only created limited employment in European transport and trade. European industry's intensive export drive would certainly have determined Europe's traditionally dominant position in the world economy. It could also have contributed to the expansion of Europe's industrial sector at the expense of industrialization in Third World countries.

The large numbers of traditional, highly-qualified European craftsmen were a third factor determining Europe's industry-intensiveness, especially when compared with the "new" societies. Many European goods were of high quality, customized and largely hand-made, promoting the traditionally strong preference among European consumers for expensive, tasteful, individualized and distinctive products. This traditional "burden" on European industry is frequently, though wrongly, regarded as simply a matter of production. Rather, it should also be viewed as a matter of consumer demand, which at the same time goes some way towards explaining the far higher levels of European industrial employment, especially when compared with the United States, Australia and Canada.

Finally, there may be links between patterns of industrial employment in Europe and the history of women's work. A comparative study with the United States and Canada reveals the striking fact that female employment in nineteenth- and early twentieth-century Europe was unusually high. Until just after World War I, about one-sixth of women worked outside the home in the United States and Canada. The corresponding average figure for Europe is more than a quarter. Variations between European countries were naturally considerable, but only in very few European countries—the Netherlands and Spain—did as few women work outside the home as did in the United States. The explanation for this probably lies within the European family where marriage occurred later in life. Early marriage in the United States siphoned women out of the labour market after a relatively short period spent working outside the home. In Europe, however, a larger reserve of women remained available for work. The change in the structure of women's work in twentieth-century Europe may have been considerably lessened by the existing European situation of commercial and agricultural work for women outside the home, as well as the social norms and restraints that this entailed. Female labour was suddenly in demand in all twentieth-century societies. In the United States, there was a sizeable reserve of unemployed women, and this resulted in a dramatic increase in female labour, chiefly in the service sector. A very high proportion of American women work in this sector today. Europe's reserve of unemployed women seems to have been smaller, on account of the longer tradition of women's work in industry. Overall, female labour increased only slightly and, even in the service sector, much more slowly than in the United States. Expressed as a European average—and there are large variations between European countries—the proportion of women working in the service sector today is significantly lower than in the United States. In Europe, the nature of women's work apparently remains more industrial.[14]

Important consequences have resulted from this European pattern of industry-intensive employment. It has limited opportunities for advancement among workers and has been a major factor in Europe's backwardness in social mobility. This subject will be dealt with later in more detail. The purely industrial city in Europe had greater character than elsewhere thanks to the employment structures, providing the history of European cities with its uniqueness. Finally, it also led to much greater numbers of industrial workers. In 1970, roughly half of all Western European workers were employed in industry. The corresponding figure for the United States and Canada was only about one-third, and for Australia two-fifths, whereas in Japan the figure was almost as high as that of Western Europe. That meant there was greater potential for membership of trade unions and greater electoral potential for European political parties representing workers. The larger number of workers also made social problems more pressing, and this factor became a prime condition for the development of social policy. Though all these consequences are only mentioned in brief here, they will be discussed later in greater detail.

3. The large European industrial concern

A third historical feature emerges in the structure of twentieth-century European enterprise. The relevant material currently available on which observations can be based results from a limited area of comparative historical research that is still in its infancy. Even so, a number of peculiarly European characteristics can be distinguished.

One feature of great importance compared with the United States appears to be the size of companies. Even at the turn of the century, the largest European companies were significantly smaller than the largest American concerns. At that time, leading European companies never had more than 200,000 employees. Those firms that were giants by European standards of the day such as Krupp (180,000 employees), Siemens (153,000) or the Gelsenkirchener Bergwerks AG (130,000) were exceptions. In pre-war Europe, any company employing between 40,000 and 60,000 workers was regarded as large. Even then, however, American firms were of a quite different order of magnitude.

In terms of scale, European firms lag far behind to this day.

Today, the largest privately-owned companies in Europe employ a maximum of 300,000 to 400,000 people (1979: Philips, 388,000; Unilever, 318,000) which puts them quite a way behind the biggest American companies (1979: General Motors, 853,000; Ford, 495,000; General Electric, 465,000). Inner European disparities in size of firms are doubtless also of importance. Currently, Europe's largest concerns are mainly British or German, much less often French, Dutch, Italian, Swedish, Belgian or Swiss, and this is a state of affairs that has persisted since the turn of the century. It must be said that within Europe, the variations in size between companies seem smaller than the jump to the American scale, which must have much to do with the far larger American home market.[15]

However, another reason for the larger American scale is the earlier and more widespread development of modern company structures. Alfred Chandler, Herman Daems and Herman van der Wee were the first to point this out. Americans not only introduced modern management methods earlier, they were also quicker than the Europeans at exploiting the advantages of vertical integration. For instance, the practice of taking over raw materials producers was more common, and American firms were also a jump ahead in buying up those companies that processed or marketed their own products. American firms have always provided the prime examples of complete integration from raw material to sales. Besides this, American companies were the first to diversify and did so more freely. Buying out firms producing quite different products resulted in a spread of risk because, on balance, where there was a crisis in one product area, success in another field could compensate for it.

Finally, American firms led the way to development and implementation of the so-called multi-divisional structure of large firms. The result was a successful compromise between the simple holding company in which all executive power lay with subsidiaries while those on the main board had little influence, and the type of over-centralized concern where individual companies had too little latitude and the senior executives were over-burdened with responsibility. This kind of multi-divisional enterprise was less common in Europe.[16]

Of course obvious differences have existed within Europe. Jürgen Kocka and Hannes Siegrist have pointed out the sizeable lead enjoyed by Germany over England in the pre- and inter-war years, and have shown that German companies were almost as heavily integrated and even, in some cases, more widely diversified than American firms. Large German firms, and possibly also those in Switzerland, seem to have occupied an intermediate position between the United States and Europe. However, in the introduction of modern methods of management and progress towards multi-divisional concerns, Germany lagged behind the United States. Despite the undeniable intra-European variations, Europe as a whole trod a more traditional path than America.[17]

Large firms in Europe have also remained longer under the control of their founding families. In America, owners have been more quickly ousted by management who ran companies without actually owning them. Corporate legal structures such as the Aktiengesellschaft gained ground, in spite of which families kept such a tight hold on increasingly complex firms that only routine daily decisions that were delegated to managers. Vital decisions such as those concerning the firm's rate of growth, acquisitions, the placing of investments, the legal form that the firm should take, how strong the bank's influence should be allowed to become and key appointments were generally taken by the European founding families than by their American counterparts.

At the turn of the century the big European companies were mostly family-owned. In the United States, the managers were dominant. Even then, of course, there were managers in Europe exemplified by men such as Rathenau, Hugenberg and Kirdorf. In their individual firms they ruled supreme, like their American opposite numbers, but in terms of the economy as a whole they were the exceptions. By contrast with the American situation, founding families in Europe have retained their power. Even when the post-war boom made inroads into such family power, it was still not fully overthrown. Although family control is the exception among large present-day companies, and though family members now have more in common with their managers in terms of training and methods, they none the less retain far more influence in Europe than in the United States.[18] The extent of their individual power and the reasons why they have retained more control of large concerns than in the United States are admittedly areas in which research has been limited.

Finally, in continental Europe at least, the mentality of entrepreneurs has been quite different to that found among American businessmen, especially in the first half of the twentieth century. Volker Berghahn's work, in particular, has illuminated this point, isolating three essential differences. First, European entrepreneurs have been far less competition-orientated. Market forces were used far less in Europe, other means being more widely used to win customers. Successful methods were, for example, price-fixing cartels with other companies, production quotas or even joint purchasing and sales through cartels and syndicates. Where national markets were relatively small, protection could be provided by tariffs, import controls, legal regulation of quality of goods or other state measures such as subsidies or the establishment of part-privatized monopolies. American entrepreneurs also naturally tried to control the markets but relied more heavily on market forces, or on the expansion, amalgamation or takeover of companies. This contrasts with the European reliance on agreements and state intervention, which leads to the second of Berghahn's points, namely that European entrepreneurs tended towards a much closer relationship with the state. They often expected more of the state, were more ready to cooperate, more understanding, sometimes even more subservient and trusting. They were also prepared to fall back on the state as an economic tool and rely on state intervention as a substitute for entrepreneurial achievement. Pressure on the state may have been greater, but in any case it was regarded as of greater importance by businessmen. Thus the interaction between economy and state in Germany appears to have been regulated by a highly-developed system of interest groups, whereas in France it was achieved through common training and extensive personal exchange between state administration and big companies. Even the geography of Europe dictated that the state was often close at hand, and this contrasted with the government in Washington that not only lacked the monarchical trappings of pomp and ceremony but was often far distant, less powerful, more intangible and generally of less consequence to American businessmen. Thirdly and finally, American business thinking has tended to identify market competition with competition in the political arena, and the market economy with parliamentary democracy. In European business circles, as in other groups in society, this notion has largely been absent.

This distinctive economic mentality among entrepreneurs has not been confined to continental Europe. British businessmen have displayed the same attitudes. It also appeared to lose a great deal of ground in Europe after World War II when American and European attitudes to the reconstruction of Europe came into conflict. There are a variety of reasons for this. Chief among them is the great attraction of the American economic model for post-war European societies. In addition, the American government intended to effect a switch in economic thinking by implementing policies targeted at the liberalization of markets in Europe, and at the stabilization of parliamentary democracies.[19] It is hard to say how far-reaching and complete this switch was intended to be. It also appears not to have taken place immediately after 1945, but when it came it was so radical that entrepreneurs themselves felt it to be a turning point.

Incidentally, I do not believe that 1945—in terms of management in Germany—was a new beginning. On the contrary, the changeover was very gradual. Respected pre-war figures stayed for a while, younger people rose more rapidly to key positions and the switch really occurred about 1960–65. By that, I mean a switch that did away with the old German nationalist thinking. I see today's attitude as one that takes all points of view into account. Today's management must prove itself in the marketplace and ensure profitability; it has to be able to cope with employees, unions, politics, the treasury and the shareholders or whoever the owners are.[20]

4. Social mobility in Europe

The history of social mobility is a fourth area in which distinct European traits can be identified, at least when Europe is compared with the United States. There can be no doubt that opportunities for advancement in Europe have been consistently misrepresented and underestimated in comparisons with "the land of unlimited opportunity". If there are any important upward paths or types of advancement in which there are differences between Europe and the United States, or between industrial societies in general—for instance among skilled workers or, in overall terms, between fathers and sons—it has so far been impossible to identify them positively. Similarly, no one has been able to provide conclusive proof that it is much easier to become an entrepreneur in the United States than in Europe, or that there is any historical substance to the expression "from dishwasher to millionaire".[21]

In a range of other very limited respects, however, it becomes apparent that social mobility has been lacking in Europe, and this is borne out especially by studies of opportunities for unskilled workers and the social backgrounds of those in academic life.

Opportunities for most population groups, but chiefly unskilled workers, have been researched in numerous studies of European and American cities covering the nineteenth and early twentieth centuries. Despite great variations within both continents, there is evidence of one clear area of differentiation between the United States and Europe. In the periods and cities studied, upward mobility of unskilled workers into white-collar careers or the ranks of the small businessman occurred substantially more frequently in the United States than in Europe. For such people, the United States was the land of greater, though not limitless, opportunity.[22]

Europe's backward position in terms of mobility is closely linked with its peculiar development in employment history already discussed: the comparatively polarized industrial and service sectors. Overall in modern societies, the service sector employs a particularly large proportion of middle-class workers, such as salaried staff and the self-employed. In those European societies that have a small service sector there are fewer middle-class opportunities for advancement. At the same time, developed twentieth-century industrial societies have a higher proportion of workers in the industrial sector than in other sectors. This creates a particularly heavy but unfulfilled demand for upward mobility in societies with high levels of industrial employment, such as those found in Europe. European-style industry-intensive employment offers relatively few opportunities for upward mobility of unskilled workers.

Another set of circumstances should also be taken into account. The European pattern of employment has been particularly unfavourable in terms of opportunities for mobility among unskilled workers because, even late in the twentieth century, the traditional unskilled jobs have played a more important role in European economies than in the United States. Workers in such jobs were usually low paid and in temporary employment and were often thrown upon an overcrowded labour market. Besides this, they tended to switch rapidly back and forth between widely varied employment, and often even between agricultural, industrial and transport jobs. For all these reasons, they would be forced to move home frequently and did not regard themselves as belonging either to a fixed trade or even a fixed sector of the economy. Because they were often from an agrarian background, they experienced great difficulties in adjusting to modern industrial and urban society. Far from knowing how to take advantage of work and education, if not for themselves then at least for their children, they lurched from one personal crisis to the next.

An important reason for the continuing presence of the traditional unskilled worker in Europe was the comparatively slow process of modernization in mass production techniques, a subject already discussed with reference to employment. Because these techniques found earlier introduction in the United States, more semi-skilled employment was available to unskilled workers in factories. This stabilized their employment position and largely did away with the kind of temporary work that often changed from day to day and contributed so heavily to the instability of the traditional unskilled worker. Unskilled workers who had secured these semi-skilled positions in the United States were therefore better able to predict and plan the course of their lives and could also take greater advantage of the opportunities that arose for training or in their jobs. So it was not only a difference in mindset that permitted greater advancement for American workers early this century. Compared with European workers, they were faced with an economic and employment structure that was more favourable to the process of advancement.

The situation in Europe was not uniform, and opportunities for upward mobility for unskilled workers were far from equal. We already know that sizeable variations could exist from city to city depending on their natures. Even when their rate of growth was high, purely industrial cities offered little prospect of advancement because the middle ground was so narrow. Proof of this can be found in studies such as those made on the German industrial cities of Bochum and Ludwigshafen. In cities in which the service sector was dominant—ports and

administrative centres—unskilled workers could actually rise
to the ranks of the lower middle classes more frequently because
this stratum was wider. This is known from studies on Rotterdam, Berlin and Copenhagen. In the long-established commercial and trading centres, the prospects for advancement for the
unskilled also seem to have been more favourable. Evidence of
this is available, for instance for Graz, Esslingen, Toulouse and
Bielefeld. What is more significant is that there was great variation between the countries of Europe. Thus it has been demonstrated that early twentieth-century Dutch society was
more open than German society. Once again, the decisive factor could be the size of the Dutch service sector which was unusually large by European standards. Despite these variations
and others within Europe, there is a striking discrepancy between American and European levels of opportunity for advancement among unskilled workers at the beginning of this
century.[23]

The numerous sociological studies of the post-1945 period
convey the same impression. On the one hand, they are further
proof of Europe's disadvantaged position in social mobility
when compared with the United States and Japan (see Table
2). In Europe as a whole, it was far less common for the sons of
unskilled workers to move into non-manual trades—unfortunately comparisons must often be made in such simplistic
terms. This theory is sometimes disputed. Social scientists often
argue that the similarities between all developed societies were
more important than the differences, and that this is still the
case. Certainly there were also European countries, Sweden for
example, that approached the American model. In any case,
the fact remains that the large, important European countries
offered significantly less opportunity for advancement for the
sons of manual workers when compared with the United States.
The position in these countries has had a great impact on
Europe's overall standing in this respect because they contain
most of the population of Europe (see Table 2). At the same
time, there is a broad consensus among social scientists that,
even as the twentieth century progressed, national variations in
opportunities for advancement were strongly dependent upon
employment patterns—in this case Europe's industry-intensive
structure. It is thus often difficult to show conclusively that variations in mentality or government policies have had any

decisive effect.[24]

On the other hand, there is ample evidence of close similarity between the countries of Europe. Especially in the very recent past, accurate and complex comparisons have been drawn between the various European societies. They plot mobility for a whole range of trades and professions and are methodologically greatly superior to transatlantic comparisons. However the material is drawn from the early 1970s, or prior to the long economic depression that lasted until the mid '80s. Besides, there exists only one three-way study of Sweden, France and England, one two-way study of England and West Germany and another two-way study of France and West Germany. In these studies, whose purpose was to seek out variations in rates of mobility between countries, the fluctuations between European societies were not considered to be very great. This was stressed particularly in the English-French and English-German studies.

In the French-German comparison, career mobility was very similar in middle- and high-ranking positions and in agriculture. France was the only country in which careers offering advancement for manual workers were significantly more common. In France, it was the progress of the worker's career that determined whether he or she was to remain unskilled or become a craftsman or skilled worker, whereas in other countries, the type of training decided the skill level. French-German variations might well be reduced if mobility is measured against parents' profession or trade. All these results are important since more than half of the population of Western Europe lives in the countries concerned and conditions within them have had a profound effect on developments in the region as a whole. Sweden has been the exception where opportunities for mobility were concerned. This is partly due to the greater openness of Swedish society where barriers between trades and social classes are less of a hindrance. However, in the 1960s and early 1970s, Sweden's rate of mobility was affected by growth in its service sector which was unusual for Europe and resulted in Sweden's departure from industry-intensive employment and an increase in opportunities for mobility, albeit for a limited time. Sweden should be regarded as a special case.[25]

It is not only in mass mobility that a distinctly European path has emerged. The same has occurred in the rapid growth

Table 2: International comparison of social mobility,

Country	Year	Employment structure White-collar	Blue-collar	Agricultural
(1)	(2)	(3)	(4)	(5)
	%	%	%	
West Germany	1970	46	49	5
Belgium	1968	54	38	8
Denmark	1972	36	42	23
France	1964	36	48	16
Great Britain	1963	38	62	–
Italy	1963/64	22	51	26
Netherlands	1954	31	69	–
Sweden	1968	34	54	8
Japan	1965	51	29	21
USA	1962	24	45	31

of education. At the beginning of the century, when only one person in every hundred was studying, this was still a marginal feature. Today, when the figure for Europe is approximately one in five, it carries far greater weight. We can only really pin down this European feature of social mobility in the development of higher education. Opportunities for entry into the academic professions offer a less accurate guide.

In the development of opportunities in higher education, most European societies have lagged behind the United States in a number of respects. Ever since the late nineteenth century, the proportion of each age group that went on to study in the United States was substantially greater than was commonly found in European societies (see Table 3). This was not only true of college education, which compares with the final years of European secondary schools, but also of American graduate schools when compared with similar European institutions. Naturally, there are major variations between European countries and besides, the countries offering numerically the best and worst opportunities underwent shifts during the course of the twentieth century. Early on, it was the smaller countries upward and downward, 1954–72

	Mobility rate			
Including	Excluding agricultural workers	Upward	Downward
(6)	(7)	(8)	(9)
%	%	%	%
37	31	32	30
39	32	43	18
39	32	35	28
40	31	28	34
30	–	27	37
35	22	21	27
27	–	20	43
48	34	32	38
47	27	45	23
48	34	38	28

such as Switzerland, Scotland and Austria which offered the opportunities. In post-war years, it has been the turn of France and the Scandinavian countries. Even so, not one of these countries with all their wealth of opportunity can approach the American level, either in range of educational facilities nor in the numbers wishing to study. Even in the post-war education explosion, disparities between Europe and the United States have only decreased slightly.

Europe has also lagged behind in the educational opportunities open to women. The foundations for this situation were also laid early on (see Table 3). The proportion of American women students has greatly exceeded the European figure since before World War II. However, we should not go too far in seeking distinct European features in this respect. There have been significant variations within Europe virtually throughout the twentieth century. Some European countries, notably France, have kept pace with American standards of equal opportunity for womens' entry into higher education, at least since the end of World War II. While differences in this respect between Europe and the United States may have been less dis-

Table 3: Educational opportunities in Western Europe and the United States, 1890–1978

Country	1890	1900	1910	1920	1930	1940	1950	1960	1970	1978
1. Proportion of Students[a]										
Belgium	1.04	0.89	1.25	1.36	1.54	2.46	3.07	9.09	18.48	25.79
West Germany[d]	0.77	0.89	1.22	2.05	1.96	1.06	4.39	6.31	13.53	25.46
Finland	1.06	1.15	1.19	1.16	2.01	2.63	4.25	2.25	13.43	20.57
France	0.62	0.93	1.32	1.50	2.31	3.46	4.34	7.39	15.81	24.11
Gt Britain	0.73	0.79	1.31	1.96	1.89	.1.15.	2.86	8.88	14.14	19.40
Greece	–	–	0.25	0.33	1.40	1.96	2.76	3.96	12.57	18.06
Ireland	–	–	–	1.65	1.88	2.44	4.27	8.95	13.77	18.32
Italy	0.76	1.02	1.05	1.64	1.25	3.99	3.56	6.52	16.97	27.46
Netherlands	0.74	0.69	1.05	1.53	2.58	3.35	7.65	13.13	19.51	28.29
Austria	0.85	1.06	3.77	4.30	3.87	2.29	4.55	7.86	11.50	21.62
Portugal	0.29	0.25	0.24	0.58	0.90	1.42	1.71	3.23	7.98	10.89
Sweden	0.91	0.65	0.88	1.12	1.69	1.99	3.68	9.02	21.32	35.56
Switzerland	0.90	1.40	2.16	1.99	1.83	2.71	3.67	5.80	8.24	16.74
Spain	–	–	1.21	1.30	1.66	1.72	2.07	3.90	8.56	24.08
W Europe	0.75	0.92	1.24	1.64	1.81	2.14	3.63	6.93	14.51	23.83
USA	1.80	2.30	2.90	4.70	7.20	9.10	16.50	20.50	30.60	40.00
2. Proportion of women among students[b]										
Belgium	–	–	–	–	10	14	16	19	29	33[c]
West Germany[d]	–	–	4	9	18	14	16	20	25	32[c]
Finland	–	–	–	–	32	33	35	46	47	49[c]
France	–	3	9	13	26	34	34	41	45	48[c]
Gt Britain	–	–	–	27	26	27	22	24	28	33[c]
Greece	–	–	–	–	8	11	–	23	31	57[c]
Ireland	–	–	–	–	29	23	25	25	34	41[c]
Italy	–	–	17	20	15	20	26	27	38	39[c]
Netherlands	–	7	14	15	18	14	15	18	20	25[c]
Austria	–	–	8	14	17	24	21	23	25	34[c]
Portugal	–	–	–	–	–	20	26	31	46	46[c]
Sweden	–	3	8	10	15	24	23	33	37	37[c]
Switzerland	–	20	22	12	12	13	13	17	23	27[c]
Spain	–	–	–	4	7	12	14	18	26	34[c]
W Europe	–	(8)	(12)	14	18	20	21	25	32	37[c]
USA	17	19	23	35	40	41	30	37	41	45[c]

(a) Proportion of students between 20 and 24 years of age (Europe) and between 18 and 24 years of age (United States) (b) Universities only (c) 1975 (d) Before 1950: German Reich tinct than in overall educational opportunities, the decrease in the extent of those differences has been much easier to define. Despite this, a comparison of Western Europe as a whole with the United States reveals a significant lack of educational and training opportunities for European women (Table 3).

Finally, high school education in America has been more open socially than in many of the countries of Europe. Since World War II, the opportunities for the sons and daughters of farmers, minor white-collar workers and labourers wishing to study at high school have been greater in the United States than in Europe. Again, there are countries in Europe to which this does not apply. Sweden, at least, was no different to the United States, and the same could also be true of those smaller European countries about which little is known. However, larger European countries lagged a good way behind the United States.[26] So far it is not clear how long this discrepancy has existed, nor is it known whether the same results would be obtained for the difficult comparison between ethnic minorities on the two sides of the Atlantic.

The shortage of opportunities for higher education has had an impact on mobility within the academic professions. Not only are there fewer posts, the consequence of a smaller academic labour market in Europe, there is also much evidence that entry in most European countries is less open than it is in America. At least in the post-war era, the proportion of academics from working-class backgrounds—should we wish to take this crude but fairly effective yardstick—has been lower in a majority of European countries than in the United States. Little is known of conditions before World War I or in the inter-war years but since 1945, this appears to be a further aspect of the disadvantage that Europe has suffered in terms of social mobility.[27]

5. Social inequality and demarcation lines in Europe

A fifth feature of twentieth-century European society, often regarded as closely associated with Europe's disadvantaged position in terms of social mobility, is the scale of social inequality and the sharpness of demarcation lines between classes and social strata. Compared with the United States, it is said that industrialized Europe exhibited less poverty and less glaring imbalances between rich and poor, together with fewer slums, less criminality and fewer social misfits and outcasts. At the same time, in their very way of life, social contacts, ambition for advancement, moral values and political tendencies, Europeans draw much sharper demarcation lines between classes, as well as between social strata, milieus and regions. In America, highly conspicuous social inequality and the belief in equality of opportunity exist as two sides of the same coin. The European situation is characterized by less striking inequalities between rich and poor, but a perceived need for making "fine distinctions".

Are these commonly-held beliefs supported by the facts? We will begin with the imbalance between rich and poor in Europe.[28]

There are a number of facts that indeed suggest that the conventional impression of Europe outlined above has come close to historical reality in the post-war era. This impression proves to be false in a number of possibly surprising respects, but ample evidence of the more even balance between rich and poor in Europe does exist. Various aspects will be considered stage by stage while attempting to ignore complex problems of theory and the quantification of inequalities, even if there is a risk of apparent over-simplification. Western Europe will be compared to the United States, as this is central to the discussion. However, as far as possible, Western Europe will also be contrasted with other western industrialized nations.

In post-war Europe at least, income variations between rich and poor have been less acute than in the United States and this appears to be one feature that distinguishes the two continents from each other. We are not concerned here with absolute variations; as may be expected in a rich country like the United States, these are greater than in less affluent post-war Europe. We are thus chiefly interested in relative figures i.e., the proportionate difference between higher incomes and lower ones.[29] Unfortunately, the necessary information is hard to come by. We can only compare the United States with West Germany and Great Britain, though it will soon be realised that these countries are not exceptional in the European context. Unfortunately, all the data consists of dry income statistics which are not easy to interpret. We must imagine ourselves faced with the problem directly. Table 4 is an attempt to do this. A comparison between the average and lowest income of the top 5 per cent and 20 per cent of earners with the average and highest income of the lowest 20 per cent of earners on either side of the Atlantic clearly reveals that relative variations in income in the United States were considerably larger than in Great Britain and Germany; this was especially true in comparison with the latter. In 1969, relative variation between these two income groups in the United States was twice as high as in Germany (see Table 4).

Only a rough indication can be given of the groups behind the statistics. They are certainly not those on the fringes of society in income terms, such as top earners and benefit claimants. If they were, the observed variations in income would not necessarily be a sound basis for conclusions about inequality within a society. Rather, they are average high earners and average low earners, and variations between these levels say much for society overall. For the lower income groups in this study, there are clear indications that the composition of the European group differed from that of the American one. The majority in this group in Britain in the 1950s and West Germany in the 1960s were pensioners, students, the unemployed and benefit claimants and therefore not in employment. In the United States, the equivalent group consisted largely of unskilled workers and poor farmers.[30] Where these groups are concerned, there was a lack of equality in American society. If whites are only compared with whites, income variations in the United States diminish (Table 4). Even then, however, they remain considerably greater than those in Britain and Germany. This subject will be dealt with again.

It would be misleading to make the hasty claim that Europe sets the standard for the scale of income variation between rich and poor. Japanese income statistics sound the note of caution. In Japan, the statistics covering income variations are compiled in such a way that they can only be compared with American statistics and not directly with those for Europe. However, variations between upper and lower incomes in Japan are far smaller than those between rich and poor in America. It can thus be suspected that they are also smaller than European variations.[31]

The proportion of national income going to low earners is another widely-acknowledged feature of European society. It was practically universal in Europe for this proportion to be significantly greater than in North America. Once again, income

Table 4: Variations in income in United States, West Germany and Great Britain, 1950–75

Income groups under comparison	Country	Year	Absolute sums higher income	lower income	Vari-ation
1. Lower limit of top decile and upper limit of bottom decile[a]	United States	1954	$7680	$1000	7.7
	Great Britain	1954	£810	£130	6.2
2. Lower limit of top quintile and upper limit of bottom quintile[b]	United States, all	1962	$8800	$2000	4.4
	United States, whites only	1962	$9100	$2250	3.9
	West Germany	1962/1963	15351DM	6115DM	2.5
	United States, all	1969	$13500	$3200	4.2
	United States, whites only	1969	$13950	$3530	4.0
	West Germany	1969	23101DM	8724DM	2.7
	Great Britain	1974/1975	£3238	£909	3.6
3. Lower limit of top half-decile and upper limit of bottom quintile	United States, all	1962	$14000	$2000	7.0
	United States, whites only	1962	$14350	$2250	6.3
	West Germany	1962/1963	24625DM	6115DM	4.0
	United States, all	1969	$21260	$3200	8.8
	United States, whites only	1969	$21900	$3530	6.3
	West Germany	1969	37484DM	8724DM	4.3
	Great Britain	1974/1975	£4983	£909	5.5

(a) Top decile: top 10 per cent of wage earners. Bottom decile: bottom 10 per cent of wage earners

(b) Top quintile: top 20 per cent of wage earners. Bottom quintile: bottom 20 per cent of wage earners.

statistics must be resorted to, however unclear and incomprehensible they may be at first glance. They show that from an uncertain point during the inter-war or immediate post-war period in Europe, the lower 10 per cent and 20 per cent of earners received a significantly larger "slice of the cake" than the same groups in the United States or Canada. For the poor, national income has thus been distributed far less unevenly in Europe than in North America (see Table 5).[32] The differences are by no means enormous. Furthermore, they should be interpreted with caution, since definitions of income are not always completely identical. Table 5 gives an overall picture. It is also not true that all European countries differed from the United States to the same degree. France and the United States, in particular, show very little variation. But where figures exist for the rest of Europe, they show that lower income groups did in fact receive a considerably larger share of national income than those on the other side of the Atlantic. For 1970 at least, income distribution is known for a very broad spectrum of European countries, from highly industrialized northern welfare states, such as Sweden and Great Britain, through to latecomers to industrialization such as Spain. With the exception of France, the picture is the same everywhere, and thus we can assume that from the point of view of low earners, there was less inequality in Europe overall than there was in America. There was no yawning gap between Europe and America, but the United States definitely lay on the outermost fringes of the European spectrum.

In the post-war age, European societies were admittedly not in the forefront of the relief of inequality for lower income groups. There are cautionary comparisons with developed societies beyond America. In Japan, there appears to have been slightly less inequality of income distribution from the point of view of the less affluent. The proportion of total national income earned by the poorer sections of that society was, if anything, slightly higher.[33] Australia seems to have much in common with Europe, at least at first sight (see Table 5). Only a highly-detailed study of comparative sizes of households reveals that the scale of inequalities in income distribution was slightly smaller in Europe.[34] The proportion of income reaching lower-income groups indicates a number of differences between Europe and other developed non-European countries. A Euro-

Table 5: Lower incomes as a proportion of total income
in Europe, North America and Japan, c. **1940–1970**
(share received by bottom **20** per cent of wage earners)

	c. 1940	c. 1950	c. 1960	c. 1970
Austria	–	5.4(BI)	4.6(BI)	3.3(BI)
Ireland	–	–	–	4.1(BH)
France	–	–	2.0(BHW)	4.3(BH)
Norway	–	–	–	4.9(BH)
Great Britain	–	7.2(BI)	6.2(BH)	5.4(BH)
Italy	–	–	–	5.1(AH)
Germany	3.0(BE)	5.4(AH)	6.2(AH)	5.9(AH)
Netherlands	5.9(BH)	3.2(BH)	4.5(BH)	5.9(BH)
Sweden	–	(4.6)(BI)	(4.4)(BI)	6.0(BH)
Spain	–	–	–	6.0(AH)
United States	3.0(BH)	3.1(BH)	3.2(BH)	3.8(BH)
Canada	–	4.7(BHT)	4.4(BH)	3.3(BH)
Australia	–	–	(6.0)(BI)	2.1(BH)
Japan	(6.3)(BI)	–	6.1(BH)	8.7(BH)

B: before tax
A: after tax
H: household income
I: individual income
W: without family supplements
    and minimum pension
T: towns only

pean pattern is discernible.

The European pattern of income distribution to the poorer sections of society is apparently connected to the development of the welfare state and consequent improvements in pensions, grants, unemployment benefits and social security in the post-war era. As will be seen in a later section, these "transfer payments" have increased greatly as the welfare state has become established throughout Europe. Lower income groups have been the main beneficiaries, which explains why they have received a higher proportion of total income in Europe than in the United States, where such payments are much lower. Comparing distribution before and after these payments, for which we regrettably have figures only for the 1970s in many cases, it is obvious that without them, lower income groups would have received a far smaller proportion of national income, practically eliminating any variation between Europe and the United States.[35] The virtual absence of a racial problem in Europe should be regarded as a second reason for the disparity between Europe and the United States. As pointed out before, a significant proportion of lower income groups in the United States consists of unskilled black labour in the north and poor black farmers in the south. Their lower share of national income is explained by economic discrimination against black Americans.[36] These differences cannot be traced back to an absence of racial prejudice among Europeans, but simply to the fact that there are hardly any blacks and few coloured people in Europe.

In all probability, at least òne other distinctive feature of European society has been responsible for the distinctive income distribution pattern observed in Europe. Time and again, studies show that the extent of inequality is heavily dependent on size of households. Inequality between single-person households is far less striking than inequality in larger households, some of which will be reliant on a single income while others are supplied by two or more.[37] The number of single-person households has been regulated by the older marrying age among Europeans which has thus helped to reduce the income gap. In America, where age at marriage has been lower, the small number of single-person households has exerted the opposite effect.

A third aspect of income distribution has been the lower proportion of national income gained by higher earners in post-

war Europe compared with the United States. It may be surprising that there is no clear proof of similar variations among
very high incomes. Comparative data concerning the "slice of
the cake" that went to the top 10 per cent, the top 5 per cent and
even the top 1 per cent of earners in the United States and
Europe are not explicit enough. According to the set of statistics
used, there is either a smaller or an equally large proportion
going to these top earning groups in Europe. By contrast, European earners in the income brackets just below this level received a noticeably lower proportion of national income.
Separating peak earners from the overall higher income group,
compared with the United States the remainder have received a
smaller proportion of national income in Europe since the
1950s or 1960s. In technical terms, it is the second-, third- and
fourth-highest 10 per cent (deciles) of earners in the United
States who have received more than their European opposite
numbers (see Figure 2).[38] There is also some indication of
growth in the proportion of income received by Europeans in
these groups. At least, this was the case in Great Britain, the
Netherlands, Sweden and, for a shorter period, Italy and Norway, all countries where the "slice of the cake" increased
slightly in the 1950s and 1960s. Against this, however, a better
position was reached by higher earners in America who seem to
have gained ground even faster, at least in the 1970s (see Figure
2).

Here again then, there is no enormous gap between the
societies of the United States and Europe. If anything, it is even
less clear than the distinction between lower-income groups
and even more dependent on varying definitions of income and
whether we take individual or family incomes before or after
tax. However, the United States is well up towards the top of
the European spectrum; in fact it matches at the very top when
looking at individuals' pre-tax income.[39] For higher earners in
Japan, the reverse is the case. Japanese higher earners received
a rather smaller proportion of national income compared with
Europeans, putting Japan at the opposite end of the European
scale to the United States.[40]

The status of this particular development as characteristic of
more equal income distribution in European societies is not so
clear-cut as in the case of the lower earners. The gains made by
higher income groups can partly be explained by saying that

Figure 2: Higher incomes by country and date

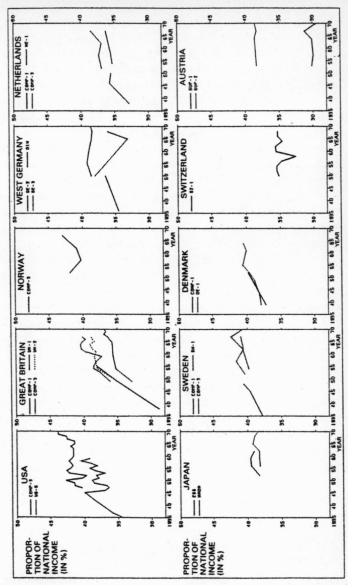

The diagrams show proportion of income received by the top 40% of wage-earners but without the proportion received by the top 10% of wage-earners.

higher earners also gained steadily in relative terms. Between 1950 and 1970 in the United States, income differentials increased substantially between professionals (administrators and officials) and most other social groups—office staff, sales people, skilled and unskilled workers.[41] Redistribution occurred between higher earners and the middle and lower incomes of the working population, so there was still some shift in the overall position. Nevertheless, incomes rose more rapidly among higher earners. This is one of the reasons for the growing share received by higher earners, which could also be observed in Europe and which tailed off in the 1970s, both in the United States and elsewhere. Higher earners thus lost some of their advantage.[42]

However, there is also some evidence which conflicts with this interpretation. Doubts first arise when surveying the development of the proportion of income received by top earners. This group—the top 10 per cent or 1 per cent of all earners—has received a progressively smaller proportion of income over the course of the twentieth century, so that groups just below that level have been in receipt of a growing proportion of national income. This reduction in the share going to the rich is a very clear development, not only in the United States but also in a whole range of European countries.[43] It would certainly be an over-simplification to equate this process to the decline of inequality. Its real nature has been a reshuffle among earners at the highest level, not between the upper and lower levels. Equally, however, the process cannot truly be seen as heightening inequality in incomes. Further weight is lent to the counterargument by the explanation put forward by Jan Tinbergen for the expansion of the proportion of national income received by higher income groups. According to him, the main reason lies in the rapid growth in academic employment and in the top managerial and administrative posts. In his view, higher earners received a greater proportion of national income because they were more numerous. In other words, according to Tinbergen, the cause lies in the redistribution of income, rather than in a change in the structure of professions.[44] This development was certainly not absent from European societies but, as was seen earlier, in the United States the rate of increase of these professional groups and the attendant growth in the number of high school students, as well as the tertiary sector overall, was far more rapid than in Europe. The more rapid change in professional structure opened up greater opportunities for advancement in the United States and may have extended its lead in social mobility over Europe. Here is a further primary cause of the greater share of national income enjoyed by higher earners on the other side of the Atlantic.

The distribution of wealth is another area in which the societies of Europe and America have differed in the twentieth century. However, despite what may have been expected from statistical evidence on income distribution, there has been substantially less inequality in the United States. Studies published in English have occasionally overestimated the extent of inequality there because they have always compared the United States with Great Britain, one European country in which the distribution of wealth is particularly unequal. Since the beginning of the twentieth century, distribution has become substantially less unequal in European societies, and this should not be overlooked. For Great Britain, France and the Netherlands at least, the evidence of this is very plain.[45] It even appears that the trends have been stronger and more sweeping in European societies than in the United States. Despite this, around 1970 the United States was still ahead in the reduction of inequality. The rich in Europe still controlled a greater proportion of national private wealth than the rich in America. Sweden was the sole exception (see Table 6). The discrepancies are no longer very great, but the United States still lies clearly at the extreme egalitarian end of societies in Europe.

The reasons for this European feature are illuminating;[46] the most important concerns the extent of home ownership. This exerts great influence on the distribution of wealth overall, because of its importance and growth as a component of national wealth. Depending on which country is examined, around 1970 it accounted for a third to almost a half of the total. Home ownership in Europe was substantially less evenly spread than in the United States. This is because the proportion of home owners in Europe has been on the increase for a long time, but still lags far behind the United States. Around the year 1950, when 45 per cent of Americans owned their own homes, the figures for Britain and West Germany were only 22 per cent and 25 per cent respectively. By 1970, the American figure had reached 63 per cent, but despite simultaneous rises in Europe it reached

Table 6: Distribution of wealth in the United States and Western Europe, 1902–75

PROPORTION OF WEALTH

Country	1902–13	1920s	1930s	1950s	1960s	1970s

1. Proportion of wealth held by richest 1%

Country	1902–13	1920s	1930s	1950s	1960s	1970s
United States	–	36%	28%	28%	29%	25%
France	50%	45%	–	31%	–	26%
England and Wales	–	61%	54%	45%	31%	32%
West Germany	31%	–	–	–	–	28%
Sweden	–	–	–	–	–	16%
Belgium	–	–	–	–	28%	–
Denmark	–	–	–	–	–	25%
Switzerland	–	–	–	–	43%	–

2. Proportion of wealth held by richest 5%

Country	1902–13	1920s	1930s	1950s	1960s	1970s
United States	–	–	–	–	–	43%
France	80%	65%	–	53%	–	45%
England and Wales	–	83%	77%	71%	56%	56%
West Germany	51%	–	–	–	–	–
Sweden	–	–	–	–	–	35%
Belgium	–	–	–	–	–	47%
Denmark	–	–	–	–	–	47%
Switzerland	–	–	–	–	63%	–

only 50 per cent in Britain, while coming to a halt at 35 per cent in Germany.[47] The remainder of the housing stock in Europe was distributed among private landlords, housing associations and local and national authorities. In any case, this means that ownership has been concentrated more heavily in the hands of the few than it has been in the United States.

Similarly, ownership of cars and individual life assurance has been more widespread in the United States. This is partly due to conditions in nineteenth- and early twentieth-century Europe, where transport and social security, like housing, was more the responsibility of public bodies. This is sometimes regarded as an ephemeral feature of Europe. It has been argued that European societies are now following the American course in the distribution of wealth, and that strong tendencies towards deconcentration of wealth in Europe are largely connected with the mounting significance of home ownership, life assurance and consumer durables, which will eventually lead to the more equal American situation. More recently, however, doubts have been raised about the decline of this European phenomenon.[48] Strong welfare state traditions in Europe might, in future, set limits to the spread of the ownership of homes, cars and private life assurance because public social security systems continue to administer a wider range of benefits than under the American system; we will return to this point.

A further consideration that emerges, when examining European wealth distribution, is that it is largely a matter of inequality between the fairly affluent. Statistics tend not to express economic differences between the haves and the have-nots, concentrating rather on differences between the haves. The term "ownership" has a variety of meanings, depending on the origin of the statistics. Savings and home ownership are usually included; but on the other hand many countries ignore life assurance and consumer durables such as cars. Lower earners, whose more advantageous position in Europe as regards income has just been examined, are largely excluded from studies of this aspect of economic inequality. More importantly, so far there is only evidence of a difference between Europe and America in the distribution of great fortunes. Twentieth-century America has only been shown to be more egalitarian where differences between the rich and the very rich are concerned. There is no current evidence that those of lesser means, for instance home owners or those with private life assurance or pensions, are in possession of a greater proportion of America's national private wealth.

Variation in life expectancy is a very different area where another feature of social inequality in European societies can be isolated. Because the sum of many social variables such as work and living conditions have a decisive impact on life expectancy, the statistics here are highly informative. Relationships are admittedly very complex and it is impossible simply to assume that better living conditions automatically lead to greater longevity. So many other factors play their part, for instance healthy or hazardous jobs and ways of life, general environmental conditions and the nature of the prevailing dominant causes of death. Despite this, variation in length of life is an important criterion for the assessment of overall social inequality.

In length of life, no specific European feature emerges. Average life expectancy has always differed quite clearly from one country to another, even among developed nations, and this is still true. The United States, Japan, Australia and Canada lie within the European life expectancy spectrum which, around 1975, showed lower and upper limits of 65 years in Portugal and 73 in Iceland respectively for males, and 73 years in Portugal and 79 in Iceland respectively for females.[49] However, in this respect, social inequality in Europe contrasts with the position in the United States. In America, variations in life expectancy have been far more pronounced than in Europe throughout the twentieth century. The advantage enjoyed by those in the administrative and liberal professions in America when compared with unskilled labour has always been far greater than in those European countries for which the relevant data are available— Great Britain, France, Austria and Denmark. In 1930 in the United States, the number of deaths among unskilled men of working age was almost twice that of males in the managerial classes, while in Britain, just as in France, the death rate among the unskilled was only slightly more than one and a half times as high, even before World War I. By 1930, the differentials had decreased even further in Great Britain. By 1950, when the death rate for unskilled men of working age in the United States was still 1.8 times the level of that for males in managerial classes, the figure for Great Britain had gone down to 1.2 times, which was about normal for other Western European countries (see Figure 3). The United States did participate in the trend towards a reduction in this kind of social inequality, but clearly lagged behind Europe right through until post-war years and possibly does so to this very day.[50] The causes of this phenomenon are not clear. There is only one thing which can be assumed with any certainty, and that is that the starkness of the inequality has a certain amount to do with the racial problems besetting American society. Around 1950 at least, black men were twice as likely as white men to die while still of working age. Because it was so common for black men to be unskilled, inequalities between types of employment were emphasized. However, the advantage enjoyed by white members of the managerial classes over white unskilled labour was far lower, and hardly differed from the situation in Europe at all. Similarly, the difference between blacks in the two groups was also lower.[51] Despite this, this very rough impression should be treated with caution; comparative research still has a long way to go in this field.

Overall then, despite reservations, there remains the impression that the notion of greater equality between rich and poor in Europe is not altogether false. Too little is known about conditions prior to World War I and in the inter-war period, so it cannot be stated with accuracy when Europe and the United States began to diverge. Nor can it be claimed that there is a peculiarly European state of affairs that obtains nowhere else in other developed countries. Above all, the survey of the distribution of income in Japan should be treated with caution. Our knowledge is, after all, largely confined to conditions in the heart of Western Europe where industrialization has been a feature of long standing. Who can say that inequality between rich and poor has not been completely differently structured on the western fringes of Europe, around the Mediterranean and Atlantic? In spite of this, at least in post-war years, the majority of Western Europeans seem to have been faced with fewer inequalities between rich and poor than the North Americans.

What of the other aspect of social inequality in Europe and North America? Is it true that Europeans have drawn more demarcation lines and erected more barriers than the Americans in their dealings with each other? Has reduced inequality in standards of living been balanced by a greater inequality in

Figure 3: Social variations in mortality rate in Europe
and the United States, 1900–60.

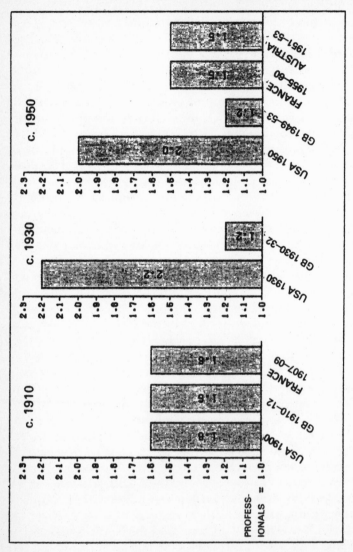

Graph compares mortality rate among those in the professional class
with the rate among unskilled workers. It shows the factor by which
mortality among the unskilled exceeded that of members of the professional class.

daily intercourse?

There can be no doubt that there is a strong tradition in European public and scientific opinion, endorsed by Alexis de Tocqueville in his observations on his numerous journeys through America:

> In the United States, even the richest citizens are very careful not to cut themselves off from the rest of the people; on the contrary, they continually seek their company, listen willingly and converse with them daily. They know that, in a democracy, the rich always need the poor, and that in a democratic age, the poor man is won over more by good manners than by charity. It is the scale of this charity which by its very nature highlights the disparities in living condition that causes hidden embarrassment among those whom it is intended to benefit; the simplicity of contact has an irresistible spell. Its familiarity is infectious.[52]

Likewise, in the twentieth century, it was widely, though not universally, considered that social contact was on a more equal footing in America. Admittedly, there is only meagre proof of the truth of this. We only have concrete indications of its correctness in three areas which confirm Tocqueville's observations, if not necessarily his conclusions. These are: the demarcation lines between white-collar and manual workers, one of the basic frontiers between the bourgeois world and the working class in the early twentieth century; in choice of marriage partners, one important measure of the "fine distinction"; and lastly, in impressions of social demarcation lines as experienced by European immigrants and visitors.

It is from comparative studies, especially those by Jürgen Kocka, that we derive our thorough knowledge of demarcation lines as they developed between white-collar and manual workers in Europe and America. Studying the first third of the twentieth century, Kocka compared social frontiers both inside and outside industrial concerns in the United States, France, Britain and Germany and, in doing so, encouraged others to undertake similar research. This was an important line drawn between the working and middle classes, though not the only one, and he concludes that in Europe it was indeed more strictly drawn than in the United States. Interestingly, he found little evidence that it was more strictly drawn in working environments in Europe or that it was connected with European working conditions. Kocka and Geoffrey Crossick discovered that the main differences between Europe and America lay in white-collar attitudes outside the working environment. In terms of clothing, trends in consumption, family life, the choice of residential areas and shops, the employment of servants and social contact, there were sharper divisions between the two groups in Europe than there were in America. The same was true of attitudes to "the boss", and social models followed by white-collar workers, such as the "gentleman" in Britain and the "official" in Germany. We may identify further differences in their attitudes to workers' political parties, their restraint in organizing along union lines in pre-World War I Britain, and the heavily anti-socialist attitudes among white-collar staff associations during the same period, at least in Germany. Also in Germany, state social and educational policies caused deep divisions that bolstered existing social boundaries rather than creating new ones.[53]

There can be no doubt that since the war, the lines drawn by European white-collar staff between themselves and the workers have been much less sharp than in the pre- and inter-war years.[54] Despite this, we should not jump to the conclusion that "fine distinctions" have vanished from European societies and brought them closer to the American example. Comparative studies of the post-war age are nowhere near as detailed or as sensitive as those conducted before the two world wars. White-collar workers are, in any case, a special group. In the course of the twentieth century, the great majority have made strides from being a component of the middle class to being a distinct employee group. There are probably other demarcation lines that have endured far longer in the post-war age in Europe where they remain sharper than in America, for instance those drawn by the commercial middle class, administrators, members of the managerial classes and officials, and the self-employed in manual trades and commerce.

A number of studies of the marriage market in the post-war era in Europe and the United States throw further light on the concept of the "fine distinction". It is quite obvious that in Europe the sections of society from which marriage partners were conventionally drawn were far more closed than they were in the United States. In Europe, daughters of families in the managerial classes were much less likely to marry into working families than in the United States. This is most evident in the case of marriages to skilled workers or craftsmen. Looking at marriages to unskilled workers, which were generally fewer in number, the sections of society in Europe were also narrower. Daughters of white-collar and public employees were far less likely to marry manual workers in Europe than in the United States. Once again, the less open European position is clear when the figures are split into marriages to skilled workers (which were quite common) and the rare cases of marriage to unskilled workers. In the United States, marriage between daughters of skilled workers and members from lower social groups provided the only example of segregation on a scale comparable with Europe. On the other side of the Atlantic, there were rather fewer marriages between daughters from the families of skilled workers and men from unskilled backgrounds. The chief cause of this is probably racial divisions in American society, because it was so common for unskilled labour to be black (see Figure 4). Even ignoring that point, choice of marriage partners also substantiates Tocqueville's observations as relevant to our post-war age, when American social divisions and barriers were less severe and fear of contact with lower social groups was less intense than in Europe.

European immigrants and visitors to the United States reported their recurrent experiences of the much more casual divisions.[55] Experience of the lower ends of European societies led to an appreciation of the greater social equality in daily contact. "It's better for us over here [in America]. Not only from the point of view of high wages and good living standards. But just think how differently we treat the boss. Is there a single one of us who so much as raises his hat to him? We wouldn't dream of it. We are just as good as he is, on the street, in the bars, everywhere. Nobody looks down on manual workers and they make no exceptions for the pen-pushers. And so they shouldn't!"[56] On the other hand, those from European middle class backgrounds sometimes found cause to lament, "I want society, not company."[57] The virtual absence of social inequality in personal contact in the United States was one of the experiences that made the greatest impression on immigrants and visitors from Europe in the nineteenth and twentieth centuries. In his widely read book *The American Commonwealth* (1888),

Figure 4: Marriage markets in Western Europe and United States, 1951–77.

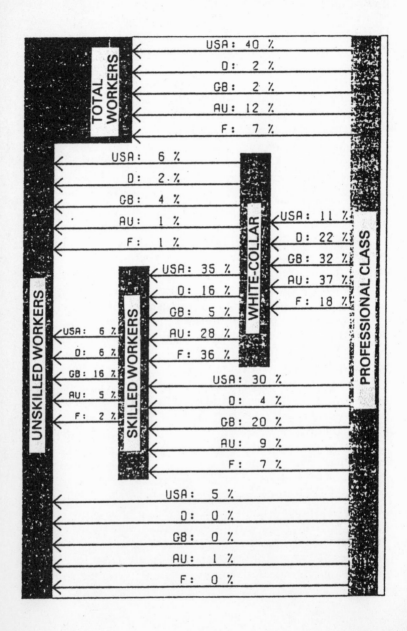

James Bryce gave a particularly vivid portrayal of the manifestations of social inequality in interpersonal contact in Europe and the very major differences from American social patterns. As he puts it:

> The second charm of American life is one which some Europeans will smile at. It is social equality. To many Europeans—to Germans, let us say, or Englishmen—the word has an odious sound. It suggests a dirty fellow in a blouse elbowing his betters in a crowd, or an ill-conditioned villager shaking his fist at the parson and the squire; or, at any rate, it suggests obtrusiveness and bad manners. The exact contrary is the truth [in America]. Equality improves manners ... it enlarges the circle of possible friendship by removing the inhibition which in most parts of Europe persons of different rank feel in exchanging their thoughts on any matters save those of business. It raises the humbler classes without lowering the upper; indeed, it improves the upper no less than the lower by expunging that latent insolence which deforms the manners of so many of the European rich or great. It relieves women in particular, who in Europe are especially apt to think of class distinctions, from that sense of constraint and uneasiness which is produced by the knowledge that other women with whom they come in contact are either looking down on them, or at any rate trying to gauge and determine their social position.[58]

Thus the impressions gained by contemporary Europeans, to which may be added any number of twentieth-century accounts, make it clear that while the new American society may have displayed more blatant social differences in living conditions, the European upper and middle classes established more severe and often more harmful social barriers to those they considered beneath them.

6. Quality of life in the European city

The modest rate of growth and better planning of cities in twentieth-century Europe has had an impact on European society, as has the improved quality of urban life. This feature is evident not only in comparisons with the United States, but also with other developed countries outside Europe and countries in the Third World. Any historical appraisal of the twentieth-century

European city benefits if one ignores the medieval and nineteenth-century roles of the city in establishing civil liberties, political activity, the origin of the middle classes and the labour movement, and upholding local political autonomy against the centralised state. These are the historical features of the European city that spring most readily to mind. Their effects would certainly have been felt well into the twentieth century, but in seeking a continuing world role for European cities, there is a tendency to overestimate their historical significance and at the same time to divert attention from other important features and past achievements.

Quality of life in European cities would certainly not have developed as it did had the rate of urban growth and the process of urbanisation matched the pace in other developed countries and the Third World. Nowhere was the rate of urban expansion so slow as in Western Europe. Of course, Western European towns grew too and direct observation of many of today's completely new cities and suburbs could provoke grave doubt about this argument, but the figures quite clearly demonstrate their modest growth. The number of city-dwellers in Europe barely doubled between the beginning of the century and 1970. By contrast, in the United States it grew fivefold; there was a sevenfold increase in Russia/the Soviet Union, while Canada saw a fivefold increase between 1900 and 1950, the Japanese figure growing sevenfold in the same period. Europe's figure was even outstripped by the threefold overall worldwide increase (see Figure 5).[59] Comparing non-European cities with those European cities that escaped war devastation, the difference can clearly be seen in the proportion of new buildings.

European cities grew at a slower rate, partly because European societies did not themselves experience the dramatic population growth that occurred in migrant countries such as the United States, Australia and Canada. But even taking account of this and comparing urbanisation in plain terms, i.e. in terms of the urban population as a proportion of the total, Europe's slow progress is still apparent when compared to developed non-European countries. In Europe in 1900 the urban population represented 41 per cent of the total and by 1970 the figure had grown to 64 per cent. The figures for the United States were 40 per cent in 1900 and 74 per cent in 1970; Russia/the Soviet Union in the same period experienced a

Figure 5: Urban growth in Western Europe, North America, Japan, Australia and the USSR. **1920–60**

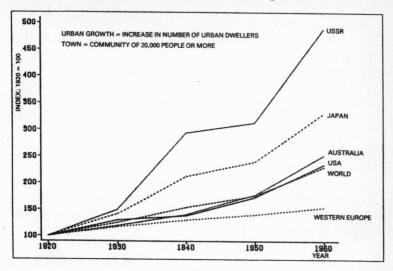

growth of from 16 per cent to 54 per cent. Between 1900 and 1960 in Canada, growth was from 37 per cent to 64 per cent, while the Japanese proportion increased from 14 per cent to 54 per cent between 1900 and 1950.[60] Most surprising is the sharp difference between Europe and Japan, a very old society and by no means a sparsely populated country.

There is no doubt that the overall figures conceal wide intra-European variations. In peripheral European countries such as Spain, Greece and Scandinavia the urban population grew particularly fast by European standards, in some cases even more rapidly than in the United States. The pace of urbanisation in those countries was also exceptionally high for Europe and approached the American rate. Admittedly, this is a somewhat lopsided comparison because the extent of urbanisation in the countries concerned at the turn of the century was very small and they were simply in the process of catching up. Naturally, it makes more sense to compare countries that share a common starting point. Contrasting America with European nations at a similar stage of expansion at the turn of the century, the European march appears considerably less hurried. Comparing the rapid expansion rates of Japan and the Soviet Union with those

European countries where urbanisation was equally unadvanced in 1900, development on the European periphery now seems far less dramatic. It can thus be claimed that, despite considerable variation within its frontiers, Europe has indeed been characterized by a more modest rate of urban growth and urbanization.[61]

One of the causes is surely that in Europe as a whole in the early twentieth century, the process of urbanization was at a considerably more advanced stage than almost anywhere else. Only North America could claim to be further ahead. Long established industrialized European countries such as Great Britain, Belgium and the Netherlands had become urbanised on a scale hitherto unseen anywhere in the world. By 1920, the most prodigious thrust of urbanisation was over in practically all of Western Europe, and several countries had even reached the upper limit of their expansion. For Western Europe as a whole, then, the age under scrutiny here is the age of advanced or even completed urbanisation. Taking a world view, even between 1850 and 1914 when Europe's cities were burgeoning, it progressed at its own stately pace. It was a remarkable time for Europe but even so, the growth of its cities and the rate of urbanisation was more subdued than in non-European countries where the process generally occurred later.[62]

The scale of the European city is another facet of urban development in Europe that was equally important in determining the quality of city life in the twentieth century. We will deal with this in some detail. The medium-sized town of between 20,000 and 100,000 inhabitants played a more significant and more enduring role in twentieth-century Europe than elsewhere. About a third of the urban population of Europe lived in towns like Cambridge, Aarhus, Lund, Delft, Liège, Tübingen, Aix-en-Provence and Ravenna. Especially in the post-war age, the figure for American and Australian towns of comparable size was lower, as it was in Japan and Canada. In the Soviet Union early this century, the urban population of medium-sized towns actually exceeded the European level. As the twentieth century wore on, however, and as far as the statistics are comparable, the Soviet cities lost a great deal of their significance as centres of population (see Figure 6). The enduring vitality of this type and scale of town is typical of Western European societies.

Figure 6: Importance of the medium-sized town in Western
Europe, North America, Japan, Australia and the USSR, 1920–60

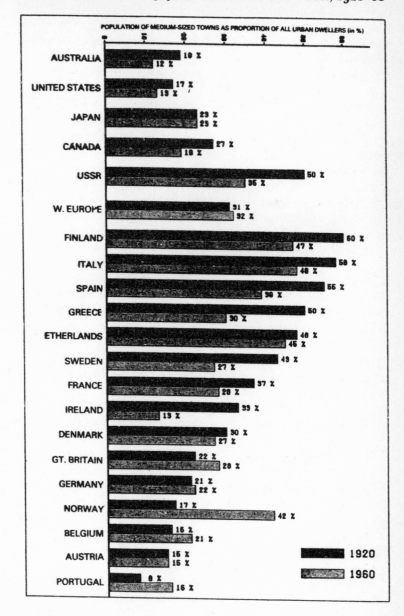

POPULATION OF MEDIUM-SIZED TOWNS AS PROPORTION OF ALL URBAN DWELLERS (in %)

AUSTRALIA — 19 %, 12 %
UNITED STATES — 17 %, 15 %
JAPAN — 23 %, 23 %
CANADA — 27 %, 18 %
USSR — 50 %, 35 %
W. EUROPE — 31 %, 32 %
FINLAND — 60 %, 47 %
ITALY — 58 %, 48 %
SPAIN — 55 %, 59 %
GREECE — 50 %, 30 %
ETHERLANDS — 48 %, 45 %
SWEDEN — 49 %, 27 %
FRANCE — 37 %, 28 %
IRELAND — 33 %, 19 %
DENMARK — 30 %, 27 %
GT. BRITAIN — 22 %, 28 %
GERMANY — 21 %, 22 %
NORWAY — 17 %, 42 %
BELGIUM — 16 %, 21 %
AUSTRIA — 15 %, 15 %
PORTUGAL — 8 %, 16 %

■ 1920
▨ 1960

This stands in direct contrast to the development of the role of the great metropolis. We have no simple, internationally comparable statistics to hand for cities of one million and more inhabitants. According to those available, in the early twentieth century such cities housed a smaller percentage of the total urban population in Europe than they did in Japan or America. Around 1920, the figure for Europe was about a third, for the United States about two-fifths, while for Japan it was as high as a half. During the twentieth century, the courses followed by developed countries in and outside Europe have diverged even further. In some non-European countries, the cities of a million or more attracted a rapidly growing proportion of the population. Whereas there had been no such cities in either Canada or Australia around 1920, by 1960 about 40 per cent of the Canadian population was living in Montreal and Toronto, and in the same year the proportion of Australians in Melbourne and Sydney was around 60 per cent. Both figures far exceed European numbers, even though the comparison should not be taken too far with countries that are so much smaller. In the Soviet Union, the populations of cities of one million inhabitants or more increased very rapidly by contrast with Europe, even though such cities never attained the significance that they had in western societies (see Figure 5). In other non-European countries, the growth rate of the major cities was less prodigious, but their power of attraction throughout the twentieth century has been much greater than in Europe, and has even continued to increase slightly. In both Japan and the United States, the number of big city dwellers rose steadily between 1920 and 1960, by which time it accounted for more than a half of the total urban population. Compared with other western countries, the attraction of Europe's big cities was quite modest and developed in a different direction. There was little growth in the number of big city dwellers as a proportion of the total urban population, the figure remaining static at around one-third. The cities of several million inhabitants actually lost some ground. Parisians, Londoners and, for political reasons, Berliners came to represent a smaller fraction of the urban population of their respective countries.[63]

The development of great cities in the rest of the world throws this European feature into relief. At the beginning of the present century, when Europe was gradually relinquishing its

Table 7: Cities of Europe among the twenty largest cities in the world, 1910–2000 (population in millions)

1910		1950		1980		2000 (estimated)	
New York	4.8	New York	12.8	Mexico City	15.0	Mexico City	31.0
London	4.5	*London*	8.4	Cairo	14.2	São Paolo	25.8
Berlin	3.7	*Moscow*	5.6	São Paolo	12.6	Shanghai	23.7
Paris	2.9	Tokyo	5.4	Shanghai	11.9	Tokyo	
Tokyo	2.2	*Paris*	5.0	Buenos Aires	10.8	Yokohama	23.1
Chicago	2.2	Shanghai	4.6	Calcutta	9.2	New York	22.4
Vienna	2.0	Bombay	4.0	Peking	9.2	Peking	20.9
St Petersburg	1.9	Chicago	3.6	New York	9.1	Rio de Janeiro	19.0
Moscow	1.5	Buenos Aires	3.0	Rio de Janeiro	9.0	Bombay	16.8
Philadelphia	1.3	*Leningrad*	3.0	*Paris*	8.5	Calcutta	16.4
Buenos Aires	1.2	Calcutta	3.0	Seoul	8.4	Djakarta	15.7
Osaka	1.0	Rio de Janeiro	2.4	Tokyo	8.3	Los Angeles	13.9
Bombay	1.0	São Paolo	2.2	*Moscow*	8.3	Seoul	13.7
Hamburg	0.9	*West Berlin*	2.1	Bombay	8.2	Cairo	2.9
Canton	0.9	Mexico City	2.1	Tientsin	7.8	Madras	12.7
Budapest	0.9	Cairo	2.1	Los Angeles	7.5	Buenos Aires	12.7
Calcutta	0.9	Philadelphia	2.1	Chicago	7.1	Karachi	11.6
Warsaw	0.9	Hongkong	2.1	*London*	6.7	Delhi	11.5
Rio de Janeiro	0.9	Los Angeles	2.0	Djakarta	6.5	Manila	11.4
Birmingham	0.8	Osaka	2.0	Teheran	6.0	Teheran	11.1
						Bagdad	11.0

Proportion of European cities

50%	20%	15%	0%

position as a world leader in urbanisation, Europe could still claim to contain half of the world's twenty largest cities. In addition to London, Paris and Berlin there were Vienna, Warsaw, Budapest, Birmingham and Hamburg. In due course, more and more European metropolises vanished from the list of super-cities, until today that list is dominated by cities in America and Asia. According to all predictions, by the end of the century not a single European city will remain on it (see Table 7).

The characteristic European development in the scale of

cities even seems to have continued, despite the reversal of the worldwide trend in urban growth and the decline of large conurbations in the recent past. In most developed western countries, areas of heavy urban concentration reached the upper limits of their expansion in the 1970s. The growth of large conglomerations, both at their centres as well as in their suburbs and satellite towns, and even in their hinterland, has been slower than that of their populations, which in some cases have even decreased. Rural areas and small towns became the new centres of dynamic growth. The shift in the employment structure, with the rise of the service sector and the slump in industrial employment, is viewed as the most important cause for the decline of the urban sprawl. It is indeed the traditional urban industrial centres that have been hardest hit by this decline. In the United States, it has affected the industrial belt which spreads over the whole of the north-east from New England to Chicago, while in Europe it has been felt from the Ruhr, through southern Belgium, into northern France and on into the English Midlands.[64]

The modest pace of other features of European urban development is reflected in the rate at which the great conurbations have lost their power of attraction. It appears that in certain respects, the relative or absolute decline of conurbations in Europe went ahead at a more subdued pace than elsewhere. While the signs of this rundown were already being keenly felt in the United States in the early 1970s, in Western Europe the first signs of the same process only really appeared in the second half of the 1980s. Prior to that, growth in the European conglomerations was still continuing. It might also be true that even in the latter half of the 1970s, developments were less dramatic in Europe than they were in the United States. It has been demonstrated by Paul Cheshire and Peter Hay that besides those conglomerations that suffered population losses, there were as many others that continued growing and as many again where the losses were exclusively from the inner cities but where the suburbs and hinterland expanded further. In the latter half of the 1970s, the decline of Europe's urban centres was thus highly ambivalent and was by no means apparent in all conurbations. It is interesting that this process had very little impact on medium-sized towns and that, if anything, their peculiar power of attraction intensified.[65]

Little thought has been given hitherto to the causes of the subdued pace of European "de-urbanisation", to use the specialists' rather emphatic term. However, one main cause could lie in the rate at which industrial employment, and therefore the European industrial city, lost its significance. As has already been shown, even in the 1970s there were considerably more wage-earners in industry in Europe than there were in developed countries in the rest of the world. For this reason, European industrialized cities did not participate in the accelerated decline seen elsewhere.

When reflecting on the size of cities, it may seem rash at first sight to lump all Western European countries together, not least because of varying national definitions of the term "town". This is certainly true for the great mass of medium-sized towns (those with between 20,000 and 100,000 inhabitants) in Europe. In the early twentieth century, quite large inner European variations were indeed apparent. In some European societies such as Germany, Belgium and Austria the total of urban dwellers in such towns was no greater than in "new" societies like the United States, Canada or Australia. Even then, however, in most European nations, the proportion of the urban population concentrated in towns of this magnitude was far higher than in other regions around the globe. Especially in countries such as Italy, Spain, Sweden and the Netherlands where industrialization was then a recent phenomenon, medium-sized towns housed anything from a third to a half of all urban dwellers. Outside Europe, this was unheard of. It should be borne in mind that the history of the European town stretches right back to the Roman era when many of today's towns were founded. However, as the twentieth century wore on, variations within Europe decreased considerably and, at the same time, European societies diverged increasingly from those of other developed countries. By 1960, only a few of the countries of Europe, and small ones at that, had such low population concentrations in their medium-sized towns that they were comparable with the United States, Canada or Australia. Only the old societies of Japan and the Soviet Union were placed on the outer fringes of the Western European spectrum. In the majority of European societies, chiefly in the larger countries such as France, Great Britain, Spain, West Germany and the Netherlands, such towns were of greater importance than in any developed country outside Europe (see Figure 6). The vitality of the medium-sized town in Europe became more and more a common European pattern.[66]

There are greater doubts about common European patterns in cities of one million or more inhabitants. Inner European variations were very large indeed, and remain so, not least because methods of enumeration vary from one country to another. Those acute contrasts that exist between small European countries are perhaps not of such great importance. On the one hand, there are those that have had no such cities right up to their very recent past, for instance, Sweden, Ireland, Switzerland, Norway and Finland. This state of affairs is largely conditioned by definitions specific to the individual countries. If we were to stipulate conurbations rather than municipalities as the standard, then the populations of Zurich, Stockholm and Dublin would certainly number over one million. On the other hand, in a range of other small countries, large urban centres exercise enormous powers of attraction and contain the majority of the country's overall population. Austria, Denmark, Greece and Portugal have all historically had cities of this nature. Admittedly, it may be argued that these small countries are more comparable to certain individual states of the United States or republics of the Soviet Union, and that similar contrasts may be observed within the United States and the USSR. It would naturally be quite unrealistic to expect that in a civilization such as that of Europe, with its range of countries of varying sizes, there could be a uniform proportion of the population living in the big cities of all the smaller countries.

Variations between the larger European countries should be looked at more critically. Here again, there are clearly contrasting cases. In the large countries around the Mediterranean, very few people have lived in big cities. Even in France, the figure has not exceeded one-third, compared with a quarter in Spain and as little as one-fifth in Italy. This may be due partly to strict geographical definitions of the city, but this cannot be the full explanation. By contrast, further north in Great Britain and the Netherlands, cities of over one million in population have been comparable only with those in western countries outside Europe in terms of their size. As early as 1920, half the total urban population of Great Britain lived in cities of this magnitude, a figure that has remained virtually static, though showing a slight downward trend.[67] Variations in the development of population centres have surely conditioned this aspect of the European city, variations that are discernible in individual states of the United States and republics of the USSR and which are quite "normal" for the whole of civilization. Besides this, throughout the twentieth century, big cities in the larger European countries grew more and more similar in terms of their importance; this subject will be addressed again later in this book. Thus, in the course of time Europe also became increasingly differentiated from other continents in terms of the size of its cities.

Overall, the rate of urban growth in Europe and the vitality of the medium-sized towns created positive conditions for the quality of European urban life. Housing, the infrastructure and services were better able to keep pace with urban growth in Europe than they were elsewhere, though individual newcomers still experienced difficulties in adjusting to the urban way of life. However, because fewer people were affected by urbanisation in Europe, such problems rarely assumed the proportions that they did elsewhere, where entire societies could experience crises in adjusting to new ways of life. Municipal authorities in twentieth-century Europe have not been as hopelessly at the mercy of the urban explosions occurring in other countries. Rather, they have been able to shape the course of development and orchestrate the process more actively. In Europe, the medium-sized town has been more prevalent; it is easier to control and simpler to administer. Thus towns in Europe were closer to the town planner's optimum size for quality of life.[68] Admittedly, the outlook has not been all rosy. During their rapid expansion in the late nineteenth century, European cities also went through a deep crisis with all the signs of over-accelerated growth, such as the breakdown of housing provision, an increase in slum properties, a burgeoning crime rate, the reduction of life expectancy among urban dwellers compared with the rural population, and increasing impotence and lack of direction in the municipality. With the twentieth century came a period of deceleration in growth which favoured European cities rather than those elsewhere because it allowed time for the lessons learnt during years of crisis to be applied more easily and more quickly in the form of practical initiatives.

Together, these form the third distinctive feature of the twentieth-century European city, besides its typical size and rate of growth as discussed above.

Compared with the United States and Third World countries in the twentieth century, public bodies in Europe have been far more influential and exercised greater determining powers in the spatial development of cities. This is due to the kind of state intervention that has typified other areas of European society and is thus by no means limited to this sphere. In dealing with spatial development of cities, however, governments in Europe have generally restricted themselves to laying down administrative structures, with local authorities being responsible for the detailed decisions. This has been a crucial role for municipal administrations in Europe, based on a range of varied customs whose origins lie in the tradition of urban administrative planning which went further back even than the formal Baroque city, to the time of the apparently organic growth of medieval and Roman towns. The thread ran right through the history of the European city, even though in most cases it could not strictly be termed municipal planning. It was also based on the vitality of urban administrations in Europe which had grown out of a quite different need. During the late Middle Ages and early modern times their function had been to provide for the poor, but they were now extending their competence. Lastly, there was the European tradition of public ownership of land and the restrictions placed by public bodies on the private ownership of land and property. In the United States at least, private ownership of land was subject to less interference and far fewer limitations.

Building on these traditions, urban authorities in post-war Europe had more effective powers of decision-making in town planning at their disposal than their American counterparts. Besides this, they also had a greater degree of autonomy, making them less answerable to central government and the interests of builders and developers, as well as home owners and tenants. In a whole range of other areas they also had more say than American authorities. They had greater legal powers in the siting of extensions to towns under their control, road layout, the conservation of green spaces, transport routing and in land use for housing, commercial, service and recreational purposes, as well as in determining architectural principles for new buildings and the conservation of historic buildings and districts. The construction of whole new districts and towns was also more closely controlled by public bodies than in America. Naturally, American cities also developed construction plans and building guidelines of their own but by contrast with the situation in Europe, it was possible for the private sector to cause amendments or waivers to be made much more easily. Besides this, municipal authorities in Europe were more active in intervention in the property market. It was not simply a case of less widespread acceptance of private property ownership in European societies. Municipal authorities bought huge direct stakes in land which they then rented or resold. The effect of this has been to quell land speculation and reduce the strictures imposed on town planning by land prices. The practice also put a brake on wastage of land which was a far greater threat in the densely-populated countries of Europe than it was in the United States. Finally, European central administrations were far more likely to undertake large-scale planning, particularly in big cities such as Paris, London and Stockholm, that transcended municipal boundaries and directed the planning of transport, industrial location, leisure facilities and new towns at regional level.[69]

Once again, there were great differences to be observed between individual European countries. In the main, however, the post-war powers enjoyed by municipal authorities in Europe had gained ground only gradually over the course of the twentieth century. One aspect highlighted by Anthony Sutcliffe in a comparative study of town planning before 1914 in France, Great Britain, Germany and the United States, was the presence of very advanced ideas in town planning, particularly in Great Britain and Germany, even though conversion to the practice of controlled urban development remained far from complete. In practice, town planning rarely extended beyond building regulations and development schemes.[70] The inter-war years, and a second burst of activity in the post-war era, saw the growth of town planning and development planning that we know today.[71]

Has the more modest rate of urban growth and more intensive planning by municipal bodies resulted in an improved quality of life in the cities of Europe? It may come as a surprise but there are few precise and concrete studies comparing

European cities with the rest of the world in terms of provision of services, quality of housing, protection from crime and life expectancy. We nevertheless have a number of indications that the quality of life in the cities of Europe has been superior.

First, the inner cities of Europe offer considerably higher standards. The impoverished, slum-ridden, and even derelict inner cities so typical of medium and larger post-war cities in America are much less common in Europe, where by complete contrast, the inner cities are frequently preferred as residential areas, and have flourishing shopping, cultural and recreational centres. The refinement of the inner cities of Europe is another feature that is rarely as strong in non-European countries. In revitalizing their city centres, the municipal authorities in Europe have been far more cautious, conserving historic sites, laying out pedestrian precincts and exercising greater restraint in driving highways through city centres, all of which has preserved their habitability and refinement much more than in the United States. It is quite likely that the attitude of Europeans to life in the city has also had an effect; they are less readily abandoned and there is greater readiness to live in towns. This is another European tradition of long standing, one that gradually extended northwards from the Mediterranean. Even the relative wealth of the rich and poor in Europe as discussed above has had an impact on the inner cities.

Secondly, there are signs that by contrast with the United States, life expectancy in urban areas of Europe has been no shorter than in the country. Since World War II at least, despite the romanticising of the rural way of life as healthier and more pleasant, average lifespan has often been as long or longer in the city than in the country. Our information covers a whole range of European nations. Even before World War I in Prussia, urban death rates were beginning to converge with those of rural areas. In West Germany, the cities lost no ground to the countryside. In strictly agrarian villages, life expectancy was even shorter than in the city. Urban dwellers in Sweden in the inter-war years lived as long as those in the country, and the same was true of post-war France, where no one had a greater life expectancy than the Parisians. In Switzerland, Finland, Ireland, Iceland and Luxembourg death rates have been lower in the cities than in the countryside since 1970, and by 1980 this group had been joined by Norway. The only countries where urban deaths remained in excess of rural ones were Great Britain, the Netherlands and Denmark.[72] Overall in Western Europe though, life expectancy in the cities appears to have been as great and sometimes even greater than in the country. In the United States the opposite has been the case. Even after World War II, death came at a lower age in the conurbations than it did in the countryside. Even infant mortality was higher in towns. The United States was similar to other developed countries in that its cities gained in life-enhancing qualities, but the old disadvantages remained to a far greater extent than they did in Europe.[73] Of course most of these town-country variations have very complex causes. They lie not only in different types of living conditions, but often also in other ways of life and differing age and social patterns. However, as indicators of Europe's lead in the quality of urban life they are worthy of study.

A more definite aspect of the superior quality of life in European cities is the level of criminality. Here again, precise comparative historical research is very rare, but it does appear that since World War II, criminality in the great cities of Europe has been well below the levels found in America. In 1970, the rate of serious crime against the person (per 100,000 inhabitants) stood at 540 for Los Angeles and 816 for Baltimore, two badly affected cities, whereas for the fifty-six largest American cities the overall average figure was 352. By comparison, the rate for London was as low as 124, and even in a badly affected city like Stockholm it did not exceed 403. Comparisons of the crime rates for 1970 between the cities of Portland and Denver in the United States, and Zurich and Stuttgart show that for a very wide range of crimes, criminality in Europe is far lower. Thus overall, life in European cities has been very different from life in American ones. Very little is known of the origins of this dichotomy or why it has always been so wide. However, life in European cities has been considerably less stressful because of the reduced threat and fear of crime.[74]

There can be no doubt that overall, the cities of twentieth-century Europe have had their problems. They also embodied threats to the quality of life. Municipal authorities often learned slowly and only through making major errors. But compared with many centres of population outside Europe, city-dwellers often led longer, better and more pleasant lives. It would be over-hasty to ascribe the superiority of city life in Europe simply to more competent urban authorities, or to city-dwellers' attitudes to the solution of the problems of their environment. Certainly, European cities have also profited greatly from the abatement in the dynamism with which they grew, frequently also from their manageability, and the consequent alleviation of crises with which they were faced. This may also have decreased the amount of suffering caused by European city life as compared with elsewhere.

7. The welfare state in Europe

Europe has been the true bastion of the modern welfare state throughout the twentieth century. Nowhere else did it grow to such proportions, nowhere else was it imbued with such vigour. Even at times of crisis, the opinions of European and overseas critics were often divided.

The prehistory of the modern welfare state can be traced back furthest in Europe. The first state systems of social security were established in the 1880s in Germany, Austria and Hungary to cover industrial accident, sickness benefits and pensions. More systems soon followed in other European countries, arising in varying forms from their different political situations. Nowhere else in the world could rival Europe where, by the outbreak of World War I, nearly all countries were equipped with the necessary basic legislation for state-run or state-supervised social security covering the three classic welfare areas named above.[75] The capacity of early forms of social security in Europe must not be exaggerated. Even in Germany, where the state system was relatively highly developed, its achievements prior to 1914 were far removed from the expectations of the post-1945 welfare state. In particular, it was anticipated that the family would provide for its elderly members. Thus the retirement allowance was intended merely as a family supplement despite the fact that, as has been seen, the family rarely took such responsibility in Europe. Pensions were not payable until the age of seventy, when many had long been incapable of continuing work, had fallen into poverty or were even dead. Health insurance covered doctors' fees, medication and hospitalization costs, but provided very little sick pay and therefore was insufficient to alleviate a family's need when income was lost through sickness. Before 1914, unemployment

European range. It appears unlikely that the present financial crisis in the welfare systems of Europe will cause erosion of Europe's advantage, or that this will be reversed to put Europe behind the rest of the world.[79]

The history of the welfare state in Europe must also be regarded as a special case because as a model and example, European social security systems had a special aura which radiated outwards. Non-European models and ideas were acknowledged by Europeans in their criticisms at the very most, but never in the way they organized their own welfare states. It was not an overall European system that served as the example to others, but rather the systems of individual European countries. Before 1914, the German model set the standard, not only in Northern Europe but also overseas. It is most interesting to note the elements of that model that continued to have an effect and those that were filtered out. A detailed appraisal is out of place here, but it does not appear to be Bismarck's carrot and stick approach that served as the model. In fear of a rising labour movement, the conservative head of government introduced national insurance as a buffer to limit workers' contact with socialist ideas and combined the measure with massive political repression against workers' organizations. The peculiar situation obtaining in Germany was not widely repeated in Europe. In Austria-Hungary and in Sweden, the more liberal politicians committed to reform took the German model as their basis, though with quite different political calculations in mind. Their idea, more often discussed than practised, was for state-administered compulsory insurance, huge by the standards of its day and apparently with great powers, which would replace the small, voluntary, mostly local and not always very efficient systems of non-state insurance. In Germany, the so-called *Kathedersozialisten* or academic socialists introduced this concept to the debate, which may be seen as the academics' contribution to the launch of workers' insurance in Germany. It seems that the effectiveness of the German model consisted in the fact that these were modern ideas advocated by middle-class social reformers, rather than a conservative power political reaction to a labour movement.[80] The academic socialists in their turn took as their starting point a broader debate that was not restricted to the Germany of the time, concerning mutual societies and private insurance. Through their solution to the debate they achieved the political conditions for a state system in Germany and, via the German system, had an impact on the discussion within Europe and overseas.[81]

After 1945, it was chiefly the British welfare state and the principles of Sir William Beveridge that served as a beacon for uniform development of the modern welfare state. The Beveridge plan was also regarded as a model system by the rest of Europe. Beveridge's reform plan had its origins in the situation of British society during World War II. It therefore comes as no surprise that the details of the British system are not widely imitated. The principles that stuck were those of insurance for all, a guaranteed minimum for subsistence, the right to benefits and equality in the eyes of the welfare state. Beveridge's ideas are founded on the broader European debate and combine general European proposals of the time. If it was the German and British models that had the greatest overall effect overseas, they were still firmly rooted in the debates in progress throughout Europe and their proposed solutions.

The impression is that in Europe there was a different range of available alternatives to the welfare state. These signalled themselves particularly during the phase when modern social security was getting established, but in periods of crisis in the welfare state they would reappear regularly in the public debate. The options were not primarily individual and neighbourly self-help as in the United States; nor primarily benefits provided by large firms or the family as in Japan; nor the incorporation of the state social security system into the umbrella state administration, which was used as a means of exerting pressure on political dissidents as in the Soviet Union. European alternatives were the non-bureaucratic, non-state administered, voluntary bodies that were often controlled and even administered by their members. Next to profit-orientated private insurance that also existed in other western countries this was the most important concept in opposition to state systems in Europe where it had a long tradition, especially in the guild movement. In the years before 1914, when European social security systems were just getting off the ground, this was a strong and effective alternative. It is estimated that during the Second Empire, the *sociétés de secours mutuels* and the *mutualités* in France insured about 800,000 workers. The numbers contributing to British friendly societies in the 1870s are put at well over a million, while the Swiss figure is around 45,000, which means that about 50 per cent of all workers were insured against personal risk. Thousands of similar societies existed during the same period in Germany.[82] The political strength of these alternatives should not be exaggerated and their technical weaknesses should certainly not be overlooked. Voluntary societies were frequently too small and therefore did not distribute the risk thinly enough. They were socially exclusive and often did not accept members from the ranks of the unskilled who would have been especially needy. The pressures on them in some areas were too great, particularly from unemployment, pensions and sometimes even epidemics. Despite this, they remained a popular and a very viable alternative in the view of European liberals and socialists. State systems incorporated a number of the features of the independent societies in order to integrate them, as well as appearing more politically acceptable themselves. There is evidence of this in trends towards cooperative administration involving insured parties, simple state funding and supervision of societies and other cooperative bodies, as well as the combination of basic state insurance provision with additional private insurance. The alternatives to state systems are still with us in today's political arguments in Europe. Political movements opposed to further expansion of the social bureaucracy in Western Europe find a natural political rallying point in these alternatives.

A number of events in the history of social security and the welfare state have brought about this specifically European situation. Several of the distinctly European features discussed earlier certainly played a crucial role here. A heavy demand for social security was created by the way in which the European family developed, a factor that has already been mentioned. It is linked to the extent of the small European family unit in which it was comparatively unusual for the elderly, relatives or unmarried offspring who could have given assistance as individual needs arose, to be included in the household. However, it is also connected with the late age at which Europeans married which left a larger section of the young adult population without strong family ties or assistance. Finally, it was conditioned by the relatively high proportion of people in Europe who never married. Consequently, when young adults and, above all, the elderly in Europe faced emergencies, they were forced to resort to public welfare agencies and social assistance more often than anywhere else. This is not to say that family support for these groups was totally lacking in Europe; nevertheless, demand on public institutions was greater.

Intensive employment in European industry also made social security appear more necessary than elsewhere. The presence of concentrated hordes of industrial workers in great factories and industrial centres engendered more fear than the scattered rural underclass or the traditional urban poor. Not only were industrial workers swarming into rapidly expanding cities; they also assumed a more dangerous image, because in large enterprises they were better able to disrupt economic development and better equipped to organize than the poor had ever been before. This is indicated by the fact that social security systems in Europe frequently started life as insurance schemes for industrial labour, even though such workers were by no means the poorest in the societies of their day. Industrial employment patterns in Europe were not merely a source of greater fear than they were elsewhere. As industry and its attendant urban expansion progressed on such a vast scale, it could be that Europeans were more directly confronted by the revolution that industrialization represented. Novel and unusual forms of industrial poverty probably got under the skin of the reformers of the day and made a greater impression than remote rural poverty, or other less public forms of poverty in small urban businesses or the service sector. It is highly doubtful if Friedrich Engels' classic work of social criticism on the condition of the working class in England would have been such a success if he had concentrated his attention on domestic servants, dockers, the rural underclass or the urban poor, instead of workers in industry. This may have caused European reformers to be more ready to accept the break that social security represented, both for the wider public consciousness and for their own. It may have been that the scale of industrial employment in Europe provoked more than just a greater amount of fear and pity than was felt elsewhere. The establishment of a large social bureaucracy was eased by the uniformity of working conditions experienced by industrial labour. The lives of industrial workers were easier to standardize and administer than those of traditional underclasses, who would take on temporary jobs here and there, sometimes had their own small businesses, perhaps owned a little land or were simply very mobile, with lives that were too erratic for an organized system to handle. The establishment of a bureaucracy to regulate social security seemed a more promising solution for industrial workers.

An established tradition of public social security was a further feature of Europe that was stronger than elsewhere. Since the late Middle Ages, the development of networks for poor relief in Europe by urban authorities, churches and foundations has been more intensive than anywhere else. Doubtless it is their negative aspects that spring most readily to mind when they are compared with modern systems of social security. Those in receipt of benefits from such traditional sources had to submit to controls so strict they would never be accepted today. Not only could they suspend citizens' rights, they also interfered more mercilessly in private matters than today's bureaucracies and recognized no legal entitlement to their assistance. Generally speaking, they were not state-run either.[83] Nevertheless, traditional poor relief gave European development a crucial headstart. Europeans adapted more quickly to the notion that welfare was also a task for public bodies and was not simply up to the individual, or to be expected from clans, patrons, feudal lords or masters. In the embryonic stages of modern social security before 1914, public welfare had already been a fixture in European societies for several hundred years. Thus in Europe, the step up to a state system was substantially smaller than anywhere else.

Finally, the strength of the European labour movement, which will be examined later, intensified the work of establishing the welfare state. Before 1914, when state systems were getting under way, considerable tensions certainly existed between the labour movement and some governments on aspects of social policy. Since the inter-war years at the latest, establishment of social security has become a central political goal for the European labour movement, which has switched its attention to the establishment of the welfare state after World War II. In developed countries outside Europe, the amount of political momentum generated was smaller. In the United States, a workers' party played only a temporary supporting role, and never rose to become a force at federal level. Japan and Canada had workers' parties of their own, but they remained weaker than those in Europe. Politically, the labour movement only generated a "European" style dynamism in Australia. This may be connected with that country's early introduction of social security and a welfare state on a European scale.

8. Labour relations in Europe

The history of labour relations, a distinctive feature of Europe, is the least well defined of all those under discussion here. Variations were far greater than in other features examined above.[84] The peculiarities of industrial relations in Europe therefore remain largely obscure and may be widely disputed. Even so, compared with the picture in most other western countries, union history in Europe appears more dramatic and eventful; there were more members, the interrelation between labour relations and politics was closer and the character of strikes was considerably different. Each of these aspects will come in for more detailed examination.

Compared with the rest of the world, industrial relations in Europe have been affected by more turbulent union history. In Europe, there has been much greater fluctuation in membership strength, supposedly one of the most crucial foundations of union power in industrial relations. In Europe, phases of far more dramatic growth than anywhere else have contrasted with periods of deeper crisis. Development of European union organization may be divided into three phases (see Table 8). The first phase, between the founding of the first unions and the period immediately after World War I, saw steady and uninterrupted growth in membership, and apparently irresistible advances in organization. In this phase, the rate of growth of European unions was almost unparalleled. Europe was in the forefront of the international union movement. In Western Europe overall around 1920, more than one-third of all wage-earners were unionized, far more than in the United States, Japan or Canada. Only the Australian union movement could boast similar success. About that time, many countries in Europe reached the peak of their unionization. In some European countries such as Great Britain, Belgium and Germany, similar levels were never reached again for several decades, if at all (see Table 8).

In the second phase, from the early 1920s until the outbreak of World War II, the European union movement was itself in a

Table 8: Degree of unionisation in Western Europe, United States, Japan, Canada and Australia 1900–80

	1900	'10	'20	'30	'40	'50	'60	'70	'80
Belgium	..	5	41	28	39	51	60	65	80
Denmark	13	15	35	32	42	52	60	63	69
Germany (Federal Republic 1950–)	5	18	53	34	–	33	37	36	38
Finland	..	..	21	12	8	32	27	58	86
France	5	8	14	15	13	31	..	31	32
Greece	..	..	..	..	..	..	..	–	..
Great Britain	13	15	45	25	33	44	44	49	53
Ireland	*	*	..	..	..	..	..	53	59
Italy	..	3	22	–	–	72	41	45	62
Netherlands	..	13	30	25	..	44	42	..	39
Norway	3	8	20	18	34	51	62	62	59
Austria	3	7	59	47	–	67	66	63	60
Portugal	..	..	..	..	–	–	–	–	40
Sweden	5	8	28	36	54	68	73	80	93
Switzerland	2	9	26	23	25	39	36	33	(37)
Spain	..	..	..	31	–	–	–	–	52
Western Europe (countries without union bans)	..	12	36	27	29	44	42	44	50[a]
Western Europe (including countries with bans)	..	*	*	24	15	41	39	41	*
United States	4	10	17	12	27	32	31	30	28
Canada	..	..	21	18	20	36	39	39	39
Japan	..	..	..	..	42	..	..	35	32
Australia	9	25	42	44	40	56	55	51	54

– = union ban   .. = no data   * = category not applicable
(a) estimated 1977–80

crisis. Even in those European countries where the movement was not suppressed or banned, membership declined heavily for almost a quarter of a century. In the democracies of Western Europe, unions lost about a quarter of their membership in the 1920s alone. Especially in Great Britain, Germany (before the Nazis' seizure of power) and Belgium, the former torchbearers of the movement, the loss of so many members was a painful blow. The impact of the crisis was felt in Scandinavia and the Netherlands too, though it was smaller and of shorter duration. Outside Europe, there were doubtless substantial setbacks in terms of membership growth, for instance in the United States, Canada and Australia, but generally they were not so serious as in Europe.

The partial collapse of the European unions appears much more complete when one considers the suppression that began in Italy and Portugal in the 1920s and later spread to Germany, Austria and Spain in the 1930s. The picture thus obtained is closer to reality. Between 1920 and 1940, overall membership losses in Western Europe amounted to nearly two-thirds; numbers fell from 28 million in 1920 to 12 million in 1940. Every second employee in Western Europe was denied the right to belong to a union of his choice, a right that was often replaced by compulsory membership of corporate pseudo-unions. These numbers illustrate the depth of this crisis in European union history. In industrialized countries outside Europe, at least in the western hemisphere, in the United States, Canada, and also Australia and New Zealand, there was none of the trauma of union bans at home or in neighbouring countries. Widespread bans on unions in Europe dramatised the history of the movement to a greater degree than in other countries, and had an even greater impact than the broader membership crisis. Above all it was this second phase that set European trade union history apart.

The third phase in Europe, between the end of World War II and the late 1960s, represented a fresh start. Peak membership in the immediate post-war years led on to a later period when membership consolidated. There was no crisis to match the one that had gone before, but at the same time there was no real growth in overall unionization. The numerical growth of organized labour in Western Europe from about 34 million in 1950 to 42 million in 1970 was almost outpaced by increased employment resulting from the boom. The proportion of unionized workers thus remained roughly static at about a half of the total. Most of the larger countries of Western Europe, such as Great Britain, France and Germany and also the Netherlands, Switzerland and Austria, survived this development. Only in Italy was a post-war peak followed by a drop in unionization. By contrast, a rising trend could be detected only in Belgium and Scandinavia. In this phase too, Western Europe differed from other industrialized regions of the world. The United States, Canada and Japan saw a gradual disintegration of union membership. Social scientists in these countries diagnosed a decline of the union movement and the fading of classic forms of industrial conflict. Variations in union development between Europe and the rest of the industrialized world are nowhere near as great as they were in the inter-war years but they nevertheless point in different directions.

Towards the end of this phase—in the late 1960s and the 1970s— existing variations tended to become greater. Union development in Europe further contradicted the earlier diagnosis of decline. In Western Europe as a whole there was a slight upward trend in unionization. As a rule, Northern European countries such as Great Britain, Belgium, Sweden, Denmark and Finland led the trend. Their numbers were swelled with the return of democracy and unionization to Spain, Portugal and Greece. By contrast, the process of disintegration continued in the United States and Japan. In Canada there was no increase. Once again, Australia alone followed the European course. It is only in recent years that most European unions have again experienced a membership crisis. Time alone will tell whether union strengths in Europe will converge on world membership levels or whether the latest crisis is merely another short interruption in Europe's otherwise unaltered long-term pattern.

Overall, development of union membership in the rest of the world is comparatively simple and linear. Growth in Canada and Australia has been continual and slow, with only the occasional hesitation; the United States saw steady increases until the middle of this century, followed by equally steady decline thereafter. The history of Western European unions, on the other hand, is one of discontinuity, occasional surges or even mass joinings, grave crises and signs of decay, and even suppression or proscription.[85]

This discontinuity occurred against a background of workers' mobilization that was more intense in every way. Since the early twentieth century, the degree of unionization in Europe has been substantially higher than in the United States, Canada or Japan. It was only in the 1930s, during the critical phase for the European movement, that North America and Europe began to drift together. At the end of the 1940s, unions in Europe had won back the advantage which they have held ever since. Australia is once again the only country that does not differ from Europe in this respect (see Table 8).

There can be no doubt that wide intra-European variations existed. There had always been European countries whose membership strengths lagged behind the pan-European average. Around 1920, the European movement's first peak, unions on the southern and northern peripheries of the continent—in Spain, Italy, Finland, Norway, and even France—were as weak or nearly as weak in membership as North American unions. Around 1980, when Europe's distinctive features once again became prominent, membership of French and Swiss trade unions was very close to levels in the United States and Japan. German, Italian and Dutch unions were similar in strength to those in Canada. Thus North America and Japan were towards the bottom of the European range of unions, which themselves were widely divergent. There was no deep, clear-cut rift between Europe on the one hand and the rest of the world on the other in the degree of unionization. Despite this fact, we should not be too hasty in discarding the notion of a specifically European course. The wide variations described for Europe can also occur between one American state and another. Differences within America were, if anything, greater than variations between the countries of Europe. In the United States, there are many old-established industrialized states such as Pennsylvania, New York, Indiana and Michigan, where levels of unionization in 1975 were similar to those in Germany and France. Side by side with these, however, were a range of southern and western states in which, again in the 1970s, the number of wage-earners who were union members would typically be around 15 per cent and could even be lower than 10 per cent.[86] Such a lack of inclination to unionise has never existed in postwar Europe.

How can this stronger overall tendency for the workers of Europe to organize be explained? Comparative research on American and European union history has usually pointed to the differences between the "new" society of America and the old of Europe. In Europe, unions had a more solid basis of old traditions on which to build, especially organization along guild lines, which in some cases transferred directly to the union system in the course of the nineteenth century. Such traditions were less secure in the United States and Japan. As discussed earlier, the rigidity of social demarcation between the upper and middle classes and the working class in Europe led to a more isolated and independent workers' culture. This culture touched most aspects of life; in many European countries it was closely associated with the labour movement and bound a worker more strongly to the unions. For that very reason, European unions could count on larger membership.[87]

However, European traditions of this kind do not fully explain why European unions continue to be stronger in numbers today. The traditions of craft guilds and workers' culture have hardly any role in most European societies today. Other circumstances must be taken into account, some of which have probably been neglected up to now and are direct results of other distinctive European features previously discussed. Larger union membership may be connected with the sheer numbers of industrial workers in Europe. Because the number of wage-earners in industry has far exceeded levels anywhere else, the potential for membership has been correspondingly higher. Weight of numbers does not necessarily determine the strength of unions, but it is an important conditioning factor. Strength of union membership could also be linked with European family patterns. The late age at marriage typical of Europe allowed a longer period of each individual worker's life for non-family ties, including union involvement, to develop more thoroughly, and these may have been more enduring in later life. This would mean that the European union movement was especially reliant, not merely on young unmarried wage-earners, but on a longer period of workers' lives when the impact on the individual of union membership was considerable. Finally, the strength of union membership in Europe has been linked to typical forms of labour conflict, as will become clearer in the arguments set out below.

Labour relations in Europe drew more of their distinct character from their close relationship with the political process. Unions did not regard themselves merely as communities of interest for the improvement of wages and working conditions. Their aims often extended to the pursuit of such goals as economic and political reform, or the revolutionization of their respective countries, usually by state measures. European unions did not just negotiate with employers and organize strikes as American unions tended to do. In Europe, as in Australia, unions always had political wings that were frequently very powerful, worked closely with workers' parties and had substantial control over legislation. The existence of Labour parties and the unions' close cooperation with them led to the unions' peculiar influence on politics. But this was a two-way process, with political pressures being exerted on union organization. In countries where Labour parties were strongly socialist—Germany, the Scandinavian countries, Austria and Great Britain—there has been a general long-term tendency towards highly uniform and often heavily-centralized unions. In European countries, where workers' parties faced strong competition from Christian parties—France, Italy, Belgium and the Netherlands—this was reflected in their division into socialist and Christian factions. In countries such as France and Italy, where the cold war brought competition between powerful Communist and Socialist parties, the union movement tended once again to divide along party lines. The closely related party and union structures observed in Europe were absent in America.

The profound difference between the "bread-and-butter" aims of American unions and the wider socio-political goals of the European movement (even though little more than lip service is often paid to them in practice) has been widely studied. The root cause of this difference is usually identified as the fundamental difference between the old societies of Europe and the "new" of America. A key characteristic of that "new" society, the political equality of all citizens and their equality in day-to-day social intercourse, has been more firmly rooted in the United States since the nineteenth century than in the old societies of Europe. As we have seen, this is borne out by the experiences of immigrants to North America. Thus although strikes were not infrequently subject to violent and bloody suppression, the argument runs that workers were not so completely shut out of society in the United States as they were in Europe; this made them less class conscious. Unions tended not to encounter political structures that were less fundamentally hostile to them. They therefore had less reason to demand basic alterations to American society, and could isolate pay and conditions as the focus of their efforts, while working to strengthen and gain recognition for their organizations. For this reason, they were less receptive to socialist ideas.[88]

Such long-term differences between the United States and Europe are naturally of great historical significance. As time goes by in our post-war age, however, they explain less than they used to do. Since World War II at least, unions have been as influential in American politics as in European. At the same time, the segregation of workers in European societies has become less severe. In spite of this, there are no signs of a breakdown in the close interplay of politics and industrial relations in Europe. Cooperation between workers' parties and unions is as close as ever.

The more turbulent history of the unions in twentieth-century Europe may be a significant cause of this. Even in recent times, the trauma of union bans had been personally experienced by many union leaders. Bans were still in place in Portugal, Spain and Greece until the 1970s. European unions had, of necessity, to involve themselves thoroughly in matters affecting their very right to exist by lobbying for basic political guarantees against union bans. This contrasted with the American and Australian situation. Admittedly, other factors were at work in European countries with long traditions of public intervention to improve living and working conditions; these were discussed in the section on the welfare state. This tradition was exploited by the unions who used it, along with strikes and threats of strikes, as a means to improve conditions for wage-earners. They worked for job protection, workers' rights, regulation of arbitration and social security. Cooperation with workers' parties was, and remains, an essential precondition for activity of this kind.

Against this characteristic background to unionization in Europe, a specifically European form of conflict has developed. The first and most striking point is that, compared with the United States in particular, the two sides in European conflicts were quite different. In America, disputes tended to be between companies and unions. Strikes were generally confined to a single company, or at the most to a small group of companies, and were organized by the works committees concerned, the "locals". Pay settlements tended to be negotiated between management and shop stewards. Conflicts tended to be in-house. Outside organizations on both the employers' and the union side had only a limited hand in the conduct and results of disputes. In Europe, however, conflicts were more often between employers' bodies and unions on a national level, and strikes were nationwide. Insofar as they were limited to individual companies, they were nationally planned or, in the case of spontaneous strikes in individual companies, there would at least be some tension between the strikers and some national organization. Pay settlements were negotiated between employers' associations and unions on a national or at least a regional basis. The control that managers and union branches had over pay settlements was at best indirect. This explains why unions in Europe were less bothered about taking control of individual businesses. They demanded closed-shop conditions to a far lesser extent, exerting less pressure on firms to employ only union members or to dismiss new employees who refused to join. On a national level, it was more important for European unions to win as many wage-earners as possible throughout the country. Therein lies an important reason for the higher degree of unionization experienced in Europe.

Furthermore, compared with the United States, the strike seems to have been used as a means to fewer ends in most European countries. Social security was less likely to be the subject of the dispute, or to be included as an element of pay settlements. Strikes were less likely to be called to secure supplements to state pensions or private health care, or accident or life insurance. By contrast with the United States, advances in these areas were more often brought about by the unions' political wings and by state measures. This kind of union policy on social security has been thoroughly effective, and has led to the much wider establishment of state systems in Europe. There has been little reason for European unions to make social security an issue in strike demands. They have also been less likely to resort to strike action to protect jobs in individual firms or branches of industry. Settlements in the United States have often contained detailed rules stating which employee groups would be the first to face dismissal, and which groups enjoy special protection within the firm. In Europe, the unions have made greater attempts at protecting jobs through support for state job-creation programmes, or else have tried to secure a direct state-regulated say in company decision-making through co-determination or works councils. Naturally these differences between European and American strike patterns are not absolute. European unions have also tried to create jobs through wage-fixing, especially in times of crisis. However, in the twentieth century, such practices have been less frequent and less in the nature of "house agreements" than in the United States.

On questions like periods of notice, job protection and procedural regulations for pay disputes, as well as the many other rules governing employer-employee relations, European unions were also less likely to strike in order to secure changes which would benefit their members. Again, they were more likely to rely on their political wings to amend national labour laws or arbitration rules. Thus, the strike in Europe has been used more rigorously to improve pay and conditions. At the same time, it has not been the chief instrument at the disposal of the unions, as it has been in America. For European unions, the important things were the potential to determine state regulation of work and social security and the ability to secure the introduction of state systems of control and welfare. As the strike weapon was more narrowly focused, cooperation with the workers' parties benefited in a corresponding measure.[89]

This is one reason why strikes in Europe and the United States have had differing economic effects since World War II. Europe is undeniably a strike-happy continent. Numerous and sometimes massive strikes, politically motivated or interpreted as such, have provoked worldwide response—but they give a false impression. Because European unions possessed and implemented so many instruments of pressure besides the strike, the number of working days lost in post-war Europe through strike action has always been much smaller than in the United States. Even in times of intense industrial strife like the 1970s, the overall number of days lost in Europe was about one-third lower than the American figure. The difference in some post-war decades was even greater. Compared with the United States, there was noticeably less strike damage done to the

European economy.[90] A final aspect of Europe compared with America, and one connected with previous points, is that strikes on either side of the Atlantic were very different in nature. Evidence of this is largely due to the work of Charles Tilly and Edward Shorter who, like most other researchers of labour disputes, have concentrated on transatlantic comparisons. In their view, since World War II there has been one kind of strike typical of North America, focusing largely on single firms and lasting an average of about two weeks. Action is carried out by a few hundred strikers, thus including only a very small proportion of all wage-earners. Typically, it never grows into a mass protest. Above all in post-war years, the researchers identify a clear tendency for strike demands to ignore political content and for responsibilities to be divided between non-political strike demands and political pressure from non-aligned unions. In this way, the unions in the United States followed the American inclination against state intervention. For them, the strike remained an essential weapon.

There was no single form of strike in post-war Western Europe. Instead we may isolate two distinct forms, and a special case in Britain. The common determining factor in the two main forms for all European countries is the status of the workers' party as either the party in power or in opposition. In those European countries where workers' parties held power for long periods after the war, strikes were fewer than in North America and were focused more on pay and conditions. When they did break out, strikes could admittedly drag on and on. In some countries, numbers joining the strikes could be enormous. In those European countries where socialist parties only held power briefly or not at all, strikes were often political demonstrations as well. By their nature, politically motivated strikes of this kind were on average short-lived, although each individual strike could rely on far greater numerical support and the mobilization of a much greater proportion of all wage-earners than in America. Overall, the last decade and a half has seen the widest differentiation between the typical Western European strike and the American pattern. The number of strikers as a proportion of all wage-earners in Europe has never been greater compared to the United States. The relative number of strikes has never been so much higher than the American figure, and never before have strikes been so much shorter in duration and therefore less economically damaging overall than those in America.[91]

To sum up, there appear at first glance to be considerable intra-European variations in union organization and labour disputes. However, one should nevertheless not lose sight of four important features common to Western Europe as a whole. First, employees are, generally speaking, more easily mobilized by the unions in Europe than anywhere else. In the first half of the century especially, this has been accompanied by more serious discontinuity in strength of membership, more dramatic growth, deeper crises, and even total bans. State intervention in the establishment of social security systems, job protection and reduction of unemployment, and regulation of industrial disputes have been viewed as more important matters by the European unions. They have attempted to achieve their aims through pressure on the state rather than through strikes, and they have been far from unsuccessful in this strategy. The danger of party political splits in the union movement, closer union ties with parties, especially workers' parties, and strikes determined by the political colour of the ruling party all reflect the impact of Europe's overall political situation in the sphere of industrial relations. Although public interest in such strongly political union activity has been much greater compared to the "bread-and-butter" type of strike in America, a survey of the post-1945 period shows that substantially fewer working days have been lost in Europe. The number of strikes and strikers has been much greater but the strikes themelves were much shorter, thus noticeably diminishing their negative economic effects.

9. Concluding remarks

Although numerous distinctive features of twentieth-century Europe have been addressed in this chapter, the survey is by no means exhaustive.[92] Sceptics may have two principal reservations which should be examined before turning to the changes undergone by these distinctive features during the twentieth century.

Some may form the impression that rather than constituting the special common character of twentieth-century European societies, the many features outlined above are a meticulous catalogue of minor coincidences. There has, of course, been an attempt to pursue correlations between the features under discussion, especially the effects of European family and industrial employment patterns. What certainly has not been done is to trace the many characteristics of twentieth-century European society back to only one or two underlying traits. The reason for this is mainly practical. It is not the historian's fear of the simple monocausal explanation which is often mocked by the argument that a single good explanation is better than many weak ones. The true reason is rather that in-depth study has so far been lacking. Even so, three more fundamental and more long-term aspects of Europe appear to be worthy of further consideration.

The sheer age of European societies could well have conditioned the features discussed above; compared with those of the United States, Canada, Australia and the Eastern Soviet Union, they are very old societies. The typical age of societies in Europe and the much denser settlement of the continent may have caused the tradition of public bodies to be stronger compared with thinly-populated new societies. At the same time, tensions between public authorities and private matters might have become more serious, causing the family sphere to act as a protective shield against long and painful experience of contact with public bodies. The enduring tradition of social divisions between old and new upper classes, between upper and middle classes and between rich and poor might also have been an effect of the age of European societies. The power and refinement of social divisions and the degree to which those affected accepted their seriousness and implications might have become more acute during the ageing process. Delays in the implementation of social changes might have been a result of the age and relative inflexibility of European societies, factors which would also account for modest rates in company growth as they developed into management-run enterprises, the slow growth of education systems and urbanisation, and delays in the complete introduction of social security systems, despite their early inception.

It would, of course, be over-hasty to equate the stately pace of social processes with backwardness. In old societies, the nature of cost-benefit calculations prior to the sweeping away of existing, functioning traditional structures will always be very different to those in new societies where new structures can be built on virgin territory with little resultant damage. In old societies, rapid changes often appear less attractive or even more dangerous and destabilising.

Long-term conquest by non-Europeans has never been experienced in Europe, nor has the continent ever been subjected to a system of wanton exploitation; this is a second fact about Europe that sets it apart from other old societies. It is the more surprising, since Europe did not enjoy the protection of the sea, like Japan for instance. It was only on the periphery of Europe that such conquests occurred over centuries, by the Arabs in Spain and Portugal, the Mongols in Russia and the Turks in Southern Europe. On the other hand, the majority of Europeans lived in societies that often experienced occupation by their European neighbours. Attitudes to public bodies could well have been affected by this historical situation. Once these bodies had developed, trust would build up and they would become accepted and often more efficient as a consequence. In occupied countries, on the other hand, ruthless exploitation and collaboration with the exploiters undermined popular respect for authority in the long term, allowing mechanisms of severe isolation to become routine. Certain public bodies doubtless assumed a class character, or became highly bureaucratized. On the other hand, in addition to this traditional defensive withdrawal into the family sphere there has been a long history of protest and revolution in Europe — not all of it unsuccessful. Of course the Europeans also waged frequent wars of conquest among themselves, but no European occupying power has been resistant enough in the long term to overcome freedom movements or military action by other European powers.

By contrast with other large old and "new" societies, Europe has retained its characteristic particularism right up to the present day. Europe is the only continent in which small and medium-sized states proliferated in the nineteenth and twentieth centuries without a single large state asserting itself. Long traditions, beyond the scope of this book, lie at the root of this phenomenon. The significance of such particularism for European society must not be overemphasized. State boundaries have imposed no greater restrictions on, say, industrialization than they have on important social changes, demographic transition, the origins of the European family, urbanisation or the rise of the labour movement, all of which drew quite different boundaries across Europe. Historians often overrate the importance of national boundaries in Europe and overlook wider European trends because of their general tendency to make studies of their own countries. Particularism has nevertheless given long-term economic and social processes their characteristic European stamp.[93] This will be dealt with at the end of the next section.

A sceptic might also query the imprecise definition of the distinctive features presented above. They were often present in most European societies, but not all. In countries outside Europe, they were often weak but not totally absent. Phenomena of a particularly European nature might often be very clear, but in comparison with some countries outside Europe—the United States for example, and sometimes the equally old society of Japan—they could be less so. The potential charge here is one of arbitrary selection. However, in a comparative study it is unreasonable to suppose that patterns of behaviour and social structures from outside Europe would be totally absent from European societies. Societies are too fluid and too mutually influential for that to occur. Crystal-clear contrasts between societies at similar stages of development with extensive exchange of people and ideas exist only as a theoretical possibility. Historical reality generally takes the form of gradual, indistinct and vague variations. This is particularly true when—as here—we compare Europe as a whole with non-European societies.

The vagueness of pan-European phenomena has been conditioned by the existence of nation-states, which offered a greater chance for general traits, processes and national features to assert themselves and to endure under their protection. This does not, of course, apply in equal measure to all the features under discussion, since they were not all equally dependent on government decisions. It is likely that without the proliferation of states, opportunities for education and the development of the welfare state would have varied less widely within Europe; however, the effect of such proliferation has not merely been to decelerate change. On the contrary, new processes which may have been suppressed in one country would at least have a chance to establish an early experimental foothold in another. Taking social security as an example, its introduction would

probably have been delayed by decades if it had not been af-
forded the protection of several nation-states in its early development.

The point of view of the observer also affects the perception of
exactly how European societies differed from non-European.
Regardless of whether or not Europe as a whole is more uniform
or more diverse than elsewhere, it is simply the norm to assess
Europe on the basis of individual states and thus to give particular attention to variations between the nations. It is similarly the norm to view the United States and the Soviet Union
as being uniform throughout, thus directing attention to common features of the two societies. What is not normal is to view
Europe and the countries in the rest of the world through a
single pair of eyes. It is this tendency that always makes what
features Europe has in common seem vague and attributable
only to a few nations, rather than appearing to be universal. In
the case of America or the Soviet Union on the other hand, even
where there are discrepancies between a whole range of individual states or republics, distinctive features tend to be more
readily accepted. There are doubtless good reasons for the application of such double standards. The particularism and,
compared with the United States (but not the Soviet Union),
the cultural diversity and polyglot nature of Europe are the
main reasons. This view distorts reality, and exaggerates intra-
European variations while neglecting the wide differences
within the United States and the Soviet Union. It is too easy to
forget that in certain crucial respects—as we shall see shortly in
employment patterns and degrees of urbanisation — present
variations between European countries are no greater than between the states of America or the republics of the Soviet
Union, and they do not necessarily extend beyond the scale
normal for a large modern state. The question must be asked: is
it so unrealistic to view twentieth-century European social history from the same perspective as the corresponding history of
the United States or the Soviet Union? It is true that the social
history of certain countries in Europe will always be of greater
importance than that of American states or Soviet republics,
but how can we disregard everything else about them?

European Social Convergence
in the Twentieth Century

The growing similarities between European societies are a subject of particular interest in the post-war era. Such similarities are revealed if one looks beyond mere static comparisons of twentieth-century European features. Moreover, it is possible to trace the ways in which distinctive features have changed and the extent to which variations within Europe, so often emphasized, have endured or weakened during the present century. Societies in Western Europe have indeed become more and more similar, especially in the post-war era. At the same time, the justification for exclusively national viewpoints on social history has become ever weaker.

Trends towards increased similarity are not evident in all social structures. They do not surface in every aspect of European life. In four absolutely crucial areas, however, they are unmistakable: industrial production and employment; education; urbanisation; and the development of the welfare state. They are less apparent in other important areas, especially family structure and labour relations. Here too, however, there is no question of very large, let alone growing, variations between European countries. I now propose to examine each of these aspects of Europe's social structure in the present century. I hope to trace the processes of convergence and to inquire into the individual causes. A number of fundamental reflections on the character and durability of these processes appears at the end of the book.

1. Economic convergence: industrial production and employment

Perhaps the foremost aspect of Europe's integration in the

twentieth century has been an increase in the similarity of production and employment structure throughout Europe. A great deal depends on this process of economic convergence, and several of its consequences will be dealt with here.

This process of convergence has chiefly been stimulated by the development of industrial production. In the course of the twentieth century, industrial production per head of population in the various countries of Western Europe has become increasingly similar. Prior to World War I, there was a great contrast between highly industrialized central countries such as Great Britain, Belgium, Switzerland or Germany, and peripheral Mediterranean or Atlantic countries such as Greece, Spain, Portugal, Ireland and Finland. There has been gradual and substantial reduction in the contrast, though even now it is not possible to speak of any enormous similarities in industrial production. Great variation still remains in an eroded form, even within the European Community which for a long time focused on its industrial centres.[1] In spite of this, the situation today is nowhere near comparable with that at the turn of the century. Another cause of change has been the continuing convergence in *per capita* industrial production even during the crisis of the 1970s (see Figure 8).

This process has, however, been far from steady. Up to the 1880s, disparities in industrial production within Europe were very acute. The gradual reversal of this trend seems to have begun thereafter, admittedly coming to a halt in the inter-war period. The true onset of convergence only came after World War II. Finland especially, but also Mediterranean countries and Ireland, made up a lot of ground on Europe's leading industrial producers. By contrast, despite its importance and the fact that its *per capita* production in 1913 and 1953 was almost twice the European average, Great Britain fell behind the overall European rate after World War II, thus decreasing intra-European variation from the opposite end (see Figure 8).[2]

The process operated within very sensitive limits however. The erosion of national disparities in industrial production had no great effect on overall disparities in economic performance. Differences between the economic performance of Western European countries have not changed to any significant extent during this century. Domestic product per head of population

Figure 8: Development of inner-European variation in production
and employment 1880–1980.

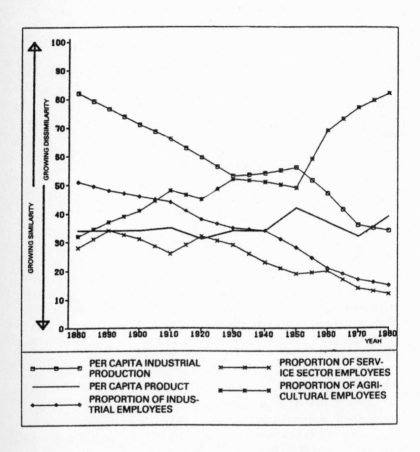

varies almost as much as ever (see Figure 8). Of course, individual countries have undergone shifts. The Scandinavian
economies performed better than the European average. On
the other hand, post-war Great Britain has lost its former position as a high achiever and has fallen to around the average.
More importantly, economic growth *per capita* in real terms was
higher than the European average in industrial late starters
such as Greece, Portugal (for a time) and Spain (in the longer
term). In spite of this, large overall variations in economic performance between the Mediterranean and the more central
countries of Europe have remained.[3]

The industrial backwardness of countries on the southern
and western periphery of Europe is chiefly, but not solely, a
consequence of their agricultural production which even until
very recently has been of great significance in their economies.
Discrepancies were preserved, among other reasons, because
agricultural output never grew to match that of industrialized
Europe, where agricultural production was on the increase in a
number of countries. In achieving high levels of self-sufficiency,
and occasionally even large surpluses, industrialized Europe
helped to maintain the gap between itself and the peripheral
countries.[4]

In the twentieth century, dissimilarities in employment
structure within Europe have shrunk even more decisively than
dissimilarities in industrial production. Early on, the proportion of wage-earners employed in industry varied greatly from
country to country. On the one hand, the old industrialized
countries—Great Britain, Belgium, Switzerland and Germany—were the leaders, with industry employing 40 per cent
to 50 per cent of wage-earners. In Great Britain, the peak of development had already been reached by this time and was
never to be exceeded. On the other hand, peripheral Mediterranean and Atlantic countries such as Greece, Spain, Portugal,
Ireland and Finland employed very small proportions of such
workers, roughly 10 per cent to 20 per cent in industry or, more
precisely, trade. In a number of these countries at that time,
employment in trade was at its lowest historical level. Growth
in industrial employment had not even begun. Variations on
this scale were eliminated over the course of the century, leading to today's situation where employment in industry is very
similar from one Western European country to the next. Again,

next. Again, the process has not been a steady one. Though variations were diminishing before World War I, and probably between the wars too, this is another process that really emerged after World War II. Uniformity in the employment structure of Western Europe can only really be said to have existed to any great extent since the 1970s (see Figure 8). This process of convergence has continued throughout the crisis of the past fifteen years, and, even as late as the early 1980s, it had neither halted nor reversed into a divergent trend.[5]

It is important to note that this process of erosion was also at work in the service sector. It would be helpful to know whether economic services such as commerce, banking, insurance or transport saw the greatest reductions in variation, or whether social or domestic services were the chief areas of change. There is currently no reliable answer to this question. It is nevertheless quite clear that in terms of the proportion of wage-earners employed in this sector, substantial convergence has occurred between the countries of Western Europe during the twentieth century. At first sight at least, variations were never very great. But closer inspection is likely to reveal greater disparities between modern services in the central countries and more traditional ones on the fringes. Even with the very rough-and-ready approach taken here, clear processes of convergence can be identified. The elimination of variation has been even more extensive than in the case of industrial employment. Once again, the main thrust of convergence came before 1945 (see Figure 8).[6]

The extraordinary acceleration of the process can be better observed in comparisons with the United States and the Soviet Union. Internal variations in employment structure between the American states and Soviet republics have also been eroded, though the resulting situation differed from that in Western Europe. Between the wars, the employment structure varied much less from one American state to the next than it did between individual European countries. Meteoric convergence in Western Europe reversed this situation. Around 1960, employment structure in Western Europe varied less than it did in the United States. In Western Europe industrial employment was fairly evenly distributed between the individual countries; not so in the United States. In the Soviet Union, contrasts between the various republics were very great, much greater than in the west. This comes as no surprise. By 1970, they had been rapidly eliminated. In spite of this, the Soviet Union has been faced with substantially greater disparities in industrial employment than Western Europe or, in its more limited sense, the European Community. In the industrialized north, the RSFSR, Estonia and Latvia each had industrial employment of roughly two-fifths of the workforce. This contrasts with the sparsely industrialized Kirghiz region and other southern Muslim regions such as Azerbaijan, Tadzhikistan and Turkmenistan, where industry accounted for roughly a quarter of employment. In Western Europe, the contrasts between the centre and the periphery were far smaller, making industrial employment more uniform overall. In this respect, social integration in Western Europe is further advanced than in the societies of either of the superpowers.[7]

There are clear limits to the extent of convergence between European countries on employment structure. Once again, opposing trends centre on the agricultural sector, an area where Western European countries have increasingly diverged. Before World War I, the numbers employed in agriculture varied greatly from one country to the next. On the one hand, there was Great Britain where only 10 per cent of wage-earners were engaged in agriculture. In this respect, Great Britain was well in advance of all its continental neighbours, even heavily industrialized ones such as Switzerland, Belgium and Germany. Finland was at the other extreme, with three-quarters of all wage-earners still employed on the land. In countries such as Spain, Portugal, Italy and even Sweden, the majority of the population still earned a living from the soil. Since then, a clear general trend has emerged, with labour abandoning agriculture and a consequent slump in employment on the land. Today, there is not a single European country in which the rate of agricultural employment exceeds one-third. Decline has progressed at differing rates from country to country and has done nothing to iron out variations within Europe, in fact quite the contrary. In Belgium and Great Britain, the countries which are the least agricultural today, less than 3 per cent of wage-earners make their living from the soil. In Portugal and Greece, on the other hand, the countries whose farming population remains highest, the figure is still almost ten times that.[8]

Overall, residual contrasts in agriculture are overshadowed

in their importance by convergence in the industrial and service sectors. The quest for causes of convergence will therefore centre on the latter areas. The conventional wisdom claims that the first effect of industrialization was the sharp variations within Europe caused by its geographically scattered beginnings. Disparities have subsequently diminished with the gradual spread of industry. Looking at Europe overall, national variations were at their most pronounced early in the twentieth century. Around 1900, countries at the heart of industrial Europe—Great Britain, France, the Netherlands, Belgium, Germany, Switzerland, several regions of northern Italy and the western section of the Habsburg Empire—contrasted greatly in economic terms with those on the Mediterranean, Scandinavian, Atlantic and eastern fringes of the continent. This analysis is not undisputed; however, there is a great deal of justification for it both in employment structure and in industrial production.[9]

There are also a number of points to be made about the consequences of economic convergence between European countries, three of which will be dealt with in more detail below. These are convergence in occupational structure, growing similarities in social mobility and, lastly, the consequences for political integration.

In the development of employment structures as sketched roughly above, individual occupations have not been discussed. Whether the numbers of doctors, metalworkers or saleswomen varies less today from country to country than it did at the turn of the century must remain unanswered. However, in the case of employee groups in the wider sense—for instance, employees in industry or public administration—the impact of convergence between employment sectors in Europe has been substantial. Variations in the scale of these larger groups also seem to have diminished in the twentieth century. Over the past fifteen years they have become negligible. Admittedly, the process of convergence has not been uniform in its intensity among all employee groups. As one would expect, it has been particularly apparent among industrial workers. Even around 1970, convergence had reduced variations between European countries to trifling levels. In the case of public employees, it was less vigorous; among self-employed farmers, it has been absent entirely. In the latter group, numbers have dwindled to minute proportions over the years and the variations are as great as ever.[10]

This convergence in the structure of work has caused social mobility between larger groups to become increasingly similar within individual Western European countries. Numerous studies of mass mobility have provided evidence of this, showing that upward and downward mobility between larger groups have overwhelmingly been conditioned by increasing similarities in working structures. Other factors have only been of minor importance. This does not, of course, necessarily apply to processes affecting only small groups in a society, for instance the mobility of teachers' sons or mobility within individual academic professions. There is, however, ample evidence of mobility between larger groups.

A number of further important points must be examined. Scrutinising the quite numerous studies of mobility that were conducted in the 1960s, using very uniform methods for whole countries, it is astonishing how small were the variations between European countries (see Table 2). The proportion of wage-earners moving between occupations is quite similar. The studies limit themselves largely to non-peripheral developed countries in Europe, but they nevertheless include the four largest countries and therefore capture the vast majority of Western Europeans. Among those large countries, France and West Germany exhibit particular similarity. Highly detailed comparative studies into changes in social mobility since World War II offer further evidence of growing similarities. Precise comparisons between countries with employment and professional structures differing as widely as those of France, Sweden and Great Britain show post-war convergence in terms of social mobility between larger occupation groups. There was particularly pronounced convergence between France and Great Britain, even though the employment history of the two countries had differed widely in the nineteenth and twentieth centuries. Convergence relative to Sweden was not quite as great; that country went through a limited period of extreme expansion in its service sector that fell far outside the typical European pattern, making it a special case. None of this constitutes a watertight case, of course, but there is convincing evidence of converging patterns of social mobility between larger occupation groups in Western Europe. A separate analysis of a similar development in upward mobility in the academic professions appears below.[11]

Finally, convergence in industrial production and employment (particularly its limits) has important effects on Europe's political integration. It may be assumed that convergence has eased the development of the European Community, and also provided favourable common ground for promotion of relations between the Community and other countries in Western Europe. It is true that convergence rarely emerges directly as a topic of political debates and decisions, which tend rather to lament the disparities that persist. Without convergence in industrial production and employment, however, problematic differences and the basis of conflicts between EC member states would in all probability have been substantially greater and less easily resolved.

The limits of convergence in Western European societies have also had an impact on political integration. There are two reasons why these limits exercise such force. Politically, every extension of Community boundaries tended to emphasise existing centre-periphery variations. In 1957, the original EC faced the problem of such variations almost exclusively within Italy, where the industrial north contrasted with the under-developed south. In 1973, the first peripheral country entered the Community—Ireland. This event was followed in 1979 by the accession of Greece, another peripheral country. Spain and Portugal were further additions in the third extension. Despite the convergence of the structure of industrial production, therefore, remaining economic differences became absorbed into the EC. The only countries staying outside the Community were those that had always been part of "inner" Europe, or else had made ground successfully during the twentieth century and would therefore have bolstered the similarities between EC countries, namely Austria, Switzerland and the non-continental countries of Scandinavia.

The limits of convergence are also important politically because in the one area where economic integration has been pushed the furthest, agriculture, the EC has become most similar to a federal government in that production and employment show negligible convergent trends. In fact, if anything the reverse trend is the stronger. The growth of disparities in agriculture is not a historical process that was halted, even for EC states, by the founding of the Community. On the contrary, the process has continued unchecked among member states even after its founding, undeniably handicapping integration.

In areas where economic convergence between European countries is particularly strong, that is to say in industrial production and employment, the Community is scarcely active at all, except in the elimination of customs barriers and in supplying aid for declining industries. Integration of the Community is making strides in areas where disparity is on the increase. Where disparity is dwindling, integration is sluggish.[12]

2. Convergence in education: literacy and college education

Education is a further area where similarities between Western European societies have grown substantially in the twentieth century. Even today the multitude of educational institutions can be confusing and difficult to grasp. Public schools in England, the *grandes écoles* in France and the dual system of professional education in Germany are completely alien to natives of other Western European countries. Convergence in examinations is still incomplete even within the European Community. The more fundamental role of secondary and further education in determining opportunities in the labour market has come nowhere near uniformity in post-war Western Europe. Some very striking differences still exist, even between close neighbours like France and Germany. In Germany today, it is during education that the groundwork for a career is laid, whereas in France, later working experience counts for much more.[13] But despite persistent contrasts of this kind, obvious convergence has taken place during the twentieth century. The best evidence is available for two widely differing educational achievements, namely basic literacy and college education.

In Europe the eradication of illiteracy is often superficially regarded as a nineteenth-century achievement. It is easy to overlook the fact that it was not uncommon for standards of literacy to be poles apart within Europe, even early in the present century. A journey through Europe from north to south would have revealed remarkable contrasts. In the northern part, Scandinavia, Britain, Germany and Switzerland, illiterates were few and far between. Tests completed by armed forces recruits and signatures on marriage certificates show that in these countries, the ability to read and write had extended, in however rudimentary a form, to practically the whole population for several decades. By that time, levels of literacy were on the whole comparable to those of today. Among the old, the picture might have looked somewhat different. Travelling on westwards or southwards from these countries into Ireland, Belgium, France, Austria or northern Italy the likelihood of encountering illiteracy grew considerably. It was probably true that among the young, the rate would have been very low, but the overall illiteracy figure would probably still have been 10 per cent to 20 per cent. Generally, that meant that amongst women and unskilled agricultural, and also factory workers, illiteracy would have been substantially higher. In southern Italy—in Calabria, Sicily, the Basilicata and on Sardinia—there was 60 per cent to 70 per cent illiteracy, while in Spain and Portugal the figures were around 50 per cent and 75 per cent respectively. Even in Southern Europe the rate was nowhere near as high as that in many African or American countries, where 80 per cent to 90 per cent illiteracy is still common today. This was the position several centuries ago in Europe; and some urban cultures around the Mediterranean had got beyond that stage as early as the Roman era, at least temporarily. Nevertheless there was a yawning divide between Northern Europe and the Mediterranean at the turn of the century. In fact it had probably never been as wide before.[14]

The gap has narrowed considerably in the twentieth century. The ability to read and write has now spread to the overwhelming majority of Europeans. While some Mediterranean countries still have illiterate sections of the population, such figures are substantially lower than at the beginning of the century. In 1981, the rate in Spain was 10 per cent, in Portugal in 1970, 29 per cent. Not only that, they largely represent historical remnants among older age groups. Literacy among younger Spaniards and Portuguese is almost as widespread as in the rest of Western Europe. The complete disappearance of variations can be foreseen and with that the end of an aspect of convergence between European societies that is frequently overlooked.[15]

The thrust of convergence in higher education in the twentieth century has been less powerful by comparison, though it too has made great progress. Throughout Europe, student populations have become increasingly similar, with consequent

Figure 9: Convergence in urbanization, education and
social security in Western Europe, 1880–1980

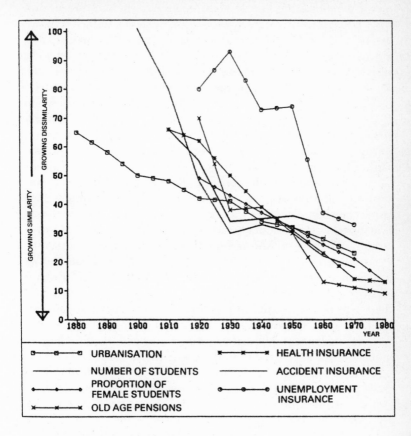

▫—▫—▫ URBANISATION	✳—✳—✳ HEALTH INSURANCE
—— NUMBER OF STUDENTS	—— ACCIDENT INSURANCE
●—●—● PROPORTION OF FEMALE STUDENTS	○—○—○ UNEMPLOYMENT INSURANCE
✕—✕—✕ OLD AGE PENSIONS	

expansion of higher education. Distribution of opportunity between young men and women of all backgrounds became increasingly uniform.[16]

Looking first at the numbers studying at the turn of the century, there was without doubt very great variation within
Europe (see Figure 9). The number of students in German-
speaking Austria and Switzerland was especially high; the
same was true of Scotland, which must be considered separately from England because of its quite independent education
system. At that time 2 per cent to 4 per cent of each age group in
each of these countries were in higher education, a figure which

in Austria's case admittedly includes many students from other parts of the Habsburg Empire. On the other hand, the numbers in higher education in peripheral countries such as Greece and Portugal were only a tenth of those for Austria and Switzerland. Such extreme cases have a distorting effect, however. Most European countries, and especially the heavily-populated ones, differed far less. Chances of entry into higher education for the majority of young Europeans did not differ nearly so widely. The variations do not appear nearly as important now when looking at the clear advantage in higher education enjoyed by the United States at that time. Nevertheless, compared with today's situation there was considerably greater variation within Europe (see Table 3).[17]

At the beginning of the century, there was even greater variation in educational opportunities open to men and women. This comes as no surprise. It was around this time that universities first opened their doors to women, and even this was not a simultaneous event throughout Europe. Some countries, liberal Switzerland and France for example, quickly came to this decision. In other countries, among them Prussia, the relaxing of restrictions was postponed for as long as possible. Thus, there was no uniformity in the universities of Western Europe. Around 1910, in Switzerland, almost a quarter of students were women, in Italy the figure was almost a sixth, in the Netherlands about a seventh, but in Germany the much-feared female accounted for only one twenty-fifth of the student population. The figures conceal even greater variation in standards of treatment of women both in teaching and in the normalization of student conditions for women.[18]

Early this century, the social background of students within Europe varied less acutely. Admittedly, there is evidence available for only about half the countries of Europe and even this is often only roughly comparable but it does include large countries such as Italy, Great Britain and Germany. There is therefore information available on the social backgrounds of the majority of students in Western Europe and it all follows a very similar basic pattern. A substantial but diminishing portion came from the upper echelons of landowning families or the families of businessmen, academics and senior officials. A growing proportion, and a substantial one, came from the lower middle class, from urban white-collar backgrounds or the ranks of minor officials, although rarely from farming backgrounds. Lastly, a very small proportion came from urban or rural working-class families.

Within this basic pattern, great variation existed between university faculties and individual institutions within individual countries, besides which contrasts also existed between European countries. The sharpest of these appear to have existed within the United Kingdom, between the very different education systems of Scotland and England. According to all the evidence, it seems that English students—taking a lead from the then highly-exclusive universities of Oxford and Cambridge—were very often products of upper-class families, whereas in Scotland they frequently came from working-class families, a situation that was unusual by contemporary standards just as it is by today's. In Aberdeen, 15 per cent of students were from such a background; in Glasgow, the figure was as high as 25 per cent. In the rest of Europe, however, there was also substantial variation.

Between the wars, these intra-European differences was already diminishing. Most obviously this occurred due to convergence in student numbers, especially because societies on the European fringes made such advances. In Austria and Switzerland, both countries with large numbers of students at the time, those numbers continued to grow but remained noticeably behind the much faster rate of growth in Europe as a whole. This was not a post-war phenomenon, as is commonly supposed. Portugal and Greece, on the other hand, where the number of students before 1914 had been especially low, started to make very rapid gains after World War I and came close to equalling the Western European average (see Table 3). Although the situation still varied widely within Europe, it was no longer as extreme as it had been around 1910.

The contrasts in womens' study within Europe were no longer so sharp either. Once again, the countries that had not participated in the European trend before 1914 started to do so. In Germany, womens' education soared until by 1930 about a sixth of students were women (the decline after 1933 was very sharp, however). This figure represents the European average at the time. In Switzerland, on the other hand, the number of women studying actually fell in the inter-war years, above all because women in other countries were now allowed entry to their home universities and had no need of a Swiss education. The convergence in womens' education remained far from complete, however, and there were still important areas of difference. Certain peripheral countries were very open to women, among them Ireland and Finland, but the same was also true of some of the larger more central countries such as Great Britain and France. Women made up more than a quarter of all students in these countries. In Mediterranean universities, such as those of Spain and Greece and probably Portugal too, female students were much less common, making up about a tenth of the total, a situation that also obtained in Belgium and Switzerland.

In the case of students' social backgrounds, the impression is that far from becoming more uniform between the wars, the picture probably became more diverse. Two trends are quite clearly identifiable. On the one hand, English, Swedish and possibly other Scandinavian universities were very open and offered the opportunity of university entry to quite a high proportion of students from working-class backgrounds. An estimate of over 20 per cent seems appropriate to England, with figures of around 15 per cent and 20 per cent for Sweden and Finland respectively. There was a link with the establishment of scholarship systems in English secondary schools, although the reasons in Scandinavia are not precisely known. On the other hand, distribution of opportunity in the rest of Europe remained largely unchanged despite an intense education debate and several educational reforms. Disregarding the overall growth of higher education, relative chances of entry for students from the working classes did not improve noticeably.

Since 1945, the overall decline in intra-European differences in educational opportunities has been even sharper. Once again, the clearest evidence for this is in attendance figures. There is no great similarity between European countries as yet but the continuity of the convergence is very clear (see Figure 9). This conceals considerable shifts in the European league table. Scandinavian countries like Sweden and Denmark rose to become leaders in terms of the numbers of students. Switzerland and, at least until the end of Franco's regime, Spain, saw numbers decline to particularly low levels, as did Portugal and Greece. In other areas variations between European countries have also changed at an extraordinary rate since 1945 and become more and more restricted in their extent.

Education for women underwent more rapid and far-reaching change. Opportunities have become steadily more uniform since 1945. Around 1975 an average of 40 per cent of European students were women, and individual countries deviated from the average less than they had between the wars. Some important differences persisted. In France and Finland, and in a dramatic late charge, Portugal, the proportion of female students rose to nearly 50 per cent by 1975. In Switzerland and the Netherlands, by contrast, the figure was only 25 per cent. West Germany also lagged well behind the European average. Nevertheless, the variations cannot be compared with the contrasts that existed between the wars or before 1914. They become even less pronounced if all institutions of higher education, including teacher training colleges and technical colleges, are included in addition to universities. The similarity between the countries of Europe then becomes very great (see Figure 9).

Distribution of opportunity may also have become less unequal since 1945. Higher education all over Europe is becoming more open than ever to members of all classes, following the pioneering lead of Great Britain and Sweden. Most countries participated in the drive to make up ground, which differed in its rapidity and extent from country to country. It seems to have begun at first in Belgium, Italy and Denmark in the 1950s, all countries where the proportion of students from the lower social classes was below the level in the pioneer countries. The process then took a hold in other Western European countries such as the Netherlands, Austria, Switzerland, France, Spain and West Germany in the 1960s and 1970s. In some of these countries at least—Germany among them—higher education for the working class was still a far slimmer hope than it was in Great Britain or Sweden, for instance. Differences that existed between the wars probably did diminish somewhat, but distribution of opportunity was not equal throughout Western Europe.

Overall then, in basic literacy and in higher education, the societies of Western Europe have drawn closer together over the course of the twentieth century. The convergence is limited to Western Europe and takes no account of the student population of Eastern European countries because of the quite different education and entry policies in force there. Once again, Western Europe shows an astonishingly advanced level of convergence when compared with the variations observed within a country the size of the United States. At least where student figures for 1970 are concerned, differences between Western European countries are as insignificant as those between individual states of the United States of America. In this respect, social integration in Europe is once more as far ahead as in the western superpower.[19]

3. Urbanization and the urban way of life
Figure 9 shows another crucial area in which Western European societies have become more and more alike, namely urbanization. Of course, very clear variations between European countries exist even today, partially conditioned by the climate of the north and the geology of Alpine countries, for instance. However these are negligible compared to the contrasts at the turn of the century. At that time, it was largely a person's nationality that determined whether he or she lived in a city or not. The countries at opposite ends of the urbanization spectrum are generally identical with those on a similar scale for industrialization. Great Britain was by far the most heavily urbanised. Even counting cities with populations upwards of 20,000 or more—which is necessary since no fully comparable figures exist for towns of smaller sizes—the majority of the British population were then living in such towns. Even in the Netherlands, built up as it was, the figure did not exceed a third. At the other extreme were the Scandinavian and Alpine countries with surprisingly low levels of urbanization for the time, and urban populations no greater than 10 per cent. The remainder lived in rural areas or small towns. Relying on individual national definitions of the term "town", which also brings smaller towns under scrutiny, there is still no great change. Great Britain was still highly urbanised, with three-quarters of its population living in built-up areas. The states of Northern Europe (no more than a quarter of the population) stand in sharp contrast, as do countries in Eastern Europe (a fifth or less). Such contrasts were very plain all over Europe even though urban growth had already been well under way since the nineteenth century.[20]

Around 1970, on the other hand, variations within Europe had diminished significantly. In Great Britain, urbanization seems to have reached its upper limit around the turn of the century and has remained static ever since. The stragglers have caught up in the course of the twentieth century, and at an unusual rate for European countries, a subject dealt with earlier. Around 1970, even in Scandinavian and Alpine countries, a third and more of the population lived in medium-sized or large towns. To judge by individual national definitions of the term, the majority of the populations of nearly every European country were town dwellers. Portugal alone had not reached such levels of urbanization. Thus overall, sharp contrasts between town and country dwellers at the turn of the century were almost universally reduced to differences in scale between majorities of city-dwellers.[21]

Convergence in urbanization was not steady throughout the twentieth century in Western Europe. By the inter-war period, the sharp contrasts that had existed were already waning, above all because there was such rapid urban growth in Scandinavia and in the Alpine countries. Between 1900 and 1940 in Sweden, the proportion of the total population living in cities doubled. In Finland the rise was threefold. After World War II, however, European societies began to converge more quickly than they had even between the wars (see Figure 9).

The historical significance of the process at work in Western Europe once again only becomes clear in a comparison with other large societies. Admittedly the results look different according to whether the United States or the Soviet Union is used for the purpose. The striking thing when comparing Europe with America is the great similarity in the scale of variations in the two continents. Around 1910, the individual states of the United States were as widely differentiated as the countries of Europe. East-coast states like New York or Pennsylvania and rural states like Texas and Kentucky were as far apart in terms of urbanization as Great Britain and Portugal at the same time. Up to the 1960s, the rate at which variation declined in the United States was no greater than that seen in Western Europe. If anything, the American variations persisted more. A highly-urbanised state like California had over 90 per cent town dwellers, whereas the figure for the predominantly rural state of Vermont was around 30 per cent; the size of the gap is comparable with the variation between Great Britain (80 per cent) and Portugal (30 per cent). Comparisons with the United States act as a corrective to the tendency to view Europe as a place of wide differentiation. In urbanization, integration advanced at least as quickly in Europe as it did in the United States.

European developments make a greater impression when placed side by side with the Soviet Union; the two trends are totally separate and anything but parallel. Around 1912, there was some variation in the scale of urbanization in Russia but this was far below the scale of contrasts between European countries. Compared with the west as it was then, there was a high level of homogeneity in Tsarist Russia. Variations in urbanization have decreased even further throughout the Soviet Union as time has gone by. The rapid rate of urbanization in Western Europe has brought the proportion of town dwellers into line with the Soviet Union. Thus, integration in Western Europe has also gained ground on the homogeneous Soviet Union.[22]

The size of towns is a further area where European societies have converged during the twentieth century. The importance of medium-sized towns with populations of between 20,000 and 100,000 has already been discussed as a feature of twentieth-century Europe. Around 1920, there were a number of countries in Europe that did not conform to the general pattern. In addition to Germany, Belgium and Austria, Norway and Portugal were countries with relatively small proportions—less than 20 per cent—of their urban population grouped in such towns. The importance of these towns grew throughout the twentieth century in all these countries and came to approach the European average. The development in countries with very high existing populations in medium-sized towns—Italy, Spain, the Netherlands and Finland—took the opposite course and their importance declined enormously. These countries converged on the European average from the other end of the range. In spite of continuing large variation, medium-sized towns have become more and more similar in their importance throughout Western Europe.[23]

The development of the conurbation in Europe over the same period resulted in a less one-sided situation. In the first decades of the century they were mainly grouped in Northern Europe; in Great Britain and the Netherlands about half of the urban population lived in cities with more than one million inhabitants. The proportion declined progressively further south; in

France it was around a third, in Spain only a quarter, and in Italy only a fifth. This could partly be due to differing systems for defining towns, but that cannot be the whole explanation. This "north-south split" diminished greatly as the twentieth century progressed. The biggest cities saw little expansion in Northern Europe. In Southern Europe, however, the number of urban dwellers in conurbations grew steadily. The inner-European convergence is especially apparent in the decline of agglomerations since the 1970s. Only the classic urban regions of Northern Europe saw a population decline. In Great Britain and West Germany, population drain became the rule. On the other hand, there was growth in the conurbations further south in the "Golden Triangle" drawn between Northern Holland, Rome and Madrid. De-urbanization was hardly noticeable at all in that region. In Italy it was one trend among many others. In France it could be observed only in a few cases. The dominant trend was one of growth and the conurbation thus became more evenly distributed throughout Europe.[24]

It seems more important that there were changes in urban life that gradually eliminated variations in Europe as the century progressed. Early in the twentieth century, the nature of the typical town dwelling—for instance, flats or detached or semi-detached family houses—largely depended on the country under observation. Houses were the special hallmark of British towns, even London, where they accounted for over 90 per cent of private accommodation. In continental Europe, flats were more common in Belgian towns, and more common still in Dutch towns, though they never constituted more than 10 per cent of all living accommodation. In Alpine and Scandinavian countries, and on the territory that now makes up West Germany, they were slightly more common. The proportion in those countries was roughly 20 per cent to 30 per cent. Flats were more common further east, in the cities of Saxony, the eastern portion of Prussia and the great cities of the Habsburg Empire, as well as in rapidly expanding Paris. Flats accounted for 30 per cent to 50 per cent of accommodation in these cases. Far ahead of all other cities, however, was Berlin: 80 per cent of accommodation in the city was comprised of the flats which dominated its landscape. Variations such as these are slow to disappear because housing stocks tend to have long lives. Despite this, the situation in Western Europe has probably increased in its uniformity since World War II. The skylines of all large Western European cities are punctuated by blocks of flats. The problems of this type of housing have become a topic of debate throughout Europe and are no longer confined to criticisms of individual cities such as "stony Berlin" as it was between the wars.[25]

It appears that the quality of living accommodation has also become more uniform in Western Europe since the end of World War II. Comparisons between quality of housing, using admittedly rough-and-ready standards such as population density, electricity and water supply and the availability of built-in baths, highlight some striking contrasts within Europe for the periods before and immediately after World War II. In the 1930s there was already great variation in the population densities of developed European countries. In Sweden or Austria, for example, population density was almost twice as high as in Belgium. Around 1950 in France or Austria, built-in baths were still very rare, in fact only half as common as in Great Britain, Denmark and Sweden. Only a half of flats and houses in Portugal and Greece had electricity, even in towns; throughout the rest of Europe, supply was virtually universal in urban areas. In the course of the 1950s and 1960s, the gap in housing quality narrowed greatly, and those that had been left behind quickly caught up. Thereafter it was the similarities that were more striking than the contrasts.[26]

Even today, Western European towns present a far from uniform picture. Countries may be identified at a glance from the construction of their buildings and the way of life of their people. Europe still has a way of developing a multitude of internal variations from which Europeans of all nationalities may derive mutual benefit. Since the war, variations between towns in Europe have nevertheless become less blatant than at any time since the beginning of the century. Urbanisation has increasingly become a feature throughout the societies of Europe. Medium-sized towns have become increasingly similar in their importance. Conurbations are more evenly spread. Quality and ways of life no longer differ so widely. Urban life is substantially more similar throughout Europe.

4. The welfare state and social security
It is not possible to make a comparative historical study of

every detail in the development of welfare state systems. However, state social security systems are one central field where ample and accurate information is available.

In the earlier discussion of the welfare state the extent of its development was highlighted as an important common feature in Western Europe. Early this century there were, however, any number of clear differences between individual European countries. Experiments were still under way with the widest possible range of state and semi-state administered systems.

Introduction of state social security was far from simultaneous throughout Europe. On the eve of World War I, social security in Germany and Austria had existed as a state system for more than a quarter of a century. However, in Germany there was no unemployment insurance, while the Austrian system lacked pension provision. At the time, most other European countries had only recently introduced their systems, and most of them encompassed only one of the three classic areas of social security—accident insurance, health insurance or pensions— as a springboard for the establishment of a welfare state. Often it was decades before there was further expansion in the scope of insurance. Here again there was great diversity throughout the continent.[27]

Up to the outbreak of World War I, political factors affecting the introduction of social security in individual European countries differed to the same degree. Bismarck's approach, in particular, was not widely emulated. He aimed to stem the advance of a burgeoning socialist workers' movement and win the workers' vote for the conservative state by introducing social security, supplemented by repression and persecution. Even in Austria, which was quick to follow the German course and also introduced accident and health insurance for workers in the 1880s, different policies were being pursued, none of them involving heavy use of repressive measures against workers' organizations. Representatives of workers' parties were directly involved in the introduction of national systems of health insurance and pensions in Great Britain and Sweden respectively. In these countries, despite controversy and tensions within parties, there were already early signs of the broad political consensus between socialists, liberals and conservatives that would later prove so essential to the expansion of the welfare state in Europe.[28]

Pre-1914 welfare institutions were so multifarious that only a few of the more important differences can be discussed here. In 1914, it was still unclear whether European governments would finally opt for compulsory insurance as in Germany where every insured worker had to become a member, or for a voluntary system as in Great Britain. It was not certain whether pure state systems, governed by law and administered by civil servants would become the norm, or whether semi-private systems would be approved to be run with state supervision and subsidies but otherwise on the lines of private or mutual companies. Sources of finance had to be finalised. The options available were employees' or employers' contributions, or funding through taxation which would give the system the appearance of a means of redistribution of income. It was unclear whether social security would be truly national, encompassing all citizens, or whether it would be dependent on status with only certain groups enjoying its benefits. Finally there was the question of how much say the system's clients or their elected representatives would have. Would a social administration evolve with clients as objects, or would they participate in fundamental decisions for which they would share responsibility? In the early days of the modern welfare state, particularism was largely responsible for the experimentation with so many types of institution and for the proposal of many other types that never got beyond the discussion phase. Thus before 1914, European countries differed very widely indeed.[29]

The groups to whom state social security was available depends chiefly on the country under scrutiny, and variations within Europe were again very great (see Figures 7 and 9). Around 1914, about a half of all wage earners in both Sweden and Great Britain were insured under the systems of the two countries. The gap to the earliest pioneers, Germany and Austria, with figures of about 40 per cent and less than 10 per cent respectively, was substantial. Greater still was the gap to countries like Finland, Italy, Switzerland and the Netherlands where state systems extended to only a small percentage of the working population. For an outsider, it would not have been easy to identify common European features as they took root. Far more striking would have been the difference in scale of the various systems.[30] In all probability this was also true of social security payments, but this is an area where information is scarce. The assistance and treatment given to individuals in need before World War I, even by the relatively large British and German systems, was apparently very different. In 1913 there were just under a million pensioners in Britain who were paid a total of about £12 million by the government, the average therefore being about £12.50 each. In 1911 the old age pension payable in Germany was 166 Reichsmarks, or the contemporary equivalent of £8.30, based on a rate of exchange of twenty Reichsmarks to the pound sterling. This was just about a fifth of the typical wage. Pensions for the disabled stood slightly higher that year, at 187 Reichsmarks. Though intended only as a family supplement, such a sum would have been an important contribution to the relief of poverty in old age. Older workers in Germany were probably not as well disposed towards Bismarck as English workers apparently were to Lloyd George who had introduced the British state pension. According to the famous report on the Salford slums by Robert Roberts, "they praised the name of Lloyd George as though he were a saint from heaven."[31]

Between the wars the great intra-European differences diminished somewhat. Social security was now beyond its earliest infancy, and for that very reason the similarities became greater. In the majority of European countries all three classic types became established although the odd country still lagged behind. There was great variation in the new types of insurance that were added to the various state systems during the 1920s and 1930s; once again in some countries, revisions never got beyond the discussion stage. Unemployment benefit, for instance, was introduced only in a minority of Western European countries. The general trend was clearly apparent however. In nearly all countries—the exceptions being Switzerland and Ireland, two of the smaller ones—at least two of the three classic types of insurance were now organised on a state basis. Nearly half the countries of Western Europe were equipped with all three. The state of flux that had prevailed before 1914 had now hardened into a trend.[32]

As far as it is possible to reduce complex political decisions to a common denominator, there also seems to have been growing uniformity in the political forces supporting the establishment of state social security. Whereas their stance on social security had frequently been ambivalent before World War I, most

European workers' parties now became the prime movers in the development of the welfare state, having overcome the internal tensions that had often barred the way. There was especially rapid development of state systems in those countries where workers' parties were in government or had a share in power. At the same time there was a consolidation of the tendency towards a consensus between workers', liberal, and conservative parties on the necessity of the concept.[33]

There was also a reduction in the number of different types of institution; here again certain common trends began to emerge. The most important was that compulsory insurance began to gain ground at the expense of state-supervised and subsidised voluntary insurance. Wherever a new system was being introduced, governments opted universally for the compulsory version. Austria (1927), Norway (1936) and Finland (1937) brought in pensions on this basis. The Dutch system of health insurance introduced in 1929 was compulsory, as were the unemployment benefit systems introduced in Austria in 1920 and Germany in 1927. Besides this a number of European governments replaced voluntary, state-supported social security with exclusively state-run systems. Norway, Denmark, France, Italy and Great Britain all took this course. Only unemployment benefit remained voluntary to the same extent as it had before 1914. Counter-developments between the wars should not be overlooked. The Nazi seizure of power in Germany had serious consequences for the welfare state. Social security became an instrument of racial discrimination and political control, thus undermining the legal right to welfare assistance, one of the most important common features of the welfare state.[34]

The final process that occurred between the wars was that state social security systems became increasingly similar in scale. There was no longer any huge disparity between the numbers covered by individual systems in different countries (see Figure 9). Around 1930, about every second or third wage earner was covered by accident insurance in most Western European countries. This figure was only exceeded in a few countries such as Great Britain and Germany. At the same time, health insurance covered about every fifth, but never more than every second member of the population of most countries; Italy and Finland were exceptional in that the number was far smaller. In most Western European countries

around 1940, at least every second wage earner was entitled to a
pension. In Germany and the Scandinavian countries the
number was considerably higher. Crucial differences still remained of course and uniformity was not a characteristic of the
European situation in terms of the three classic areas of social
security provision. Unemployment benefit systems in particular varied greatly in the number of wage earners covered. In
Great Britain and Germany about every second worker was insured against unemployment; in France and Scandinavia, on
the other hand, it was only a few per cent.[35] Overall, however,
contrasts in the scale of social security systems decreased somewhat in the years up to the outbreak of World War II.

The thrust of convergence after World War II was very much
greater. The highly developed welfare state finally emerged as a
tangible feature of Western European societies, spreading to
every country. Only then did it become more than just a
phenomenon apparent only to the historian with the benefit of
hindsight.

This was primarily because after World War II the welfare
state was expanded at a hitherto inconceivable rate. The
number of people benefiting from social security grew faster
than ever. For the first time, the situation was reached where
certain systems covered almost the whole of the population of
their country. Social security expenditure mushroomed,
boosted by cost-intensive innovations such as housing benefit,
family allowances, educational grants, index-linked pensions,
higher levels of pensions, and sickness and unemployment benefits which narrowed the gap on an employee's normal earn-
ings. Throughout Europe, social security payments came to account for ever higher percentages of national income. Whereas
the European average around 1950 was roughly 6 per cent, this
had grown to 14 per cent by 1975. The European average for
total state expenditure on social security was 14 per cent of national product in 1960; this grew to 30 per cent by 1981. Development of state expenditure on social security thus became
an increasingly important element of overall social and
economic policy. Changes, for instance in pension levels, that
had previously only affected minorities now became central to
election campaign planning.

There is a definite link between the welfare state's dramatic
rate of expansion and the earlier economic crisis and World

War II, both of which had shaken belief in the capacity of economies to mend themselves, thus slackening a crucial restraint on welfare state policies. Besides this, the post-war boom had given such policies extended room for manoeuvre, simultaneously creating conditions whereby social security would become unavoidable because of the growth of dependent labour in industry. This unprecedented expansion swept away many of the persisting variations in social security within Europe at a stroke.[36]

The introduction of the three main areas of insurance gradually reached completion throughout Western Europe in the decades after World War II. Accident insurance was established in Belgium, France and Great Britain. Pensions came to Switzerland and Ireland. Belgium, Finland and Sweden voted for state health insurance; Switzerland was alone in Western Europe in rejecting this type of insurance, having opted for both industrial accident insurance and state pensions. State unemployment insurance, a late introduction even in pioneering countries, was far from universal. As late as the 1970s, it was still unavailable in Scandinavia. Today, however, the overwhelming majority of Western Europeans have state cover against unemployment, though this still varies from country to country.[37]

Between the wars and after World War II, the political champions of the welfare state were essentially the same. Throughout Europe, welfare state policies contained in the manifestoes of workers', liberal and conservative parties differed very clearly. After 1945, when the foundations of social security were being laid, political attitudes to the issue also differed widely, particularly in France, Great Britain and West Germany. But the actual decisions themselves did not differ greatly, and the expansion of the welfare state followed similar lines throughout the continent. Whether power was in the hands of conservative and liberal politicians who tended to hold the process in check, or politicians of the workers' parties who drove the welfare state ever onward, there were few great variations in the practicalities. With nests well feathered by the economic boom, the general consensus on the necessity of state social security lasted until the early 1970s.[38]

The institutions themselves also became more and more similar. Compulsory insurance was more favoured than it had been between the wars, and it was exceptional for voluntary systems with state funding to be retained. National insurance, that is to say, insurance of all citizens under one system, spread increasingly as the British example became recognized, though admittedly it did not become universal. The very oldest system was particularly resistant. In post-war West Germany, the division between blue-collar and white-collar insurance was retained, and certain self-employed groups were exempted from the state system. Proposed reforms inspired by the British example fell before conservative government policies of the day, but also because of inertia within insurance institutions and opposition from insured parties and the unions. In general, the most popular system was the national system, embracing the whole population regardless of status. Sources of finance were as varied as they had ever been before 1914—taxation, employee contributions and employers' payments were all favoured as means of raising finance. Participatory administration never became the norm. Overall, however, there was less variation in the institutions of state social security than there had been before World War I or between the wars. The age of experimentation came to an end in Western Europe.[39]

After 1945, the scale of state social security in Western Europe converged so rapidly and to such a degree that it is possible to describe today's position as highly uniform. Nearly all wage earners came to enjoy insurance of all three main types under state systems. By 1975, nearly all Western European countries had reached this ultimate situation for health insurance and pensions. The only exceptions were in Germany, Austria, Ireland and—with particular regard to health insurance—the Netherlands. About 10 per cent to 20 per cent of wage earners, mostly the self-employed, were still not under the state umbrella of health insurance and pensions. In the case of accident insurance, the extension of cover to all workers was a later development, but European societies were also converging in this respect too. In the area where overall European development came late, namely in unemployment insurance, the number of wage earners that were protected still varied widely from country to country. Even here, convergent trends may be identified (see Figure 9). This was the period when convergence was resulting in true similarities in the scale of social security systems in individual countries.

It is difficult to say whether there was also convergence in the benefits offered by various systems. The effects of social security on the people it serves is a very sensitive point in the history of social security. It has hitherto been neglected by researchers, or else has only been dealt with in laborious preliminary studies. Financial assistance given by social security systems and the welfare state in general gives a rough indication, even though it obscures certain aspects that are important from the citizen's point of view, for instance distribution of payments, non-financial services, efficiency and personal contact with the administrative machinery. Since World War II, Western European social security systems have offered increasingly similar levels of financial assistance, and this convergence has extended to social services in general. Around 1950, benefit levels varied greatly. Taking the economic strength of individual countries into account, benefit levels in Austria, Germany and Belgium were about twice as high as in Norway, Finland or Switzerland. By 1975 this gap had narrowed substantially.[40]

There are thus any number of indicators that state systems of social security have converged dramatically over the course of the twentieth century. The sharp contrasts that existed in all aspects of the welfare state before 1914 have undergone constant change resulting in greater uniformity, even though there is no absolute uniformity in Western Europe even today. There are still differences from which lessons may be learned. They are, however, only variations on a fundamentally similar system that has developed further in Europe than anywhere else in the world.

5. Similarities and differences in family structure
In family structure—as in industrial relations (a subject for later discussion)—the processes of convergence have not been as apparent as in the cases described above, which are among the best-researched. In other areas the extent of research does not allow precise theories to be advanced.

Convergent processes are by no means absent from developments in the European family, and this is especially true of women's work. Between the wars and before 1914 above all, the extent of women's work varied greatly from country to country. Around the turn of the century in Austria two-fifths of wage earners were women. In France, Switzerland and Finland the figure exceeded one-third. By contrast, females accounted for less than a quarter of wage earners in the Netherlands, and less than one-sixth in Spain. Between the wars the contrasts became, if anything, even greater. Portugal and Finland then had the highest proportions of female wage earners, while in Spain the proportion dropped even lower than before. Admittedly, knowledge of methods used by the various national statistical bureaux is still inadequate, and the figures must therefore be treated with some caution. In those cases where historians have traced statistical methods more accurately, however, there is no indication whatsoever that the differences observed before 1914, and subsequently between the wars, were only a product of methods of survey and compilation. By contrast, today the extent of women's work outside the home is fairly uniform throughout Western Europe. In countries with the highest figures for women's work, they still constitute around two-fifths of the workforce. This is the predominant case in Scandinavia. In countries where the proportion had formerly been lower, increases and convergence have taken place, so that today women account for almost one-third of all wage earners in countries such as Spain and the Netherlands. In these countries growth has continued right up until the past few years. In the four biggest and most populous European countries, France, Great Britain, West Germany and Italy, similarities in the extent of women's work are startling.[41] The impression of convergence is reinforced by the growing similarity of women's education in Western Europe, which has become decisive in the later careers of so many young European women.

Convergence in women's work has brought more than just an improvement in career opportunity. Aspirations and values have also grown in similarity. Present day surveys show a very similar underlying pattern in all Western European countries. Only a relatively small overall proportion idealises a housewife's existence of marriage, an abandoned career and a life of devotion to the home and the rearing of children. The majority of Europeans of both sexes, and with very small variation from one country to the next, is in favour of the example of the woman who continues to work outside the home even after marriage and the birth of her children; admittedly in most countries this ideal is still combined with a perceived division of a man's and a woman's work in the home, leading to a considerable extra burden on the woman working outside the home. Even in this respect there is no great variation within Europe.[42]

It is important not to overstress this aspect of convergence. It has been by no means as dramatic as that witnessed in employment structure, education, urbanisation or the welfare state. Before World War I it appeared that women's work was set to become very similar in nature throughout Europe. Between the wars there was a period of divergence, a possible consequence of the "labour service" undertaken by women during World War II which differed greatly from country to country, though it could also be connected with labour policies pursued during the recession. Far from changing radically since 1914, inner-European differences today are only marginally smaller than they were then (see Appendix for Table 9).

This must be qualified by observing that even as late as 1975 only certain special age groups were showing real signs of convergence in the extent of work for women. Among young adults (20–24 years old, before the typical marrying age), the proportion of working women was indeed very similar from one European country to the next. This was true for EC countries at least; information on others is lacking. Throughout the Community—except for Italy—about two-thirds of women worked for a living at this age, the rest being in education. Italy was the only country where there were significantly fewer women going out to work at this age. Beyond the typical marrying age for women, striking differences begin to emerge within Europe (see Figure 10) which must be partly due to the history of women's work in individual European countries. Its effect was greater on older age groups than on younger. In the Netherlands, where women's work was increasing all the time, it became more widespread among younger than among older women. In Germany where women's work had seen little change since the war, the differences between older and younger age groups were smaller. There are also traces of differing life cycles for working women from country to country. Women in Belgium typically abandoned their careers for good after getting married or giving birth to their first child. In Great Britain, and to a lesser extent in West Germany, work outside the home was dropped only while children were small and resumed once they had reached school age. The most common pattern in Denmark was for women to continue working despite childbirth, the woman's cycle thus becoming similar to a man's (see Figure 10).[43] It is only after pensionable age that differences begin to disappear again.

Closer inspection gives the impression that convergence in the nature of women's work in European countries has been greatly affected by the state of labour markets, educational opportunities, the welfare state and the family. Among young adult women there was great similarity before marriage, the age when labour market and educational opportunities are particularly keenly felt, and the family role has little (and increasingly smaller) impact on a woman's working life. Similarities increase around pensionable age, an effect of welfare state provision which has tended to iron out differences within Europe. Similarities were smaller after marriage and the birth of children. During this phase of a woman's life a mother's working conditions (nursery school, school and mealtimes, opening hours at the shops and the amount of time spent and family help received in doing housework) has a far greater impact on her outside occupation. These conditions still apparently differ greatly from country to country; the variations in the character of women's work around the age of thirty are surprisingly great. There is thus little indication that the variations are growing out as time progresses. Instead the process of convergence has come up against an unmistakable barrier. Variations have diminished but only slowly because of their evident durability.

The impression of an almost static situation is reinforced by more detailed study of other elements of twentieth-century family development.

Relationships between marriage partners show few signs of the rapid growth in similarity that has characterised some of the other aspects of European life under discussion here; similarity in this respect was probably always greater. Today the typical age of marriage differs as greatly from one country to the next in Europe as it did early this century. The high age at marriage which characterises and conditions so much of European society remains largely unchanged. Certain differences, not very great admittedly, between Austria and Ireland on the one hand (as countries where marriage is typically late) and France on the other, have existed since before 1914 and have been evident in the post-war age too. Around 1970 the Germans and

Figure 10: Employment among female population by age group in Western European countries, 1975.

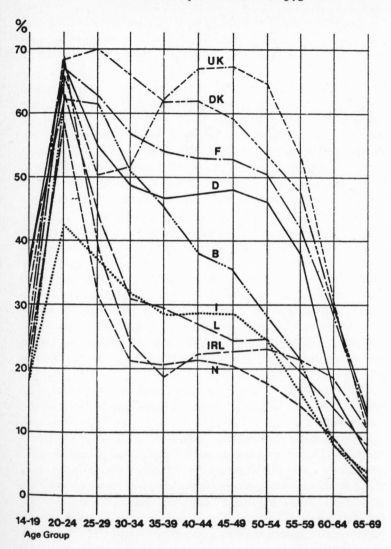

UK = United Kingdom; DK = Denmark; F = France; D = West Germany; B = Belgium; I = Italy; L = Luxemburg; IRL = Ireland; N = Netherlands

Italians tended to marry late, Austrians and Britons typically slightly earlier (see Table 1). Today the variation in the extent of divorce is about as great as it was at the turn of the century (see Appendix for Table 9). Around 1910 divorce in the countries with the highest rates—especially Switzerland, France and Austria—could be twenty times more common than in countries with low rates such as Great Britain. Since World War II the contrasts have not become any less sharp. By 1970, divorce was most common in Denmark, where it was similarly about twenty times more common than in Portugal at the other end of the European scale. Hence there is nothing to suggest that relationships between marriage partners have become more uniform over the course of the twentieth century, or that there has been any dramatic reduction of distinctive national features.

Today, with the exception of certain situations, inner European variations in relationships between marriage partners are small. Just as at the turn of the century, the typical age at marriage today varies surprisingly little from one European country to the next. Disregarding certain exceptions, it varies by only a few years. The variation in the age at which marriages typically terminate with the death of one marriage partner is also surprisingly small. In the countries for which comparative studies are available, the age was typically around seventy years for women and uniformly around eighty-five years for men. Thus the number of years of marriage which Europeans could typically expect to spend was much more similar than might have been expected. The uniformity of attitudes towards marriage in individual European countries is also surprising. Surveys in a range of countries concerning the value placed on marriage, the importance of mutual respect, tolerance and sexual satisfaction for a successful marriage and the unimportance of material wealth and social background have highlighted some very similar attitudes. Even now, contrasts within Europe can be sharp in those cases where politics or the law have a determining influence. Divorce is the best example here; there are enormous differences because divorce laws, proceedings and the material consequences of divorce vary so greatly from one European country to the next. However, in those aspects of the family where politics and the law exert less power over relationships, married life shows great similarity and has probably changed little since the turn of the century.[44]

The situation with parent-child relationships is practically the same, with no radical process of convergence being discernible this century. Variations in birth rates are no greater today than they were a hundred years ago. Early this century, peripheral countries such as Finland, Portugal, Spain and Italy were the ones with the highest birth rates; at that time France had the lowest rate. The gap between them was no greater than that which exists today between France, Ireland, Spain, Portugal and Greece with their high birth rates and West Germany, Denmark and Italy at the other end of the range. Infant mortality shows a similar trend and incidentally reveals the importance of parent-child relationships as well as advances in public health, infant care and medical provision. Over a century of prodigious reductions in infant mortality have nevertheless preserved the inner European hierarchy to a surprising extent. Around the turn of the century, the level of infant mortality in Germany, Austria and Spain was very high by European standards. In these countries, one-fifth of children would die in their first year of life. In Scandinavia, especially Norway and Sweden, the rate was less than half as high; about one in ten children would die before the age of one. Infant mortality has without doubt decreased massively since then, but such variation continues almost unchanged to the present day. As well as two peripheral countries, Portugal and Greece, West Germany and Austria also have above average infant mortality rates. In these countries around one child in seventy died in its first year. The Scandinavian countries have been joined by Switzerland and the Netherlands as the countries with particularly low levels of infant mortality. In 1980 in Sweden, only one in every 150 children died before the age of one. As far as these figures allow statements to be made about family life, inner European variation has not balanced out and is still regrettably clear.

The inner European variations that exist today in parent-child relationships are by no means vast, and were probably not as great as the variations that once existed in other areas of society which have been examined in these pages. A hundred years ago European countries had very similar birth rates—disregarding France, a special case. Today there is a certain tendency for European countries to drift apart, even close neighbours such as France and West Germany. Nevertheless, the variations are small compared with third world countries. Whatever infant mortality figures may reveal about relationships between parents and children, this is another area where intra-European variation has persisted over the past hundred years just as it has in other areas of society. Attitudes to children are today very similar throughout Western Europe. The ideal size for a family is virtually the same throughout the EC—with the exception of France and Ireland. The aims that parents have for the upbringing of their children vary to a surprisingly small extent. Honesty, tolerance, responsibility and good manners, attitudes to parental authority, parental care and education are all highly regarded by parents. The consensus reached by Western Europeans is especially striking. Contrasts between European countries only really exist in those cases where the law or politics, including local public services, play a part; this could be the case in infant mortality which is also determined by quality of maternity hospitals and infant care. Variations within Europe are more obvious in the type of arrangements made by parents for the supervision of their children which have an impact on contact with their children in daily life. There are great variations in the extent to which grandmothers, creches or paid child minders are made use of, and this is evidently connected with standards of public services and therefore local and national government decisions.[45]

The family is therefore not an island where differences between European societies have been fossilised or a sanctuary for distinctive national features. The opposite is rather the case. Sharp contrasts exist only where the law and politics strike at the heart of the family. The family does not present an obstacle to the social integration of Western Europe and has for some time shared many common characteristics in a range of European countries.

6. Divergence of industrial relations
In terms of industrial relations there has been little growth in the similarity of Western European countries. This might be looked at as a barrier to social integration. Degrees of unionization, types of unions and strikes differ widely even today. During the twentieth century some of these differences have become even more marked.

The extent of unionization among workers differed as much

at the turn of the century as it does today. Around 1910, unionization was many times higher in Great Britain, a heavily industrialised country, than it was in Italy, a largely agrarian nation; however union membership varied greatly even in the main industrialised countries of Europe. Around 1910, union membership among British or German workers was three times as high as it was in Belgium or Switzerland. Even in the late 1970s, it was the variations between countries that were most striking. In Sweden, Denmark and Finland, and Belgium too, the overwhelming majority of workers were unionized. In Great Britain, Spain, Ireland and Austria the majority was smaller but present nevertheless. In France, West Germany and Switzerland on the other hand, only about one-third of workers belonged to unions (see Table 8). There are doubtless very clear differences between Western Europe as a whole and North America or Japan. However European countries have not really become more similar in the extent of unionization in the course of the twentieth century.

In the types of trade unions that are encountered in Europe, it is once again the differences that are most apparent. The typical Central and Northern European unified trade union (not aligned with political parties or with churches) as seen in Scandinavia, Great Britain, Austria and West Germany differs very clearly from the unions defined as socialist, communist or Christian in Italy, France, Switzerland, Belgium or the Netherlands. Since the lifting of union bans, Spanish and Portuguese unions have also been cast in the latter mould. In fact, it is possible to say that contrasts within Europe have been heightened. Between the wars there were communist, socialist and Christian unions in most countries, certainly Germany and Austria. This split between "aligned" unions characterized the European scene even though their principles were far from uniform from one country to the next. The unified unions which first appeared between the wars were something of a curiosity; it is only since the war that European unions have become polarized into unified and aligned blocks. Another post-war development has been the split between heavily centralized bureaucratic unions (typical of Central and Northern Europe), and the British grassroots model. In the former type of union, the bureaucracy tended to wield the power at the expense of the rank and file; disputes lacked spontaneity and were largely planned and directed by union officials. The British unions tended to concentrate more power in the hands of members and shop stewards within individual plants who therefore had much greater control over planning, conduct and conclusion of disputes. A further important difference that has been preserved within Europe throughout the twentieth century has been in the extent of integration of white-collar, self-employed and civil service staff associations into the union movement. In central and northern countries such as Switzerland, Denmark and Sweden such organizations distanced themselves from the unified unions. In Germany, the divide between white-collar and blue-collar unions had been particularly large before 1914; even late in the inter-war period, this divide was never fully closed. Integration of white-collar unions and associations had been much more advanced in Belgium and Italy where alignment was more important than status as an element of unionization.[46]

It is the huge variation in types of strike that is the chief cause of breakdown in the social integration of Europe. Before 1914 and between the wars the variations were already considerable. At that time, however, one particular type of strike quite clearly held sway while a further two types were of significantly smaller importance, as Tilly and Shorter have shown. There were the frequent long drawn out strikes with few participating strikers in large countries like France, Italy, Germany, Spain and Belgium. Then there were the even longer and more frequent strikes with substantially smaller support in Scandinavia and the Netherlands. Finally there was the modern type of infrequent but lengthy and very heavily supported strike which at the time was typical only of Great Britain.

By contrast, after World War II there has been no dominant form of strike. As in the organization of unions, a great divide grew up in Western Europe between two very different types of strike of similar importance, and a third special case. There was the typical Central and Northern European strike that occurred very infrequently, lasted a long time and often received massive support. Such strikes tended to be strictly limited to securing reviews of pay and conditions and were typical of Scandinavia, the Netherlands, West Germany and Austria. In France and Italy strikes tended to be short, very frequent and well-supported, being very often more in the nature of

political demonstrations than disputes over material conditions. Lastly there was the British strike, typified by frequent,
short and small-scale disputes which often revolved around
matters of authority within an isolated firm.

The differences between these types of strike are much more
stark than before 1914 or between the wars (see Appendix for
Table 9). Tilly and Shorter believe that the cause of the variations lies in the status of workers' parties in national and regional parliaments. In countries where workers' parties had a
long tradition of power in national or state governments,
strikes receded and became less and less political. Unions had
more opportunity to achieve their political aims via their political wings. In countries such as France and Italy where, right up
to the early 1980s, socialist parties were rarely in power and in
any case not for long, strikes remained an instrument of political control and were frequently used as such.[47] With socialist
governments installed in nearly every Mediterranean country
in the 1980s a test is available for this theory, and time will tell if
labour relations gradually grow in similarity as a result.

The very persistent diversity of strike forms and types of
union organization has had a heavy impact on the European
union movement's political integration. This diversity has been
an essential cause of long-term difficulties in the establishment
of a union organization for the whole of the European Community—the European Trades Union Confederation—which
has taken far longer to set up than either the European industrial organizations or the European farmers' association and is
still weaker in membership terms. However, these differences
have also meant first that social policy, labour law and company law have never been acknowledged as being central to
European integration in the wider sense, and secondly that
Europe-wide wage agreements must still be regarded as a
difficult nut to crack.[48] The heterogeneity of unions is a prime
cause of their weakness at European level.

A few convergent trends must not go unacknowledged, however. Throughout the twentieth century, the economically dependent have become more similar in the extent to which they
have become unionised. Tracing developments in democratic
countries with no limitations on the right to unionise, the differences showed first signs of waning quite early in the century.
During and directly after World War I there was a massive

surge in union membership which resulted in a slight reduction of the variations in the extent of unionisation. A second surge directly after World War II seems to have ironed out the irregularities still further. Admittedly, no further convergent trends have been initiated (see Tables 8 and 9). Bringing all Western European countries into the survey, variation in membership of free trade unions becomes wider still in the 1920s and 1930s because there were no trade unions left in Italy and Portugal, nor later in Spain, Germany and Austria. In the 1970s Western European countries at last began to converge on each other again. Most recently the extent of unionisation has become more similar than ever before (see Tables 8 and 9). This is without doubt a fundamental and decisive dismantling of variation within Europe.

Besides this there are, in the short term, indications from events of the last decade and a half that variations in types of union organisation have been on the decrease. Comparative studies of Great Britain and West Germany have shown that while union organisations in the two countries have not exactly fallen into line with each other, they have become slightly more similar. Spontaneous unplanned strikes and members' influence have increased in Germany, making that country's unions more similar to the British model. In the 1970s British unions became increasingly ready to cooperate with government economic policy and with plans to amend rules governing industrial relations, making them more similar to the typical Northern European union. In Italy there was closer cooperation between the different shades of union; the power of the division into secular and clerical unions diminished and there was a growth in overall similarities with unified trade unions. There were also changes in the formerly Catholic French and Dutch trade unions which may be interpreted in these terms. Though admittedly weak in terms of organisation, the unified European Trades Union Confederation was founded in 1973 after lengthy negotiations reflecting the trend towards a bridging of the divide between secular and clerical unions. These beginnings are all the more important because the ETUC represents not only nearly all unions in the European Community, but also those in other countries such as Sweden, Austria and Switzerland.[49]

The final question that must be raised concerns the extent to which variations in strike forms were limited to the average daily strike and whether this conceals a common European propensity to conflict that has surfaced in serious disputes since World War II. It is significant that the two great waves of strikes immediately following the war and in the late 1960s affected the whole of Europe and thus illuminated similarities in industrial relations throughout the continent. The period immediately after World War II was a time of peak strike activity in nearly all Western European countries. In Sweden, Denmark, Finland, West Germany, Austria, Switzerland and the Netherlands, the late 1940s were a time when the Central and Northern European variety of strike was put into action on a massive scale, and with a frequency never witnessed before or since. In countries like France, Belgium and Italy, where the nature of strikes was typically different from this, the number of strikes also showed unusual increases during this period. Precise timing, political background and extent and consequences of strikes were by no means identical of course, but the late 1940s were an important era in the history of industrial relations. The exception here is again Great Britain.

The events of the late 1960s and early 1970s were similar. The wave of strikes was independent of differences in the industrial relations patterns of individual countries and is without doubt crucial to the history of at least two countries, France and Italy. Strike activity also peaked in Belgium, Finland, West Germany and this time in Great Britain too. The vast majority of Western Europeans once again saw a wave of strikes sweep their countries. It was only in Switzerland, Austria, the Netherlands and most of Scandinavia that the unrest was significantly less keenly felt.[50]

None of this can conceal the fact that even today, industrial relations differ to an extraordinary degree from one European country to the next. *National* features may be less significant now, but the contrasts between *groups* of countries since World War II have remained sharper than in employment structure, production, education, urbanisation, the welfare state or even the family. Types of union and strikes varied greatly especially in the years directly after World War II and in the climate of the cold war, chiefly because a country's political culture has a greater impact on industrial relations than it does on the other areas of European social history under examination in these pages. Strikes are also dependent on political events, economic crises and wars, and the often short-term tactical decisions of unions and their members. This is why industrial relations in the United States vary to approximately the same extent from one state to the next as they do in Europe. It is therefore impossible to expect any great similarity in union development or the development of industrial relations. The fact that there were signs of convergence in this area in Europe in the late 1960s and 1970s therefore seems all the more significant, albeit the increases in similarity stopped short of any great achievement in absolute terms.

7. Causes of convergence: four explanations

The marked general convergence of Western European societies in the twentieth century has reduced differences between those societies to a scale comparable with regional differences in the United States and the Soviet Union. But what are the causes of and background to this convergence? Do they possess long-term effects which allow the prediction of a continuing process of social integration in future? On the other hand, are they short-term developments which might be reversed, allowing a possible future decay of social integration? Is social integration connected with political integration or might its history be regarded as following an independent course, affecting the Europe beyond EC boundaries and subject to other forces? The causes of and background to convergence are, without doubt, central to the resolution of these questions. To put it simply, there is no guaranteed answer. There are a number of possible explanations which will be briefly presented and discussed here. But before turning to them, it is necessary to make some further preliminary remarks.

Where there is evidence of marked convergence between the societies of Europe, it is unmistakable that it has commonly occurred in areas that have undergone a re-appraisal in the past ten years and where former trends have simultaneously been reversed. Until about a decade ago, industrialization, higher education, urbanisation and the welfare state were growing at an unprecedented rate and were undisputedly the key factors in social advancement. All that has since changed. Growth in industrial employment has tailed off in many regions of Europe. It is not only agricultural centres that now present the problems but industrial centres such as Glasgow, the English Midlands, southern Belgium, Lorraine and the Ruhr. Education is expanding rapidly but it is outpacing the economic and structural capacity of the labour market, and the threat of unemployment hangs over many university leavers. Throughout Europe growth of the great cities has run its course. There are even the first signs of migration away from the conurbations. The welfare state has come up against financial and political barriers. In many European countries either its growth has stopped or else it is being actively dismantled. At the same time many Europeans have come to scorn the glamour of industry and shun the city. Higher education is regarded with suspicion. There are concerted attacks on the welfare state and the social bureaucracy. Thus there are two unavoidable questions: does social integration centre on those areas of society that have now fallen deepest into crisis, and will it not in all probability come to an end or go into reverse because different countries in Europe will map their own individual escape routes? A further question is this: would integration be re-evaluated by Europeans if it was no longer regarded as the product of modernity and social advancement but rather that of crises, burdens on the individual and on society, and frequently also hopelessness? The quest for the causes of and background to social convergence is important for this reason too.

In current research four approaches attempt to explain the convergence of European societies in the twentieth century, though they are not always applied to the subject of social integration. First, there is the politically directed approach that cites the end of the division of Europe by nation-states. The second approach regards the economic boom of the 1950s and 1960s as the most important engine of convergence. The third approach assigns the process to the demise of social diversity within the European *ancien régime* which was a product of industrialization and its social consequences. Finally, there is the view that divergent socio-historical developments originating in similar pre-industrial societies in Europe gave rise to sharp contrasts between European societies during a long period of industrialization, but finally ran their course to re-emerge in similar modern societies.

There is reason to regard the nation-state as a significant factor conditioning intra-European variation between the late nineteenth century and the end of World War II. One may also trace post-war convergence back to the discrediting and weakening of the nation-state which occurred especially in ex-fascist countries and in those that suffered occupation in World War II.[51] There is no doubt that the emergence of the nation-state had enormous impact on social development throughout Europe. As well as affecting economies to varying and ever greater extents, it had an impact on educational institutions, town and regional planning, the origins of state social insurance, family law, arbitration in labour disputes and labour law. The nation-state reinforced variation within Europe because power was in the hands of such diverse political groupings. In the conservative German empire under the Kaiser, circumstances differed greatly from those in republican France. Besides this, governments at the time were not only engaged in building up trade barriers against their European competitors but also tended to reject other European social and political models as being alien. They therefore reinforced real or imagined national characteristics as part of their social policy. This was not the only pattern, of course. The European brand of nationalism was very sensitive to the real or supposed superiority of other nations, a fact that led to German imitation of the British pattern of industrialization and French copying of the German education system. However, the tendency of nation-states in Europe to seal off their territory from other countries was not limited to the economic sphere. The trend was heightened between the wars when Europe was divided into parliamentary democracies on the one hand and authoritarian and fascist states on the other. The division has made a crucial difference not only to political rights but also to social policy and its repercussions; a wedge has thus been driven between European societies.

Nevertheless, there does not seem to have been a proportional relationship between growth in social convergence and the decline in the credibility of the nation-state since World War II. There are several arguments supporting this analysis. First, and most importantly, convergence appears to have possessed a dynamic of its own. Patterns of family and industrial relations have not grown more similar since 1945 compared with the golden age of the nation-state. Similarly, in urbanisation, employment structure, and even in educational opportunity and the welfare state—both areas that are heavily dependent on political factors—the variations were already on the wane before the outbreak of World War II. The decline of nationalism in Europe does not always parallel the history of social integration and the historical connections that do emerge are not particularly close. Besides this, in the last forty years or so, when convergence has been at its height, it was not the nation-state that became discredited as such. Rather, it was the nationalism of the earlier part of the century. National governments, on the other hand, have seen anything but a decline in the last forty years. Their authority reached new heights during the establishment of the welfare state and with the resounding success of post-war economic policies. The establishment of the European Community meant that in some economic fields, certain countries did not enjoy the full benefits of this new found authority. However, in terms of formulating social policy which has given national governments more control over social developments in the last forty years than at any other time in the twentieth century, the EC has little authority. There are no indications that European governments have steered a conscious course towards convergence with other European countries, but at the same time convergence does not seem to have been handicapped by the growth in the powers of national governments. In the last forty years, there is ample evidence of a driving force for social integration in Europe but little evidence of a close connection with intervention by European national governments and administrations. It would be wrong to trivialise the contribution to the history of social integration made by nation-states and nationalism. In Germany, for instance, they played a vital role in that country's split with the main current of European development before 1945. They may also have hindered and delayed the process of convergence, but there is no proof that they constitute the main reason for the dramatic convergence that has occurred especially in the post-war age.

The economic boom of the 1950s and 1960s is often regarded as a central cause of convergence in European societies.[52] There is no doubt that it coincided with the accelerated convergence of European societies in terms of industrial production, employment structure, education and social security. There are a number of reasons why the post-war boom might have been responsible for that acceleration. On the southern, western and northern peripheries of Europe the recovery led to the rapid establishment of industries, bringing industrial employment in

Ireland, Spain, Portugal and Finland into line with levels common in the rest of Europe. The variations in the extent of industrialization within Europe were thus considerably reduced. The boom made the elimination of trade barriers within Europe more politically realistic; internal political pressure for the protection of home markets and markets within the EC were relatively slight. Thus it was also politically feasible for governments to moderate customs barriers to allow competition from other Western European countries outside the EC, without automatically giving the impression of playing a political game as might have been the case during an economic crisis. With European markets interacting to a greater extent, a likely consequence was a more even spread of industrialization throughout Europe. The boom also extended the range of financial options available to European governments. Countries whose social and educational policies were underdeveloped for a great variety of historical reasons were now presented with an unprecedented opportunity to gain ground vis à vis the pioneers, for instance by establishing a system of social security. The boom was therefore an essential precondition for convergence of educational opportunity and social insurance systems in Western Europe. Another effect was to mobilize all available reserves of labour, thereby not only improving education and career prospects for women, but also making substantial inroads into the differences existing between the societies of Europe. These were all effects of the levelling and integrating power of the economic boom. It may be assumed that without this phase of prosperity in the 1950s and 1960s, social integration would not be as far advanced as it is today.

It would be an exaggeration to regard convergence merely as a child of the boom, and to expect the divergence or even social disintegration from the economic crises of the last fifteen years. The developments since the early 1970s give no indication of an end to social integration. In those areas of society in which integration has been a strong historical process, it has continued even during times of crisis and there has been continued reduction of differences in industrial production and employment structure. Student figures show less differentiation. Educational opportunities for women grew ever more similar. Urbanization showed no signs of re-emerging differences. Systems of social security were without doubt more similar after the onset of the crisis than they had ever been in the twentieth century. So far, there are no clues to the long-term effects of the period under discussion here which runs for approximately ten years after the oil crisis of 1973 (see Figures 8 and 9, and Appendix for Table 9). Over the course of this decade or so, European societies have become steadily more similar.[53] The boom can therefore hardly be regarded as the true engine of social integration.

Besides this, examination of conditions before 1945 does not show that periods of economic prosperity were necessarily accompanied by social integration, nor does it show that economic crises necessarily caused European societies to drift apart. During the last real boom, from the 1890s to the outbreak of World War I, intra-European variations, especially in employment structure and urbanisation, did diminish slightly. However, similar trends may be identified between the wars, when the economic outlook was generally poor (see Appendix for Table 9). Thus there is nothing to indicate that convergence and divergence are closely linked to economic cycles. If convergence occurred particularly rapidly during the 1950s and 1960s and if societies actually did become very similar, then there must be more behind the phenomenon than just the boom.

The third approach establishes industrialization as the instrument whereby intra-European variations were gradually whittled away in a long process resulting in increasingly uniform social conditions for all Europeans. That process was final. Local and regional autonomy and characteristics that persisted before and throughout the industrial revolution—subsistence economies, bad transport networks and lack of information on the outside world—were gradually supplanted by increasing dependence on market forces, transport systems reaching into every last valley in Europe and the proliferation of modern systems of mass communication. Industrialization and industrial societies became the norm throughout Europe. There is a considerable weight of evidence in support of this approach. Compared with knowledge of twentieth-century societies, information on the differences between societies further back in history is imprecise. It is therefore only possible to observe differences being trimmed in the latter stages of a process that began in the eighteenth century. However, where such a process did occur it is startlingly continuous. This is the power of such long-term explanations when compared with weaker explanations such as the post-war boom or the decline in the credibility of the nation-state. The progress of convergence in Western European societies supports the notion of industrialization as a long-term leveller of variations. Prior to 1914, differences first began to disappear in countries that had been in the forefront of industrialization. Employment, urbanization, education and the welfare state were generally more similar in those countries than in other less heavily industrialized countries such as Italy, Sweden, Norway and Denmark which subsequently began to make up ground in the first half of this century. After World War II, it was the turn of the remaining peripheral countries, Greece, Spain, Portugal, Ireland and Finland, to bring their social structures more into line with the underlying Western European norm. Geographical spread of industrialization and convergence of European societies often run surprisingly parallel. This adds plausibility to the approach that regards industrialization as the long-term motivation for social integration in Europe.

That approach does not exclude the post-war decline of the nation-state as an accelerator of convergence, neither does it rule out the possible effects of booms and depressions on convergence; rather it throws the special nature of the post-war boom into relief. Whereas earlier booms, in the 1850s and 1860s and directly prior to World War I, had led to integration only in parts of Europe, the post-war effect was felt throughout Western Europe. Neither of the other approaches highlights the durability of social integration to the same degree, nor does it show up the independence of the process on political integration.

There are also weaknesses in this attempt at an explanation, however. First it cannot handle reverse developments. It does not explain why many variations within Europe have become greater in the twentieth century, for instance in politically linked fields such as strike procedures, or in economically connected areas such as agricultural employment. Neither can it explain why some variations, like those in family or population structure, remained constant or else increased slightly only to slip back again to their old levels, but never underwent continuous decrease (see Appendix for Table 9). It remains unclear

why the levelling effects of industrialization should have failed
to apply to developments in agricultural employment, the family, population and strikes. Secondly, this approach has great
difficulty explaining the rapid changes that occurred in individual countries as part of the overall European development.
In the course of this study of social integration in Europe it has
become clear that in areas of political interest such as education
or the welfare state, there were neither enduring leaders nor
laggards among the countries of Europe, but there was a rapid
rotation at the head and in the rearguard of developments. In
attempting to follow the course of social integration by observing only individual European countries, many will be seen to
stray from the European norm, leaving confusion in their wake
(see, for example, Figure 7). This is another phenomenon that a
long-term levelling effect of industrialization cannot explain because the degree of industrialization within European countries
has been organized into rigid hierarchies that have been slow to
change.

The fourth approach is perhaps more helpful in this respect.
It assumes that every far-reaching social revision—whether it
be industrialization, the introduction of social security or the
rise of women's education—at first caused great, and sometimes even growing, variations between the societies of Europe.
In the case of the development of industrial production in particular, there is evidence of this in comparisons between individual countries, as well as between different regions of Europe.
There are a number of reasons for this drifting apart that occurs
in the early stages of important social change. Political and
economic conditions may be favourable in one country, but not
in the next. Also, very different national traditions form the
foundations of such change. Thus, in Germany, a strong history
of bureaucratic development favoured an early introduction of
state social security, whereas in Switzerland the process was
more lengthy because of the absence of such a tradition. Faced
with a problem such as social security for instance, the great
range of available solutions should not be forgotten as a possible cause of variation. It has already been demonstrated that
the early stages were often characterised by experimentation.

The proliferation of states in Europe is another cause of variation. It was easier for individual countries to detach themselves from developments using the protective shield of the state

than it was for the states of the United States or the Soviet republics. To begin with, compared with the United States or the USSR, social change would thus necessarily bring about greater variation within Europe, resulting in the subsequent process of convergence taking longer. The central pillar of this approach is that every social change will bring about intranational variation and only gradually force imitation which later leads to greater similarity. This process has been seen at work in employment structure, urbanisation, education and the development of the welfare state. The approach also explains why processes of convergence are continuous, but at the same time allow more room for the great variety of developments taking place in individual countries. Variation is thus not assumed to be a legacy either of the *ancien régime* or of modernization. Rather, internal differences developed from this beginning through social change.

Accepting this final approach then, the outlook for convergence does not appear conclusive. Future social change may be expected to drive a wedge between the societies of Europe and reinforce the differences between them. At the same time, it is likely that disintegrating effects are no longer as powerful as they were early this century because the nation-state no longer provides such protective cover, because solutions originated by one country can be adapted more rapidly by other European countries and again because the European Community exerts a certain amount of pressure in the direction of uniform solutions. One cannot exclude the possibility that new internal European social differences will arise, but the likelihood is that their disintegrating effects will be weaker than in the past.[54]

4

Conclusion

Is there an emergent society that may be termed truly European? Are its structures and ways of life different from those of industrial countries in America and Asia? Are Western European societies really becoming increasingly similar? In crossing European national frontiers, does the traveller find fewer and fewer different social structures and forms of life? Are Europeans revising their outlook? Do they really think on an increasingly European scale and regard themselves as Europeans rather than Frenchmen, Germans, Britons? Besides economic integration of markets and political integration of institutions, is there a latent, covert process of social integration that implies a host of consequences?

The surprising, possibly unbelievable answer is that on close examination, social integration of Europe is proceeding largely unnoticed by social historians and sociologists, with the result that its existence is neither recognized nor discussed. This study has dealt with eight crucial and well-documented areas of comparative twentieth-century research. Nevertheless, in nearly all these fields, the information is neither comprehensive nor precise. The divisions between European and non-European structures and ways of life are not always very sharp; neither are all these areas characterised by obvious convergence between European societies. There are other essential areas of twentieth-century European social history where knowledge is even less complete.[1] However, where the information is available, social integration has been surprisingly clear in Western Europe. One may summarise by noting that there are three main results.

1. In the twentieth century, there have been many features which are common to all European societies and set them

clearly apart from American, Japanese and Soviet societies. These features are by no means as clearly present in all European societies, and in certain countries they are entirely absent. There are not always sharp differences between Europe and other continents. Also, in the case of the United States there is ample comparative evidence which is often not matched by information on Japan, the USSR or smaller "new" societies such as Australia or Canada. Despite these qualifications, however, a whole range of distinctive European features emerges in the twentieth century. There is a particular European family structure. The nuclear family is more clearly dominant in Europe than in Japan or the USSR. It has been less common for married couples to live together with their parents or other relatives in the same household. At the same time, marriage and the founding of families has been a relatively late event in the life of the average European. As a rule, men and women have remained single for a few years longer than elsewhere, the consequences of which are many and often still unclear. Family life after marriage has probably been more withdrawn, private and intimate in Europe, with stronger and more exclusive emotional ties between parents and children.

Employment structure in Europe is very distinctive, with industrial employment much more common than elsewhere. Industry employs a relatively greater number of wage-earners, while service sector employment was less common. Europe was thus the only continent where industrial society endured for any length of time, and where industry has been the biggest employer. Even after losing its leading position in recent years, industrial employment has remained more important than in most non-European countries. European societies have not simply lagged behind the "modernity" of the United States as is often supposed. Rather, its course in the twentieth century has followed a distinctive industry-intensive pattern. This is another feature that has been rich in consequences, for instance in terms of social mobility, urban development, social conflict and the welfare state.

It also seems that in Europe there has been a characteristic approach to the management of large concerns. Families have tended to keep control longer than in the United States where managers were quicker to reach key positions; the same was true of Japan in a modified form. Modern techniques of management were generally introduced less quickly than in the United States. Right up to the post-war era, businessmen at the helm of large companies relied more heavily on agreements with other firms and on state intervention than on their power to make the grade in the market.

Social mobility was an area where Europe trailed the United States considerably, though this is often overestimated. In urban America, unskilled workers, in particular, had better chances of upward mobility than their counterparts in Europe. This was especially clear early this century. Access to further education was an increasingly important area and was, in general, more open in the United States than in Europe, making entry into academic professions that much simpler. In the past, Europeans have undoubtedly exaggerated social mobility in the "land of unlimited opportunity", but the United States has indeed enjoyed a limited advantage in this respect.

The nature of social inequality on the other hand was entirely different. At least in the very recent past, material differences between social classes in Europe appear to have been less sharp, and the contrasts between rich and poor less blatant than in the United States. The welfare state seems to have been a vital factor in reducing social inequality, as has the relative absence of racial problems. At the same time, lines of social demarcation drawn by members of the upper and middle classes between themselves and members of the lower classes were stricter and more exclusive than in the United States. Knowledge on this subject is very limited but there are a number of indications to go by.

Urban development in Europe has been more favourable. Urban growth in Europe did not occur at such a precipitate rate as in other developed countries. Towns on a manageable scale were most favoured so that crises during the era of most rapid urban expansion were easier to cope with than they were in other continents. Town-planning was developing faster at the same time. Its impact was greater and contributed to making life more bearable, more sophisticated and more agreeable in Europe's cities.

Public social insurance in Europe developed to a degree not witnessed anywhere else, and was generally introduced earlier too. It became more firmly established and has remained so to the present day. The proportion of annual financial capacity expended on social security has always been higher in Europe than anywhere else. More European citizens were covered by the state at all times. All of this meant that European social security systems often served as models for the rest of the world, but never the other way around.

Finally, industrial relations in Europe developed in a characteristic fashion. Despite great variations within Europe, the degree of unionisation among wage earners was generally higher in Europe than in the United States or Japan, though the twentieth-century situation was far less continuous and was affected by dramatic fluctuations between peak and crisis, the latter including total bans in certain countries. At the same time, because political boundaries between Christian and secular, socialist and communist parties were generally reflected in European trade union confederations, they also had a peculiar impact on the nature of industrial relations in Europe. More importantly, many objectives were left to the political wing of the union movement; in this respect Europe differed from the United States in particular. In Europe, the aims of strikes were often less extensive because the unions attempted to achieve more through state channels; in the case of the development of the welfare state their actual achievements were also greater. In consequence, union behaviour was strongly influenced by the colour of the ruling political party. Increased success for the parliamentary representatives of the union movement generally led to fewer working days lost through strikes. Since World War II, the wheels of industry have been idle less often in Western Europe than they have been in the United States.

Each of these distinctive features is heavily dependent on the others. However, so far, attempts at isolating their common causes are little more than speculation. It is safe to assume that the age of European societies, especially when compared to the United States, the absence of long-term occupation by foreign powers (compared with the Soviet Union especially) and the diversity of states and nations in Europe made all the difference between them and other industrialized countries, and exercised considerable power over socio-historical developments in the twentieth century. There is little sense in viewing all these features as signs of the backwardness and traditional nature of European societies, or on the other hand of regarding them as marks of their superiority. In many respects European societies have simply trodden their own distinctive path.

2. European societies have become substantially more alike over the course of the twentieth century. The process of convergence was particularly rapid after World War II although it was common for it to have begun between the wars. Occasionally the process swept away only the most extreme international differences, but it was not uncommon for very strong similarities to result. The convergence of Western European societies can be observed in a number of areas.

Industrialization no longer remained concentrated in the centre of Europe but gradually extended to peripheral areas of Scandinavia, the Atlantic and Mediterranean. *Per capita* industrial production varied less and less over time.

A result of this was that employment structure became very similar indeed from country to country, and probably from region to region too. The proportion of workers in industry also grew more similar, though the same was true of the service sector. The process was so rapid and sweeping that intra-European variations have shrunk below the level of variation between the states of America and the republics of the USSR.

In education, the whittling away of the north-south divide in illiteracy has not been the only change. The extent of college attendance, educational opportunities for women and also—though to a lesser degree—class distribution of opportunities for further education also has also grown in similarity.

The development of towns and cities is an area where variations between European countries had previously been enormous. Here too, they no longer exceed the American or Soviet regional scales. The average size of towns in each of the countries of Europe also grew more similar. Convergence in the quality of urban life is an area where information is limited, but in the standard of urban dwellings—the only area where historical surveys exist—variations have also become substantially smaller.

Lastly, European societies have grown increasingly similar in the development of their welfare states. In the last twenty years, social security institutions have come to vary less than they did early in the century. Since World War II, social expenditure has converged noticeably. For the last ten years, the number of citizens covered by state social security provisions has hardly varied from country to country; this is in stark contrast to the situation early in the century.

Convergence in the development of the family within European societies has been less vigorous, chiefly because at the turn of the century, variations within Europe were in general not very great, certainly not as great as in employment, education, urbanisation or social security.

There is no doubt that counter-trends exist too. Two such trends are of particular significance. The differences in the proportion of employment in agriculture have not diminished over the course of this century. In fact, the reverse is true. In the area where political integration has been pushed almost furthest of all by the common agricultural policy, social integration has run in the opposite direction. In the past decade, types of union organization and strike forms have differed as much as ever, especially between north and south, and this is of even greater importance. Variations in strike forms have become even greater than at any time since the end of World War II. Industrial relations have therefore been the stumbling block to the social integration of Europe. Convergence, such as it is, is so far too insignificant to warrant much attention. Despite this, in some areas of social history, the available data permits identification of a dominant trend towards convergence that is, in some cases, so strong that the differences within Europe are no greater than those found within the United States or the USSR.

A range of causes lie behind the process of convergence. Above all, long-term social changes should be viewed as the starting point because short-term explanations on the basis of isolated events are of no use in tackling such a lengthy process of development. Social integration is more than anything else a result of the ironing out of pre-industrial variations between countries and regions caused by industrialization and the gradual emergence of industrial society. In the overall timescale from the Industrial Revolution in Great Britain in the late eighteenth century to the industrialization of peripheral countries such as Spain, Portugal, Ireland and Finland after World War II, the slow pace of the process cannot be overstressed. Once this ironing out had finished, it did not leave an identical structure to those found in the United States, the USSR or Japan. If anything, European features as discussed earlier surfaced even more clearly.

Another factor affecting convergence is the special nature of social change in Western Europe. The early stages of social change in Europe universally led to to particularly sharp differentiation because of the multitude of nation-states and the great regional diversity in the continent; the age of European societies was also a factor since they were less adaptable to change than "new" societies overseas. The protective shield of nation-states and regional characteristics in Europe therefore preserved wide discrepancies in the early stages of industrialization, during the establishment of state social security, the beginnings of urbanization, the onset of expansion in education and the infancy of modern trade unions; this did not happen to the same degree elsewhere. Thereafter the variation dropped back to "normal" levels, as are found in the United States or the USSR. Twentieth-century social history embraces exactly that period between the era of the most glaring gaps early in the century, and the "normalization" that occurred after World War II.

There are two short-term events and reversals that are important enough to be added to these long-term considerations. The post-war boom did not actually cause, but certainly accelerated, social integration in Europe. European societies would probably not have grown so similar had it not occurred. Secondly, World War II caused nationalism to be discredited; thereafter rapid exchange of social institutions and ideas between European countries was facilitated, and this contributed to convergence between European societies.

3. The attitudes of Europeans to their neighbouring countries underwent a fundamental change. Social integration has extended beyond mere characteristics common to all and the convergence of social structures and ways of life. It also surfaced in more open attitudes towards social integration. It has not been possible here to make a detailed examination of this phenomenon, largely because there is little detailed information on the attitudes of the average European before the 1950s, when modern opinion polls were introduced. However, it is possible roughly to isolate some far-reaching developments.

Relations between Western Europeans of different nationalities are today no longer characterized by hostility and mistrust, but by trust and a sense of affinity. Questions about the reliability and trustworthiness of other Western European nations tend to elicit basically positive responses. The old feelings of national *angst* and fear of isolation or outside threat hardly exist at all in the average European, who no longer regards his or her own nation as a wolf among wolves. This sea-change in attitudes to other Western Europeans has made a deep impression on intra-European relations. Tensions and threats of war have thereby been largely deprived of their social seedbed which no longer nourishes the old enmities. Peace-oriented European foreign policy must no longer be regarded as a laborious and hazardous juggling act between adversarial nations with little in common except their hostility and mistrust of each other. In the consciousness of the average European, peaceful relations between Western European nations are seen to be normal and not just the achievement of artful politicians. Integration of Europe through conquest and exploitation by more powerful European nations has also been rendered impossible by the removal of its social breeding ground. Political integration by force failed in the forms envisaged both by Napoleon and the Nazis; both were largely based on preconceived enmities and nationalist assumptions of superiority. Conquest and exploitation of other nations appeared as a law of nature. Most Europeans today find cooperation and a sense of common purpose natural and normal within Europe, and have left behind the aberrations of the past era of conquest.

This change in attitudes probably did not occur overnight following World War II, but was a gradual process spanning the past few decades and even the last few years. Attitudes to West Germany in particular were slow to change because much of the rest of Europe was still mindful of the painful experience of total war and occupation by the Germans. For a long time, findings from surveys were dominated by expressions of mistrust. It was not until the 1970s that West Germany attained the status of a trustworthy neighbour. Trust of some southern European countries seems less well developed, but with the exception of these few, the protracted history of nationalist *angst* and perceived enmity in Western Europe has gradually come to an end over the last thirty or forty years. This historical fact surely had its deepest impact on Franco-German attitudes.[2]

The post-war era has seen a shift in the way that Europeans perceive the sovereignty and independence of their own states. The experience of World War II may have caused many Western Europeans to change their attitudes to these building blocks of the nation-state, and to curb nationalist reservations in the face of supranational European integration. Surveys provide clearer evidence that younger Europeans growing up in the post-war climate have been more prepared to support supranational institutions than older Europeans who spent their youth during times when nationalism was open and unbridled. The social basis for such institutions was thus strengthened as post-war generations attained voting age and began to occupy places among the political decision-makers. It must be said that post-war generations evidently did not regard a unified centralized European state as an option; the most they would consider was a supranational government alongside their own national body. They were more open to the concept of supranational integration, but most certainly did not lend their indiscriminate support to every policy advanced by European institutions.[3]

Since the founding of the European Community, the supporters of European integration in the forms promoted by the EC have been in the majority in most member states. It is true that this was no blank cheque either. Survey findings demonstrate very clearly that Western Europeans' assessments of Community policy have fluctuated widely and developed differently from one country to the next. There were positive reactions to successes such as the founding of the EC and its first expansion when Great Britain came into the fold. On the other hand, scepticism tended to be fuelled by breakdowns in integration such as the failure of the European Defence Community in 1954, the veto against Great Britain's entry in 1963, the failure of the Monetary System since 1973 and the financial crisis that has endured throughout the 1970s and the early 1980s. But even since 1973, there has been a majority in favour of European integration in most European countries.[4]

On the basis of the evidence that I have presented, social integration in Europe is clear, continuous and highly advanced. Social developments in Europe have typically followed a separate path from that followed in North America, Japan, Australia or the USSR. Convergence between European societies has increased steadily, leading in some aspects to very close similarities between some European countries that far exceed the results of such processes in the United States or USSR. Finally, Western Europeans have gradually broadened their horizons beyond exclusive national considerations and into a dimension where there is consciousness of a common European situation and identity.[5]

As a note of caution, it should be added that social integration is more than just the history of social causes of political integration, or social consequences of economic integration. Equally, the history of social integration is not merely to be taken as a social history of the European Community. In many respects, it has its own underlying dynamic. In the first place, common features and convergence of European societies are not restricted to countries in the EC; they nearly always apply to all of Western Europe, which includes the Alpine countries and non-continental Scandinavia that have often no intention of joining the European Community. Many features also extend into Eastern, Central and South-Eastern Europe, regions dealt with only briefly because relevant research is largely rendered inaccessible by the language barrier. Ignoring specifically national features, where intra-European variation is to be observed, its lines of division tend to run through the original territory of the European Community—even more so after expansion to the Iberian peninsula. Neither past nor present Community frontiers can therefore be said to have played a tangible role in social integration. The geographical differences between social integration on the one hand and the corresponding political process on the other have naturally diminished as the Community has expanded. With the addition of Spain and Portugal, only one-tenth of the population of Western Europe remains outside the European Community. Nevertheless this difference should not be taken too lightly. Countries such as Switzerland and Sweden that have provided effective social and political models in the past remain outside Community boundaries but still share common features and have participated in the European trend.

Secondly, social and political integration followed separate historical courses in Europe. Even between the wars and in the immediate post-war period when the Common Market was not yet in existence, or was taking its first faltering steps, European societies already shared common features and the first convergent trends could already be identified. Social integration reaches back further than the past three decades of political integration. It is therefore problematic to view it as a consequence or achievement of the Common Market. On the other hand, it was not until the 1960s or 1970s that similarities finally grew to be as substantial and impressive as they currently are. Social integration can therefore be regarded neither as an essential determinant for the inception of the European Community, nor as a powerful agent in its development. Social integration cannot, of course, be said to lack political consequences. Its strength may have lain in stabilising the Community, or at least preventing additional problems from adding their weight to existing crises and tensions. Even this connection must be viewed with caution because European Community politicians have evidently been unaware of the existence of social integration, and have therefore been powerless to make use of it. As has been demonstrated earlier in the case of trade unions and labour relations, wherever social integration has tended to be weak it has left an unmistakable impression on policies pursued within the Community. Social policies and labour and company law play only a supporting role, while wage agreements binding throughout Europe still lie on a very distant horizon.

Finally, crises and successes in social integration have not been mirrored by events surrounding the European Community. Especially in the 1970s, developments were quite separate. While the European Community got into deeper and deeper financial water and threatened to sink under problems of political decision-making, Europe was making continuous convergent headway in matters of central importance to society such as development of employment structure, education, urbanisation and the welfare state. Family structure and labour relations at least showed no signs of disintegration. Crises and reversals in political integration therefore had no adverse outcome in terms of advances in social integration.

The long-term view thus confirms that a truly European society is emerging to a far greater extent than has previously been demonstrated or recorded. To me, this is a novel and fascinating conclusion. However it needs to be tested against further social and economic data than are at present available. It should also not deceive the observer into thinking that a political community will rise from the growing common ground of European societies without further cultivation. The same long-term perspective shows national political structures and culture to be much hardier and less easily integrated than the economies and societies of Europe. Political integration is therefore still more than just a matter of structural change; it is as much to do with political decision as anything else. From the political angle, the extent of social convergence as it stands should not be expected to grow much further, especially bearing in mind that the United States and the USSR manage to handle far greater variation within their own countries. The social preconditions for political integration may therefore be assumed to be as far distant as ever. The political nut will be the toughest one to crack.

Appendix

	1880	1890	1900
1. *Economic growth*			
Per capita product	34	34	34
Per capita industrial product	82	–	71
2. *Employment*			
Industrial	51	48	46
Service sector	28	24	31
Agricultural	32	37	41
Income quota	19	17	14
Women's work	21	21	19
3. *Family and population*			
Infant mortality	26	25	24
Divorce	..	..	44
Birthrate	13	12	12
Population growth	32	35	31
Age structure			
Proportion of juveniles up to 15 years old	11	10	8
Proportion of elderly (65 years and over)	23	22	21
4. *Education*			
Male students	..	..	..
Female students	..	..	..
5. *Urbanisation*			
Proportion of urban dwellers	65	58	50
6. *Welfare state*			
Accident insurance	..	..	101
Health insurance	..	..	..
Old age pensions	..	..	..
Unemployment insurance	..	..	..
Social expenditure	..	..	..
Social security expenditure	..	..	..
7. *Social conflict*			
Unionisation			
(a)	..	..	..
(b)	..	..	..
Strikes	..	..	..

.. = No or insufficient information
(a) Only those countries without union bans

Table 9: Similarities and differences between Western European countries 1880–1980 (coefficients of variation in %).

1910	1920	1930	1940	1950	1960	1970	1980
35	31	34	34	42	37	32	39
66	–	53	54	56	47	36	34
44	38	35	34	28	21	17	15
26	32	29	23	19	20	14	12
48	45	52	51	49	69	77	82
11	11	10	11	9	9	10	12
22	14	16	16	15	12	19	15
29	31	31	39	42	50	47	34
63	56	51	50	49	51	54	..
15	16	24	18	15	12	15	20
37	59	56	73	45	31	37	101
9	11	12	15	11	11	10	13
20	17	16	15	17	16	13	14
66	55	34	35	36	33	27	24
..	49	43	37	32	26	21	13
48	42	41	34	32	28	23	..
80	48	30	33	30	22	18	..
66	62	50	39	31	23	14	13
..	70	38	39	30	13	11	9
..	80	93	73	74	37	33	..
..	..	..	..	31	21	19	19
..	..	..	..	33	20	17	18
50	44	40	49	30	31	28	33
50	44	53	94	55	57	52	33
63	51	69	135	141	125	187	..

(b) Including countries with union bans (unionization = 0)

Notes on Table 9

The coefficient of variation is the most common method of measuring differences between countries. It calculates the individual countries' variations from the European average and expresses them as percentages of the average. The greater the coefficient of variation, the greater the difference between the European countries. The smaller it is, the greater the similarity. If the coefficient goes below 10 per cent, statisticians describe the position as very similar. The thinking behind the use of such a rigid statistical method in historical analysis may be questioned. As a supplement at least, some real historical comparison of differences within a large nation should be used, for instance a comparison between states of the United States or the republics in the Soviet Union, as was done in Chapter 2. Such a comparison gives a point of reference for the coefficients of variation that may be expected in historical reality.

It is essential to point out that the coefficient of variation expresses absolutely nothing about the development of individual countries. If one country approaches the European average another compensates by drifting away from it, the coefficient does not alter. It is therefore necessary to keep the development of individual countries in view as well as the coefficient.

Unless otherwise indicated, the coefficient is calculated without weighting. In the cases where it is weighted by the size of the individual countries, there are few discernible differences in the trends between unweighted and weighted coefficients. These are probably no greater than the influence of varying statistical definitions such as are unavoidable in comparisons involving many countries. Where data was unavailable for all sixteen countries, the coefficient was determined by a sample standard deviation. This increases the coefficient slightly compared with the normal procedure. In the case of temporal deviations, linear interpolation of the base data was carried out relative to the key years listed in the table (calculations: Rüdiger Hohls).

Notes and References

Chapter 1: Introduction (pp. 1–11)

1. Compare with white-collar staff: J. Kocka (ed) *Angestellte im europäischen Vergleich*, Göttingen 1981; id., *White Collar Workers in America 1890–1940*, London 1980. College education: F. K. Ringer, *Education and Society in Modern Europe*, Bloomington 1979; A. J. Heidenheimer, "Education and Social Security Entitlements in Europe and America", in: P. Flora and A. J. Heidenheimer (eds) *The Development of Welfare States in Europe and America*, New Brunswick 1981; K. H. Jarausch, "Higher Education and Social Change: some Comparative Perspectives", in: id. (ed), *The Transformation of Higher Learning 1860–1930*, Stuttgart 1983; H. Kaelble, *Social Mobility in the Nineteenth and Twentieth Centuries: Europe and America in Comparative Perspective*, Leamington Spa 1985. Social policy e.g.: G. V. Rimlinger, *Welfare Policy and Industrialization in Europe, America and Russia*, New York 1971; W. Fischer, "Wirtschaftliche Bedingungen und Faktoren bei der Entstehung und Entwicklung von Sozialversicherungen", in: H. F. Zacher (ed), *Bedingungen für die Entstehung und Entwicklung von Sozialversicherungen*, Berlin 1979; P. Flora and J. Alber, "Modernization, Democratization and the Development of Welfare States in Western Europe", in: P. Flora and A. J. Heidenheimer (eds); J. Alber, *Vom Armenhaus zum Wohlfahrtsstaat*, Frankfurt 1982; G. A. Ritter, *Social Welfare in Germany and Britain*, Leamington Spa 1986; id., *Der Sozialstaat: Enstehung und Entwicklung im internationalen Vergleich*, Munich 1989.

2. Good summaries of the ideas of Europe's pioneering role: S. Rokkan, "Dimensions of State Formation and Nation-building", in: C. Tilly (ed) *The Formation of National States in Europe*, Princeton 1975 (cf. on this point P. Flora, "Stein Rokkans Makro-Modell der Politischen Entwicklung Europas", in: *Kölner Zeitschrift für Soziologie und Sozialpsychologie* 33, 1981); A. J. Toynbee, *A Study of History*, Vol 4, London 1951; K. W. Deutsch, "On Nationalism, World Regions and the West", in: O. Torsvik (ed), *Mobilization, Center-Periphery Structure*

and Nation-building: A Volume in Commemoration of Stein Rokkan, Bergen 1981; J. Baechler, John H. Hall and Michael Mann (eds) Europe and the Rise of Capitalism, Oxford 1988; Michael Mann, The Sources of Social Power, 2 vols, Cambridge 1986; John H. Hall, Powers and Liberties: the Causes and Consequences of the Rise of the West, Oxford 1985; Eric L. Jones, The European Miracle, Cambridge 1981.

3. G. Barraclough, European Unity in Thought and Action, Oxford 1983; P. Renouvin, L'idée de la fédération européenne dans la pensée politique du XIXe siècle, Oxford 1949; H. Gollwitzer, Europabild und Europagedanke, Munich 1964.

4. Cf. e.g.: H. S. Commager (ed), America in Perspective: the United States through Foreign Eyes, New York 1947 (consists almost exclusively of travelogues written by Europeans); C. Erickson, Invisible Immigrants, Leicester, Leicester University Press 1972; E. W. Chester (ed), Europe Views America, Washington 1962; E. Fraenkel, Amerika im Spiegel des politischen Denkens, Cologne 1959; M. F. Joseph (ed), As Others See Us: the United States through Foreign Eyes, Princeton 1959.

5. One of the very few studies dealing with the social side of European integration is Wolfram Elsner, Die socialökonomische Lage und ihre Beeinflussung durch die westeuropäische Integration, Berlin 1978. It deals, however, with a different and much more specialised question than our study. It asks to what extent European integration led to greater welfare provision for Europeans. To this end, it surveys theories both of welfare and integration, and also summarises empirical results while making suggestions for future research. In this work, it is evident how little theories and research on integration are concerned with that which we here understand to be social integration.

6. A preliminary survey such as the above must limit itself to differences between countries. It is clear from studies of individual countries how far-reaching regional differences have been in the twentieth century, and that observation of political boundaries often gives artificial results in socio-historical surveys; nevertheless, the socio-historical basis of inter-regional differences and common features within Europe still lies obscured behind a mountain of technical problems whose solution is one of the central tasks of research into the social history of Europe. The most important and impressive attempt at writing an economic history of Europe from the regional angle is: S. Pollard, Peaceful Conquest: the Industrialisation of Europe 1760–1970, Oxford 1981; the main period dealt with is, however, the years up to 1914. Long-term examinations of the development of regional disparities in twentieth-century Europe are so far lacking. Even the influential study by J. Williamson ("Regional Inequality and the Process of National Development: a Description of Patterns", in: Economic Development and Cultural Change 13, 1965) deals only with individual European

countries in themselves and not the wider European development. An overall short-term study: D. Biehl et al, "Zur regionalen Einkommensverteilung in der europäischen Wirtschaftsgemeinschaft", in: *Weltwirtschaft* 1972, No 2; cf. also W. Molle, *Regional Disparity and Economic Development in the European Community*, London 1980.

Chapter 2: Distinctive Features of European Societies in the Twentieth Century (pp. 12–99)

1. Cf. most recent publication: R. Wall et al. (eds), *Family Forms in Historic Europe*, Cambridge 1983 (especially relevant are the contributions by P. Laslett and R. Wall); also P. Laslett, *Family Life and Illicit Love in Earlier Generations*, Cambridge 1977, chap. 1; J. Hajnal, "European Marriage Patterns in Perspective", in: D. V. Glass et al (eds), *Population in History*, London 1965, pp. 101–47; M. Mitterauer, *Sozialgeschichte der Jugend*, Frankfurt 1986, pp. 19ff, an excellent recent survey; Z. Szeman, "Die Herausbildung und Auflösung der Grossfamilie in Ungarn", in: *Zeitschrift für Soziologie* 10, 1981; F. F. Mendels, "Proto-Industrialisation: Theory and Reality", in: *Eighth International Economic History Congress*, A Themes, Budapest 1982, p. 95; R. Pipes, *Russia under the Old Regime*, London 1987; T. Shanin, *The Awkward Class. Political Sociology of Peasantry in a Developing Society: Russia 1910–1924*, Oxford 1972, pp. 28ff; D. L. Randel (ed), *The Family in Imperial Russia*, Urbana 1976. A very stimulating contribution is M. Mitterauer, "Gesindedienst und Jugendphase im europäischen Vergleich", in: *Geschichte und Gesellschaft* 11, 1985. For a condensed summary of criticism on Laslett cf. M. Barbagli, *Sotto lo stesso tetto*, Bologna 1984, pp. 35ff. Most points are not relevant to the twentieth century.
2. Laslett differentiates between four European family types: the "western" in which the "European" family is evident in its purest form, and is typically found in Britain; the Central European in which the European family is not so evident, and frequently includes non-relatives in a single household; the Southern European, which includes a range of extended family types (three generations or families consisting of several brothers) where the age at marriage is considerably lower; the Eastern European type, where the three-generation family is more common than in Western and Central Europe and age at marriage is also low. Cf. Laslett, "Family", in: Wall et al. (eds), pp. 256f. Laslett stresses that the Central European type is actually only a variety of the western type, for which reason the two actually constitute a single type (p. 528).
3. Cf. R. Wall, "Introduction", in: Wall et al. (eds), pp. 46ff; M. Biskup et al. (eds), *Family and its Culture: an Investigation in Seven East and West European Countries*, Budapest 1984, pp. 164, 292, 389f.
4. This is also substantiated by the marriage rates (number of mar-

riages per inhabitant) most commonly recorded in international reference works. It is a rough indicator of age at marriage because—in countries with comparable age structure—it is lower the higher the age at marriage (though it is also affected by frequency of divorce and re-marriage, and the age structure itself). In Western Europe, marriage rates are substantially lower than in Eastern Europe and developed countries outside Europe. Cf. UN Statistical Yearbook 1981, pp. 72ff.

5. Cf. L. Roussel, "Les ménages d'une personne: l'évolution récente", in: *Population* 38, 1983, pp. 999, 1002: proportion of single person households around 1950 in Western Europe (average) 13%, in USA 9%, in Canada 6%; in 1960 Western Europe (average of fourteen countries) 16%, in USA 13%, in Canada 9%; in 1970 in Western Europe (average of fourteen countries) 19%, in USA 18%, in Canada 13%. Unmarried heads of household as a proportion of all households in 1970: Federal Republic of Germany 12%, France 11%, Switzerland 11%, the Netherlands 9%, USA 7%, Canada 7%; comparison with Japan: A. Imhof, "Individualismus und Lebenserwartung in Japan", in: *Leriathan* 14, 1986, pp. 380ff. (Reprinted in: id., *Von der unsicheren zur sicheren Lebenszeit*, Darmstadt 1988).

6. Cf. P. Ariès, "Pour une histoire de la vie privée", unpublished paper. Seminar "A propos de l'histoire de l'espace privée", 9–11 May 1983. Wissenschaftskolleg Berlin. Collected conference papers, pp. 11f, 23f. Another strongly argued study: E. Shorter, *The Making of the Modern Family*, London 1976; overall there has been little comparative research into family relationships in twentieth-century Europe.

7. Cf. as examples Commager (ed), pp. 155f; Helbig, in: *Protokolle des 20. Historikertags*, Sonderheft der GWU, pp. 191ff; G. Schmoller, "Sozialpolitische Rückblicke auf Nordamerika", in: *Preussische Jahrbücher* 17, 1866, pp. 520ff; L. Fulda, *Amerikanische Eindrücke*, 4th edn, Stuttgart 1914, pp. 200ff; M. J. Bonn, *Die Kultur der Vereinigten Staaten von Amerika*, Berlin 1930, pp. 267ff.

8. G. Birmingham (alias Canon Hannay) quoted in: H. S. Commager (ed), *America in Perspective*, New York 1947, pp. 282–3; M. Young and P. Willmott, *Family and Kinship in East London*, London 1957, p. 142 quoted in: E. Shorter, *The Making...*, p. 239

9. Cf. similar attempts at an explanation: Mitterauer and Sieder, pp. 57ff; Hajnal, p. 34; Ariès, *Vie privée*; P. Laslett, "Family and Household as Work Group", in: Wall et al. (ed), pp. 556ff; Pipes, pp. 26ff.

10. Cf. for this consequence of the European family some stimulating points in P. Laslett, "Family and Household as Work Group", in: Wall et al. (ed), pp. 435ff; for historical change in the high number of single elderly: J. Ehmer, "Zur Stellung alter Menschen in Haushalt und Familie—Thesen zur Grundlage von quantitativen Quellen aus

europäischen Städten seit dem 17. Jahrhundert", in: H. Konrad (ed), *Der alte Mensch in der Geschichte*, Vienna 1982, pp. 90f.

11. This argument and the following points on industry-intensive employment structure in Europe are dealt with in more detail in: H. Kaelble, "Was Prometheus Most Unbound in Europe? Labour Force in Europe during the 19th and 20th Centuries", in: *Journal of European Economic History*, 18, 1989.

12. It must be stressed that this theory is partly dependent on the definition of industrial sector and service sector. In the above case the "International Standard Classification of Occupations" of the ILO is used, which is also the basis of OECD and UN statistics. It is especially important that in this work, transport and communications are assigned to the service and not the industrial sector. It will justifiably be argued that these services are for the most part services to manufacturers and therefore belong to the industrial sector. The pivotal point in the decision to make this assignment was that the special European feature of intense industrial employment that is at the core of the discussion would be unaltered by any other definition. Besides, it would have been a mammoth technical task to recalculate the ILO classification so widely used in international data compilations and come up with other definitions which would be dubious without time-consuming recourse to original sets of national statistics. In any case transport and communications are not solely services to manufacturers.

13. Trade within Europe is best ignored here because the problem of scale is a factor. The bigger the country, the smaller the export-orientation, at least among developed countries. It is therefore necessary for total exports of the European economy, but excluding trade within Europe, to be included in comparisons with large countries such as the USA, the Soviet Union and Japan. It then becomes impossible to compare Europe with smaller countries such as Australia or Canada.

14. The plausibility of these explanations is supported by important empirical indications which cannot be examined here for reasons of space. Cf. Kaelble, "Prometheus". Wage earners in industry as a proportion of all wage earners (industry includes mining, construction and utilities) based on: OECD, *Labour Force Statistics 1970–81*, Paris 1983, Table IV. Western Europe 46%, USA and Canada 34%, Australia 40%, Japan 45%.

15. Cf. for the early twentieth century: J. Kocka and H. Siegrist, "Die 100 grössten Industrieunternehmen im späten 19. und frühen 20. Jahrhundert", in: N. Horn and J. Kocka (eds), *Recht und Entwicklung der Grossunternehmen im 19. und 20. Jahrhundert*, Göttingen 1979, pp. 84ff; cf. for the present: *Diercke Weltstatistik 82/83*, Munich 1982, p. 251 (number of employees); "Top 500 1986", in: *Financial Times*

26.11.1986 (top European companies).

16. Cf. most recent summary: H. van der Wee, *Prosperity and Upheaval, The World Economy 1975–1980*, Harmondsworth 1987, pp. 213ff; A. D. Chandler and H. Daems, "The Rise of Managerial Capitalism and its Impact on Investment Strategy in the Western World", in: H. Daems and H. van der Wee (eds), *The Rise of Managerial Capitalism*, Louvain 1974, pp. 1–34; A. D. Chandler, *The Visible Hand. The Managerial Revolution in American Business*, Cambridge/Mass. 1977; A. D. Chandler and H. Daems (eds), *Managerial Hierarchies*, Cambridge 1980.

17. Kocka and Siegrist, "Industrieunternehmen", pp. 84ff.

18. Cf. van der Wee, *Prosperity*, pp. 224ff; P. L. Payne, "Family Business in Britain: A Historical and Analytical Survey", in: A. Okochi and S. Yasuoka (eds), *Family Business in the Era of Industrial Growth*, Tokyo 1984, pp. 188ff; M. Lévy-Leboyer, "Le patronat français, 1912–72", in: id., *Le patronat de la seconde industrialisation*, Paris 1979; H. Siegrist, "Deutsche Grossunternehmen vom späten 19. Jahrhundert bis zur Weimarer Republik", in: *Geschichte und Gesellschaft* 6, 1980, p. 88.

19. Cf. on this point: V. Berghahn, "Montanunion und Wettbewerb", in: H. Berding (ed), *Wirtschaftliche und politische Integration in Europa im 19. und 20. Jahrhundert*, Göttingen 1984; id., *The Americanisation of West German Industry, 1945–73*, Leamington Spa 1986 (especially Introduction); also: H. Weber, *Le parti des patrons*, Paris 1986.

20. A. Kleffel, "Diskussionsbeitrag", in: H. Pohl (ed), *Legitimation des Managements im Wandel*, Wiesbaden 1983, pp. 42f.

21. Cf. H. Kaelble, *Social Mobility in Comparative Perspective*, Leamington Spa 1985, pp. 6ff. Regrettably there are no studies for the first half of the twentieth century comparing Europe with Japan, Australia, Canada or the Soviet Union. The question of whether Europe has suffered limited disadvantage with respect to these countries as well as the United States must therefore remain open for the time being; in support of the argument that social mobility is very similar in all modern societies: R. Ericson and H. Goldthorpe, "Are American Rates of Social Mobility Exceptionally High?" in: *European Sociological Review* 1, 1985. Id., "Trends in Class Mobility: A Test of Hypothesis Against the European Experience", Casmin Working Paper No. 13, Mannheim 1988.

22. Cf. for the comparison between North American and European towns and more precise evidence for the explanations: Kaelble, *Social Mobility*, pp. 5ff.

23. Cf. for rate of upward mobility: Kaelble, *Social Mobility*, pp. 8ff; the only comparative study of European countries so far (the Netherlands and Germany): H. van Dijk et al., "Regional Differences in Mobility Patterns in the Netherlands 1810–1940", in: *Journal of Social History*,

March 1984.

24. Cf. for differences between USA and Europe: S. M. Lipset and R. Bendix, *Social Mobility in Industrial Society*, Berkeley 1967, pp. 11ff; S. M. Miller, "Comparative Social Mobility", in: *Current Sociology* 3, 1960; more recent studies: K. U. Mayer, "Class Formation and Social Reproduction—Current Comparative Research on Social Mobility", in: R. F. Geyer (ed), *Cross-national and Cross-cultural Comparative Research in the Social Sciences*, Oxford 1979 (also refers to comparisons of the USA with Japan, Canada and Brazil); L. E. Hazelrigg and M. Garnier, "Occupational Mobility in Industrial Societies: a Comparative Analysis of Differential Access to Occupational Rank in Seventeen Countries", in: *American Sociological Review* 17, 1976; D. J. Treiman, "United States and Great Britain", in: *American Journal of Sociology* 81, 1975; M. Seaman, "Some Real and Imaginary Consequences of Social Mobility: A French-American comparison", in: *American Journal of Sociology* 82, 1977; D. B. Grusky and R. M. Hauser, "Comparative Social Mobility Revisited: Models of Convergence and Divergence in Sixteen Countries", in: *American Sociological Review* 49, 1984 (a good round-up of research trends); W. Müller, "Soziale Mobilität: Die Bundesrepublik im internationalen Vergleich", in: M. Kaase (ed), *Politische Wissenschaft und politische Ordnung*, Opladen 1986; Ericson and Goldthorpe, "American Rates"; it should be noted that Europe's disadvantaged position early in the century is not necessarily comparable with that after 1945, because at the turn of the century studies of individual towns were used to compare mobility between generations, whereas after 1945 national studies were used.

25. Cf. more recent comparative studies for Europe, which nevertheless make no attempt at tackling social mobility in Europe as a whole: K. U. Mayer, "Berufsstruktur und Mobilitätsprozess. Probleme des internationalen Vergleichs objektiver Indikatoren zwischen England/Wales und der Bundesrepublik Deutschland", in: H.-J. Hoffmann-Novotny (ed), *Soziale Indikatoren im internationalen Vergleich*, Frankfurt 1980; R. Erikson et al., "Intergenerational Class Mobility in Three Western European Societies: England, France and Sweden", in: *British Journal of Sociology* 30, 1979 (stresses the interest of differences pp. 1ff); id., "Social Fluidity in Industrial Nations: England, France and Sweden", in: *ibid.* 33, 1982; id., "Intergenerational Class Mobility and the Convergence Thesis: England, France and Sweden", in: *ibid.* 34, 1983 (study of trends since inter-war period); W. Koenig and W. Müller, "Educational Systems and Labour Markets as determinants of Worklife Mobility in France and West Germany: a Comparison of Men's Career Mobility, 1965–70", in: *European Sociological Review* 2, 1986 (by contrast with other researchers, Koenig and Müller examine career mobility over five-year periods, not mobil-

ity between fathers and sons. Career mobility often highlights greater differences between countries).

26. For a compilation of European data: Kaelble, *Social Mobility* pp. 40ff; for United States cf. M. Trow (ed), *Teachers and Students. Aspects of American Higher Education*, New York 1975, pp. 11-13.

27. Comparative studies on access to academic professions are very scarce. However, a group that closely resembles the academic professions crops up in a number of studies of mobility. Cf. S. M. Miller, "Comparative Social Mobility", in: *Current Sociology* 9, 1960, pp. 36ff; Erikson and Goldthorpe, "American Rates", pp. 17f; (United States' substantial headstart on all European countries under study with respect to access to the upper middle classes both from working families and middle-class families).

28. This section on the history of social inequality has to be subjected to two limits because of a lack of comparative historical study. First, it can only deal with the situation after 1945. Secondly, it only tackles inequality in incomes, wealth and life expectancy, unfortunately ignoring crucial areas such as inequality in living conditions, workplace conditions, education, solution of personal crises and legal entitlements. Despite these gaps, incomes, wealth and life expectancy enable the necessary generalisation to be made. Cf. a justifiably restrained international comparison: W. Fischer, *Armut in der Geschichte*, Göttingen 1982; a very good survey of social inequality in the USA but with European comparisons in mind: H.-J. Puhle, "Soziale Ungleichheit und Klassenstrukturen in den USA", in: H.-U. Wehler (ed), *Klassen in der europäischen Geschichte*, Göttingen 1979, pp. 233-77.

29. The distinction between proportion of income and income differentials is, unfortunately, all too often disregarded in literature on the subject. For historical change and historical comparisons the distinction is a crucial one. The factor by which the income received by members of a given higher income group exceeds that received by members of a given lower income group represents the income differential. This is what the present discussion is concerned with. Absolute variation in terms of dollars, marks or francs is not as important as relative variation. Compilations of historical developments and international comparisons of income differentials are very uncommon. Where they do exist, a confusing range of indicators are used. Income differentials have the great advantage of being very concrete, and as with wealth differentials are almost certainly understood by those to whom they apply and really do have an impact on their ways of life. Income proportions define the "slice of the cake" received by a given income or occupational group. Statistical income groups as they are presented here, usually lie at their heart. There has been a great deal of study of this problem. Processing of data is widely standardised, making com-

parisons quite simple. A range of well thought-out indicators has been developed (Sawyers, *Income Distribution* contains a good round-up). However, it is often overlooked that the indicators express nothing about income differentials. They also lack concreteness, giving results that are certainly of interest to the social scientist or the historian, but at the same time hardly form part of the consciousness of the people to whom they apply and are therefore not used so exclusively for socio-historical research.

30. The social group forming the bottom income group in British-American comparison, in: K. F. Lydall and J. B. Lansing, "A Comparison of the Distribution of Income and Wealth in the United States and Great Britain", in: A. B. Atkinson (ed), *Wealth, Income and Inequality*, Harmondsworth 1979, p. 147; information on the make-up of the bottom 20% of income-receivers in West Germany in the 1960s, in: G. Schmaus, "Personelle Einkommensverteilung im Vergleich 1962/63 und 1969", in: H.-J. Krupp and W. Glatzer (eds), *Umverteilung im Sozialstaat*, Frankfurt 1978, p. 93

31. For Japan, Nakamura has calculated the degree of spread of average income between the top 20% and bottom 20% of income-receivers for the years 1951–74. In 1951 the degree of spread was about 80%; in 1961, after amendment of income statistics, it stood at 60%, and in 1974 at around 50%. Cf. T. Nakamura, *The Postwar Japanese Economy*, Tokyo 1982, p. 120 (diagram only; method of calculation also explained). The relevant figures for the USA are, 1950 209%, 1961 202% and 1970 209% (calculated from: *The Statistical History of the United States*, New York 1976, p. 292: Families and Unrelated Individuals).

32. This thesis is also supported in comparisons between individual European countries and the USA by: H. van der Wee, *Prosperity*, pp. 254ff; Royal Commission on the Distribution of Income and Wealth. "The International Comparison of Income Distributions", in: Atkinson (ed), 1980, pp. 71ff; Lydall and J. B. Lansing, in: *ibid.*, 1973; T. Stark, *The Distribution of Income in Eight Countries*, London 1977, pp. 177ff (USA and Great Britain); E. Smolensky et al., *Postfisc Income Inequality: a Comparison of the United States and West Germany*, Lexington/Mass. 1979, pp. 69ff; M. Sawyers, *Income Distribution in OECD Countries*, OECD Economic Outlook, Occasional Papers, July 1976, pp. 14ff; contrast with: M. Schnitzer, *Income Distribution: a Comparative Study of the United States, Sweden, West Germany, East Germany, the United Kingdom and Japan*, New York 1974, pp. 111ff, (income in Germany less equally distributed than in the USA).

33. Cf. Stark, pp. 134f (with reservations); van der Wee, *Prosperity*, pp. 256f; Sawyers, pp. 14f. There is no great difference with Japan either. Japan is at the opposite end of the range to the USA. General mea-

sures of income inequality such as Gini coefficients have been shunned because they do not allow identification of the actual area of the incomes hierarchy in which various countries differ. For the period around 1970 Sawyers calculated the usual indicators for a range of European countries, the USA, Canada and Australia. These also show tangibly greater income inequality in the USA compared with the European average and a substantially smaller degree of inequality in Japan.

34. Cf. van der Wee, *Prosperity*, pp. 256ff; Stark, p. 16 (comparison of Great Britain with Australia only); Sawyers, pp. 14f, 18f (comparison of size of households).

35. Cf. Sawyers, pp. 22f, 34f.

36. Cf. Lydall and Lansing, pp. 148ff; Stark, p. 182 (very brief); foreigners in West Germany are no more likely than natives to be among the lowest 20% of income-receivers. They tend to be grouped among the second-lowest 40% (Schmaus, p. 95).

37. Cf. for example: *ibid.*, p. 96.

38. Cf. F. Kraus, "The Historical Development of Income Inequality in Western Europe and the United States", in: P. Flora and A. J. Heidenheimer (eds), pp. 194ff, 215ff (general trend towards decline; proportion of top decile in USA in 1970 at bottom end of range); Sawyers, pp. 17ff (USA in top position in 1970 before tax, after tax in top end of range of countries examined by OECD).

39. Cf. on this point the instructive selection of various definitions of income that appears in Sawyers, pp. 14–19.

40. Sawyers, p. 14.

41. Cf. P. Henle, "Exploring the Distribution of Earned Income", in: *Monthly Labour Review* 95, 1972, pp. 23f; *Statistical History of the United States*, pp. 304f.

42. Cf. *Statistical Abstracts of the United States*; for France: *Données sociales*, édition 1981, Paris INSEE 1981, p. 215.

43. Good survey in: Kraus, pp. 199ff; supplementary for France: Sawyers, pp. 26ff; for Japan, Ireland, Australia and Canada: Stark.

44. Jan Tinbergen, *Einkommensverteilung. Auf dem Weg zur neuen Einkommensgerechtigkeit*, Wiesbaden 1978.

45. Netherlands: cf. van Dijk, *Wealth and Property in the Netherlands in Modern Times*, Rotterdam 1980, p. 9; J. M. M. de Meere, "Long-term Trends in Income and Wealth Inequality in the Netherlands, 1908–40", in: *Historische Sozialforschung* 27, 1983, pp. 28ff (taxed wealth only); France: A. Daumard, "Wealth and Affluence in France since the Beginning of the Nineteenth Century", in: W. D. Rubinstein (ed), *Wealth and the Wealthy in the Modern World*, London 1980, pp. 115ff; A. Babeau and D. Strauss-Kahn, *La richesse des français*, Paris 1977; Great Britain: A. B. Atkinson and A. J. Harrison, *The Distribution of Wealth*

in Britain, Cambridge 1978, p. 165.

46. The following argument is best presented in: A. B. Atkinson, *The Economics of Inequality*, Oxford 1983, pp. 167ff; cf. also: Lydal and Lansing, pp. 150ff (also home-owners in Great Britain and the United States 1954); E. Ballerstedt et al., *Soziologischer Almanach*, Frankfurt 1975, p. 166; for the general rise of home-ownership, with USA still leading the field: *Statistical History of the United States*, p. 646; *Social Indicators for the European Community 1960–75*, Luxemburg 1977, pp. 219ff.

47. A. H. Halsey (ed), *Trends in British Society*, London 1972, p. 307; Ballerstedt et al., p. 166; *Statistical History of the United States*, p. 646; *Social Indicators for the European Community 1960–75*, Luxemburg 1977, pp. 242f. For the proportion of property values included in national wealth cf. Babeau and Strauss-Kahn, pp. 6off.

48. Atkinson, *Economics of Inequality*, pp. 167ff.

49. Cf. J. Vallin, "Tendences récentes de la mortalité française", in: *Population* 38, 1983, p. 81; id. and J. C. Chesnais, "Evolution récente de la mortalité en Europe, dans les pays anglo-saxons et en union soviétique 1960–70", in: *ibid.*29, 1974, pp. 861–98.

50. Cf. the only historical international comparison: L. Guralnick, "Socio-economic Differences in Mortality by Cause of Death: United States 1950, and England and Wales 1949–53", in: *International Population Conference*, Ottawa 1963, pp. 287–313; on long-term trends: A. Antonovsky, "Social Class Life Expectancy and Overall Mortality", in: *Millbank Memorial Fund Quarterly* 45 (2/1), 1967, pp. 31/73. Informative: UN, *The Determinants and Consequences of Population Trends*, New York 1973, pp. 137–40.

51. Calculated from I. B. Täubner and C. Täubner, *People of the United States in the Twentieth Century*, Washington D.C., p. 528.

52. A. de Tocqueville, *Democracy in America*.

53. Cf. J. Kocka, *Angestellte zwischen Faschismus und Demokratie*, pp. 120ff, 296ff, 319ff; G. Crossick, "The Emergence of the Lower Middle Class in Britain", in: id., *The Lower Middle Class in Britain 1870–1914*, London 1977; also: Kocka (ed), *Angestellte im europäischen Vergleich*; in summary: H. Kaelble, *Industrialisation and Social Inequality in Nineteenth-Century Europe*, Leamington Spa 1986, pp. 172ff.

54. Cf. Kocka, *Die Angestellten in der deutschen Geschichte 1850–1980*, Göttingen 1981, pp. 193ff.

55. Cf. on this point: C. Erickson, *Invisible Immigrants: the Adaption of English and Scottish Immigrants in Nineteenth-Century America*, Leicester 1972, pp. 67f, 255; cf. also W. Helbich, "Letters from America: Documents of the Adjustment Process of German Immigrants in the United States", in: *Anglistik und Englischunterricht* 1985; id., "Immigrant Letters as Sources: a Contribution to Research in Social History", in: C. Harzig and D. Hoerder (eds), *The Press of Labor Immigrants in Europe*

and North America, Bremen 1985.

56. A. Kolb, *Als Arbeiter in Amerika. Unter deutsch-amerikanischen Grossstadt-Proletariern*, Berlin 1904, p. 90, quoted in Kocka (ed), *White-collar Workers*, p. 165.

57. Quoted from Erickson, p. 68.

58. J. Bryce, "The Faults and Strength of American Democracy", in: H. S. Commager (ed), *America in Perspective*, New York 1947, pp. 233–234.

59. Cf. for Europe and Soviet Union: P. Bairoch, "Population urbaine et taille des villes en Europe de 1600 à 1970", in: *Revue d'histoire économique et sociale* 54, 1976, p. 309 (communities of over 5,000); USA: *Statistical History of the United States*, p. 11 (national definition of town: communities of over 2,500, excepting certain larger rural communities and with the addition of certain smaller urban communities); Canada: M. C. Urquhart et al., *Historical statistics of Canada*, Cambridge 1965, p. 14 (communities of 1,000 and over, including certain smaller communities within agglomerations 1901–56); Japan: P. Flora, *Indikatoren der Modernisierung*, Opladen 1975, pp. 22f, 36 (communities of 10,000 upwards, 1898–1950); worldwide growth: UN, "Growth of the World's Urban and Rural Population, 1920–2000", *Population Studies* No. 44, New York 1969, p. 24 (communities over 20,000). To capture towns with populations below 20,000 in international comparisons, non-uniform definitions must be taken into consideration. Even with other definitions the same picture of relatively slow urban growth in Europe emerges.

60. Calculated from data, *ibid.*

61. Comparison here with European exceptions that did not affect overall development in Europe. Between 1920 and 1960 the number of urban dwellers in Spain rose by 149%, in Greece by 233% and in Finland by 240%, extraordinarily rapid compared with the 64% rise throughout Western Europe. In the Soviet Union the number rose even quicker than in these few European "prodigies", by 388%. The figure for Japan was 230%, in the USA it was "only" 133%, in Canada 220% and in Australia 156% (calculated from: UN, "Growth of the World's Urban and Rural Population", pp. 98f).

62. Between 1850 and 1914 the number of urban dwellers in Europe (not inc. Russia) multiplied only three times. Urbanisation increased from 19% to 36% and thus remained some way behind the North American rate at the time; it was also slower than the rate of urbanisation this century in Japan and the Soviet Union. At the time there were only a few European countries where the rapidity of urban growth was of "un-European" proportions; among them were Germany, Switzerland and the countries of Scandinavia. Cf. urbanisation rates 1850–1910 in: H. Kaelble, "Der Mythos der rapiden Indus-

trialisierung in Deutschland", in: *Geschichte und Gesellschaft*9, 1983, p. 117; P. Bairoch, *Tailles des villes, conditions de vie et développement économique*, Paris 1977, pp. 17ff; for 1920–60 comparable rates of growth can be readily calculated from: UN, "Growth of the World's Urban and Rural Population", pp. 105ff.

63. The proportion of urban dwellers living in cities of a million and more inhabitants grew between 1920 and 1960 in the United States from 40% to 51%, in Japan from 47% to 52%, in the Soviet Union from 0% to 15%, in Australia from 0% to 59%, in Canada from 0% to 39%, but in Western Europe from 32% to just 35%. The proportion of urban dwellers living in cities of 2.5 million or more inhabitants grew from 25% to 34% in the USA between 1920 and 1960, in Japan from 32% to 43% and in the Soviet Union from 0% to 12%. In Europe it dropped from 20% to 13%, in France it fell from 35% to 32%, in Great Britain from 26% to 23%. Because of the peculiar position of Berlin, Germany is a special case (calculated from: UN, "Growth of the World's Urban and Rural Population", pp. 98ff, 107ff).

64. Cf: B. J. L. Berry and Q. Gillard, *The Changing Shape of Metropolitan America, Commuting Patterns, Urban Fields and Decentralisation Processes 1960–1970*, Cambridge/Mass. 1977; G. Sternlieb and J. W. Hughes (eds), *Post-Industrial America: Metropolitan Decline and Inter-Regional Job Shifts*, New Brunswick 1975; id. and C. O. Hughes, *Demographic Trends and Economic Reality*, New Brunswick 1982, pp. 125ff (USA 1960–80); for Europe: P. Hall, *Growth Centres in the European Urban System*, London 1980, pp. 144ff, 211ff.

65. Cf. for European development especially: P. Cheshire and D. Hay, "The Development of the European Urban System, 1971–81", Paper at the Conference on the Future of the Metropolis, Berlin 1984. Cf. for urbanisation in Europe 1960–80 (EC): *The Regions of Europe*, ed. by the Commission of the European Community, Luxemburg 1981, pp. 23ff.

66. Cf: UN, "Growth of the World's Urban and Rural Population", pp. 98ff, 100ff.

67. Cf. on the other hand: *ibid.*, pp. 1097ff.

68. A round-up of optimal scales in: Bairoch, Taille, pp. 249ff.

69. P. Hall, *Urban and Regional Planning*, Harmondsworth 1974; C. T. Adams, "Urban Planning" in: A. J. Heidenheimer et al., *Comparative Public Policy*, London 1983; J. A. Dunn, *Miles to Go: European and American Transportation Policies*, Cambridge/Mass. 1981; F. Ribert, "Comparative Urban Policy and Performance", in: F. Greenstein and N. Polsby (eds), *Policies and Policymaking*, Reading/Mass. 1975; N. Glickmann and M. White, "Urban Land-Use Patterns: an International Comparison", in: *Environment and Planning* 11, 1979; A. L. Strong, *Land Banking: European Reality, American Prospect*, Baltimore

1979; J. Sundquist, *Dispersing Population: What America Can Learn from Europe*, Washington D.C., 1975; cf. J. Reulecke, *Geschichte der Urbanisierung in Deutschland*, Frankfurt 1985.
70. A. Suthcliffe, *Towards the Planned City. Germany, Britain, the United States and France 1780–1914*, Oxford 1981.
71. Suthcliffe; Hall; Matzerath and I. Thienel, "Stadtentwicklung, Stadtplanung, Stadtentwicklungsplanung. Probleme im 19. und 20. Jahrhundert am Beispiel der Stadt Berlin", in: *Die Verwaltung* 10, 1977.
72. UN, *Determinants and Consequences of Population Trends* I, New York 1973, pp. 132ff (Sweden, Norway); H. Matzerath, *Urbanisierung in Preussen 1815–1914*, Stuttgart 1985; *Wirtschaft und Statistik* 1968, pp. 150ff; J.-N. Biraben, "Quelques aspects de la mortalité en milieu urbain", in: *Population* 30, 1975, pp. 509–522; B. Benjamin, "The Urban Background to Public Health Changes in England and Wales 1900–50", in: *Population Studies* 1964, pp. 225–48; *UN Demographic Yearbook* 1971, pp. 693ff; 1982 pp. 350ff (Austria, Finland, Iceland, Ireland, Luxemburg, the Netherlands, Norway, Switzerland, Great Britain and Denmark); M. Natale and A. Bernassola, *La mortalità per causa nelle regioni italiane*, Rome 1973.
73. Cf. Täubner and C. Täubner, pp. 518ff; W. Nugent, *Structures of American History*, Bloomington 1981; UN, *Determinants and Consequences*, p. 133; A. Weber, *The Growth of Cities in the Nineteenth Century*, ND Ithaca 1963, p. 343; P. Bairoch, *De Jéricho à Mexico*, Paris 1985, p. 307.
74. Cf. T. R. Gurr, "On the History of Violent Crime in Europe and America", in: H. D. Graham and T. R. Gurr (eds), *Violence in America*, Beverley Hills 1979, pp. 363ff; id., "Crime Trends in Modern Democracies Since 1945", in: *International Annals of Criminology* 16, 1977; *Statistical Abstract of the US*, ed. by US Department of Commerce 93, 1972, pp. 143–5; cf. M. E. Wolfgang, "Urban Crime", in: J. O. Wilson (ed), *The Metropolitan Enigma*, Cambridge 1968 (USA); V. V. Stanciu, *La criminalité à Paris*, Paris 1968; D. Szabo, *Crimes et villes*, Paris 1960 (France and Belgium since World War II); F. H. McLintock and N. Howard Avison, *Crime in England and Wales*, London 1968; M. B. Clinard, *Cities with Little Crime: A Comparative Study of Switzerland with Sweden and the United States*, Cambridge 1977 (Portland, Denver, Zurich, Stuttgart); *Städtebau und Kriminalität*, ed. by Bundeskriminalamt, Wiesbaden 1979 (West Germany 1960–72); K. O. Christiansen, "Industrialization and Urbanization in Relation to Crime and Juvenile Delinquency", in: *International Review of Criminality Policy* 16, 1960 (Denmark around 1960).
75. Cf. a chronological summary of all legal foundations of social security in Western Europe (exc. Greece, Portugal and Spain): P. Flora and J. Alber, "Modernization, Democratization and the Develop-

ment of Welfare States in Western Europe", in: Flora and Heidenheimer (eds), p. 59. These are naturally not all cases of a fully developed system according to the current definition. Europe's headstart would be even greater if state systems restricted to individual occupations, such as mining, were taken into account.

76. Cf. for the limits to the capacity of social security before 1914: Ritter, pp. 62ff; Fischer, pp. 83ff; for the proportion of wage earners covered by insurance cf. Flora and Alber, p. 55. The figure given there is an average that gives no clue to the differences in the development of various branches of social security. The four types of insurance are weighted differently within the average: old age pensions are weighted at three times that of accident and unemployment insurance, health insurance is weighted double; id., "Modernization", pp. 54–6.

77. Cf. R. T. Kuderle and T. R. Marmor, "The Development of Welfare States in North America", in: Flora and Heidenheimer, pp. 82ff, 108; T. Fukutake, *The Japanese Social Structure. Its Evolution in the Modern Structure*, Tokyo 1982, pp. 197f; L. Tierney, "The Pattern of Social Welfare", in: A. F. Davies and S. Eucel (eds), *Australian Society*, New York 1965, pp. 114ff.

78. Cf. more recent surveys in this unusually extensive comparative field: Ritter; Flora and Heidenheimer (eds); Alber; P. Flora, *Growth to Limits: the Western European Welfare State since World War II*, 5 vols, Berlin, New York 1986; H. G. Hockerts, "Die Entwicklung vom Zweiten Weltkrieg bis zur Gegenwart", in: P. A. Koehler and H. F. Zacher (eds), *Beiträge zur Geschichte und zur aktuellen Situation der Sozialversicherung*, Berlin 1983; P. A. Köhler and H. F. Zacher (eds), *Ein Jahrhundert Sozialversicherung in der Bundesrepublik Deutschland, Frankreich, Grossbritannien, Österreich und der Schweiz*, Berlin 1981; W. J. Mommsen (ed), *The Emergence of the Welfare State in Britain and Germany*, London 1981; Rimlinger; Zacher (ed), *Bedingungen*; S. Kuhnle, "The Beginning of the Nordic Welfare States: similarities and differences", in: *Acta Sociologica* 21, 1978, supplement.

79. Social expenditure as proportion of national product calculated from J. Kohl, "Trends and Problems in Post-war Public Expenditure Development in Western Europe and North America", in: Flora and Heidenheimer (eds), pp. 317, 339. Cf. also for comparison between some European countries and USA, Canada, Australia, New Zealand: P. R. Kaim-Caudle, *Comparative Social Policy and Social Security*, London 1973, pp. 300ff; for Japan cf. Fukutake, p. 200. For the number of people covered by the Japanese state system around 1970 cf: *Japan Statistical Yearbook* 1972, pp. 512–15. Cf. also for most recent developments: OECD, *Social Expenditure* 1960–90: problems of Growth and Control, Paris 1985.

80. For the impact of German social security on other countries cf. H.

Heclo, *Modern Social Politics in Britain and Sweden*, New Haven 1974, pp. 172ff, 177ff (Britain), pp. 178ff (Sweden); Ritter, pp. 83, 103 (Britain); E. P. Hennock, "The Origins of British National Insurance and the German Precedent 1800–1914", in: W. Mommsen (ed), pp. 84–104; M. Braun, *Die luxemburgische Sozialversicherung bis zum Zweiten Weltkrieg*, Stuttgart 1983; K. Ebert, *Die Anfänge der modernen Sozialpolitik in Österreich*, Vienna 1977; K. Emi, *Essays on the Service Industry and Social Security in Japan*, Tokyo 1976.

81. For wider discussions in Europe before passing of legislation in Germany: G. Perrin, "L'assurance sociale, ses particularités, son rôle dans le passé, le présent et l'avenir" in: Köhler and Zacher (eds), *Beiträge*, pp. 30–7; a retrospective look at the European debate through the eyes of the most important of the Kathedersozialisten on social security: G. Schmoller, *Grundriss der allgemeinen Volkswirtschaftslehre*, II, Leipzig 1923, pp. 407–17; a very well balanced account of the role of the Kathedersozialisten and Bismarck's power policy: Ritter, pp. 24–36.

82. Cf. Y. Saint-Jours, "Landesbericht Frankreich", in: Köhler and Zacher (eds), *Ein Jahrhundert*, p. 204; A. I. Ogus, "Landesbericht Grossbritannien", in *ibid.*, pp. 299f; A. Maurer, Landesbericht Schweiz, in *ibid.*, p. 764; Fischer, *Armut*, p. 87.

83. *Ibid.*, pp. 33f; C. Sachsse and F. Tennstedt, *Geschichte der Armenfürsorge in Deutschland*, Stuttgart 1980, pp. 30ff; W. K. Jordan, *Philanthropy in England 1480–1660*, Westport 1978; M. Mollat (ed), *Etudes sur l'histoire de la pauvreté*, 2 vols, Paris 1974.

84. The following is supported by a range of stimulating studies on distinctive features of industrial relations in Europe: E. Shorter and C. Tilly, *Strikes in France 1830–1968*, Cambridge 1974, chap 12; E. M. Kassalow, *Trade Unions and Industrial Relations: an International Comparison*, New York 1969, pp. 5–28; B. C. Roberts, *Towards Industrial Democracy. Europe, Japan and the United States*, London 1979, pp. 1–22; E. Jacobs, *European Trade Unionism*, London 1983; A. M. Ross and P. T. Hartmann, *Changing Patterns of Industrial Conflict*, New York 1960; P. Lösche, "Vereinigte Staaten von America", in: S. Mielke (ed), *Internationales Gewerkschaftshandbuch*, Opladen 1983, pp. 1157ff (exceptional account including comparisons with Europe); J. T. Dunlop and W. Galenson (eds), *Labor in the Twentieth Century*, New York 1978; S. M. Lipset, *The First New Nation*, New York 1967, pp. 193–233; H. Mommsen, "Arbeiterbewegung", in: *Sowjetsystem und Demokratische Gesellschaft*, I, Freiburg 1966; D. Geary, *European Labour Protest 1848–1939*, London 1981; P. N. Stearns, *Lives of Labour: work in Maturing Industrial Society*, London 1975; M. Shalev and W. Korpi, "Working-Class Mobilization and American Exceptionalism", in: *Economic and Industrial Democracy* 1, 1980; also: K. Tenfelde (ed), *Arbeiter und*

Arbeiterbewegung im Vergleich, Munich 1986.

85. Membership figures for European trade unions calculated from data contained in Table 8.

86. In 1974 the coefficient of variation for unionisation in America stood at 39%; in the latter half of the 1970s in Western Europe it stood at 35% cf. for Europe: Appendix for Table 9; for the USA: G. S. Bain and R. Price, *Profiles of Union Growth: A Comparative Statistical Portrait of Eight Countries*, London 1980, p. 92.

87. Cf. Kassalow, pp. 12ff; Lipset, *Nation*, pp. 193ff.

88. Kassalow; Lipset, pp. 178ff.

89. Cf. best summary on this subject: Lösche, pp. 1181ff.

90. H. Kaelble, "The Dissolution of a European Strike Pattern? Disparities and Convergences in Twentieth-Century European Industrial Relations", forthcoming, in: *International Review of Social History*, 1990.

91. op. cit., p. 13.

92. There is a range of important areas where information is currently too scarce to allow concrete characteristics of European societies to be traced: the European middle classes, workers, officials, farmers; European life cycles and attitudes to infancy, youth and death; relationships between the sexes and the social position of women; European attitudes to work, also attitudes to daily, weekly, yearly and lifelong periods of unemployment; migration within Europe and the condition of newly-arrived migrants in the heart of Europe in the twentieth century; European intellectuals and their role in politics and society; European villages, and the European's preference for confined regions which is especially evident in speech and dialect, architecture, clothing, eating and drinking habits, festivals and political structures.

93. Cf. also: J. Baechler, J. Hall and M. Mann (eds), *Europe and the Rise of Capitalism*, Oxford 1988; M. Mann, *The Sources of Social Power*, 2 vols, Cambridge 1986; J. H. Hall, *Powers and Liberties: the Causes and Consequences of the Rise of the West*, Oxford 1985; Eric L. Jones, *The European Miracle*, Cambridge 1984.

Chapter 3: European Social Convergence in the Twentieth Century (pp. 100–149)

1. The coefficient of variation for *per capita* industrial production (inc. energy and construction) in European Community countries in 1973 was 33%; in 1980 still as high as 30% (not inc. Greece. Calculated from *Eurostat. Revue* 1973–82, Luxemburg 1984, pp. 53, 103). Figures for *per capita* industrial production are of similar relevance to proportions of workforce employed in industry; both provide a guide to the degree of industrialisation in given Western European countries;

neither express anything about the development of industrial productivity.

2. Cf. on growing disparities before 1880 and on developments in individual countries: P. Bairoch, "International Industrialisation Levels from 1750 to 1980", in: *Journal of European Economic History* 11, 1982, pp. 293ff.

3. Cf. for the development of individual countries compared with European average: Bairoch, "Levels"; OECD, *Historical Statistics 1960–85*, Paris 1987, p. 47.

4. Cf. for development of *per capita* agricultural production among agricultural workers: OECD, *Historical Statistics 1960–85*, p. 47.

5. For development of individual European countries cf. H. Kaelble, "Prometheus"; up to 1985: OECD, *Historical Statistics 1960–85*, p. 37.

6. For individual countries: Kaelble, "Prometheus"; OECD, *Historical Statistics 1960–85*; a comparison between various branches of the service sector by H. van Dijk: "The Development of the Service Sector in Germany and the Netherlands", in: *Historical Social Research* 44, Oct. 1987. Similar differentiated comparisons should be prepared for the whole of Western Europe.

7. In 1930 the coefficient of variation between individual states of America for proportions of industrial employment was 32%; in 1950 it stood at 26% and in 1960 29%. The corresponding figures for service sector employment differed only slightly from the European figures: 1930, 18%; 1950, 14%; 1960, 12%. Calculated from: W. Fuchs, *The Service Economy*, New York NBER 1968, pp. 26–8. It would be wrong to expect too much of these figures however, because definitions of sectors differ somewhat, and above all because the number of states of America is far higher than the number of countries in Western Europe; internal differences therefore appear much greater within the USA. Coefficient of variation between Soviet republics for industrial employment was 60% in 1940 and 21% in 1970. This was substantially greater than the Western European value, but probably below the American. Calculated from data supplied by S. Merl from: *Narodnoe khozjajstvo SSSR 1922–72 gg. Jubilejnij statističeskij ežegodnik*, Moscow 1972. For precise European coefficients of variation cf. Table 9 in appendix. Comparison of regions of Europe also reveals an astonishing level of similarity between industrial and service employment: 1981, 21% and 15% respectively. Cf. *Die Regionen Europas*, Brussels 1984, second periodical report on the socio-economic situation and development of the regions of the European Community, Part D. After the accession of Spain and Portugal the similarities remained virtually unchanged: 1985, 22% and 16% respectively. *Third periodical report on the socio-economic situation and development of the regions of the European Community*, Brussels 1987, p. 169.

8. Cf. for survey of the development of agricultural employees as a proportion of the total of all employees: P. Flora, *Quantitative Historical Sociology*, The Hague 1977, pp. 48f; *Eurostat Review 1977–86*, Luxemburg 1988, p. 110; OECD *Historical Statistics 1960–85*, Paris OECD 1987, p. 36; for regional distribution cf: *Die Regionen Europas. Second periodical report*, Part D (coefficient of variation 86%); *Third periodical report*, p. 165 (coefficient of variation 1985: 105%).

9. Cf. for this thesis: S. Pollard, "Industrialisation and the European Economy", in: *Economic History Review* 26, 1973; Williamson, *Regional Inequality* (classic work on this subject); G. L. de Brabander, *Regional Specialisation. Employment and Economic Growth between 1846 and 1970*, New York 1981 (detailed evidence for this theory from Belgian employment history); H. Kaelble and R. Hohls, "The Regional Structure of Employment in Germany 1895–1970", in: *Historical Social Research* 44, 1987 (evidence for Germany/the Federal Republic).

10. The coefficient of variation for industrial employees as a proportion of total wage earners in Western Europe was only 9% in 1970. Similarity was therefore very great. Calculated from: OECD, *Labour Force Statistics 1970–81*, Paris 1983, Table IV (industry inc. mining, construction and utilities). In 1973 and 1982 by contrast, the coefficient of variation for self-employed farmers was very high at 76% and 79%. Calculated from: *Eurostat Review 1973–1982*, pp. 118, 123 (Norway, Finland, Austria and Switzerland not included).

11. Table 2 taken as basis for mobility rates in the 1960s. Coefficient of variation for mobility rates in Western European countries was only 18%. For change in social mobility since World War II cf. R. Erickson et al, "Intergenerational Class Mobility and the Convergence Thesis, England, France and Sweden", in: *British Journal for Sociology* 34, 1983; cf. also comparative works cited in Chapter 2, notes 21, 24 and 25.

12. For growing disparity in agricultural employment in the European Community: coefficient of variation rose from 45% in 1960 to 19% in 1972, after entry of Great Britain, Ireland and Denmark in 1973 it rose to 65%. Before entry of Greece in 1979 it stood at 62%, in 1980 it rose to 76% (calculated from: *OECD Historical Statistics 1960–80*, Paris OECD 1982, p. 34).

13. Cf. Koenig and Mueller, "Educational Systems and Labour Markets as Determinants of Worklife Mobility in France and West Germany", in: *European Sociological Review* 2, 1986.; B. Lutz, "Bildungssystem und Beschäftigungsstruktur in Deutschland und Frankreich. Zum Einfluss des Bildungssystems auf die Gliederung betrieblicher Arbeitskräftestrukturen", in: H. G. Mendius et al., *Betrieb, Arbeitsmarkt, Qualifikation*, Frankfurt 1976; cf. also intra-European comparisons: F. K. Ringer, *Education and Society in Modern Europe*,

Bloomington 1979; A. J. Heidenheimer, "Education and Social Security Entitlements in Europe and America", in: P. Flora and id., (eds); K. H. Jarausch, "Introduction", in: id. (eds), *Transformation of Higher Learning 1860–1930*, Stuttgart 1983; R. Premfors, *The Politics of Higher Education in a Comparative Perspective, France, Sweden, United Kingdom*, Stockholm 1980; R. L. Geiger, "The Changing Demand for Higher Education in the Seventies: adaption within Three National Systems", in: *Higher Education* 9, 1980, pp. 255–76.

14. Cf. for a round-up of illiteracy rates in the nineteenth and early twentieth centuries in Western Europe: Kaelble, *Industrialisation and Social Inequality*, p. 90.

15. Cf. for illiteracy rates in Spain and Portugal: *Anuario estadístico España 1982*, tab. 1.1.3 (illiteracy rates 1900–70); *Anuário estadístico Portugal 1961*, 1, tab. 10 (illiteracy rates 1878–1950, though extended to cover whole population inc. one- to five-year olds); UNESCO, *Statistical Yearbook 1984*, pp. 1–20.

16. In order to be able to compare numbers of students in different European countries the following arguments will be based on student proportions of the various age groups.

17. For similar summaries with slightly different definitions: Flora, *Quantitative Historical Sociology*, pp. 56f; id., *State, Economy and Society in Western Europe 1815–1975*, Frankfurt 1983, pp. 553ff; R. Schneider, "Die Bildungsentwicklung in den westeuropäischen Staaten 1870–1979", in: *Zeitschrift für Soziologie* 10, 1982.

18. Cf. for this and following accounts of growth in similarity in Western European college education: Kaelble, *Social Mobility*, ch. 2; for Scotland cf. R. D. Anderson, *Education and Opportunity in Victorian Scotland*, Oxford 1983, pp. 310ff.

19. Coefficient of variation for students in higher education in the states of America in 1970 stood at 25%. Numbers of students are not absolute but related to age groups. The relevant age group—18–20-year olds—was only roughly appropriate. Because it is coefficients of variation that are being compared here, not absolute numbers of students, this rough age group does not handicap the results. It could also be that for 1970 for the USA the value is an extreme, and that during periods of slower growth in education, differences within America were substantially lower. Here it is only relevant to point out that differences exist between European countries today that are also present within a country such as the United States. Calculated from: *Statistical Abstracts of the United States* 92, 1971, ed. by U. S. Department of Commerce, pp. 25, 107.

20. For towns with populations above 20,000 cf. Flora, *Sociology*, p. 40; id., *State*, vol. II, pp. 247ff; for towns according to national definitions cf. P. Bairoch, *Population urbaine*, pp. 307ff. As Bairoch shows, even

today, the definition of a town can vary greatly from one European country to another. They are defined sometimes by size of community, by housing density, by town charter and even by prevailing employment structure (proportion of wage earners in agricultural occupations); cf. a more recent attempt by Bairoch at calculating proportions of town dwellers using a more universal definition (towns of over 5,000 inhabitants): P. Bairoch, *De Jéricho à Mexico*, Paris 1985, p. 288.

21. Cf. Flora, *Sociology*, p. 40; Bairoch, *Population urbaine*, pp. 307ff.

22. Coefficient of variation for proportion of urban dwellers (communities of over 2,500) in the states of America for 1900 was 64%, 1930 45%, 1970 23%. Calculated from: *Statistical History of the United States*, pp. 24–37. Coefficient of variation for the proportion of urban dwellers in the republics of the USSR (not inc. Estonia, Latvia, Lithuania or Moldavia up to 1940) was 36% in 1913, 20% in 1940 and 20% in 1970 (without the additional republics resulting from World War II only 17%). Calculated from summaries by S. Merl from: *Narodnoe khozjajstvo SSSR 1922–72 gg. Jubilejnij statističeskij ežegodnik*, Moscow 1972; for definition of towns cf. S. Merl, "Russland und die Sowjetunion 1914–1980", in: W. Fischer (ed), *Handbuch der europäischen Wirtschafts- und Sozialgeschichte*, vol. 6, Stuttgart 1987, p. 171.

23. Coefficient of variation for the proportion of urban dwellers living in medium-sized towns in Western European countries fell from 49% in 1920 to 38% in 1960. Calculated from values given in Figure 6.

24. Cf. UN, *Growth of the World's Urban and Rural Population*, pp. 107ff; Hall, p. 156; Cheshire and Hay, *European Urban Systems*.

25. Account of life in housing blocks early this century: R. Eberstadt, *Handbuch des Wohnungswesens*, Jena 1920, quoted from W. Hegemann, *Das steinerne Berlin* 1930, ND 1963, p. 333.

26. Cf. A. D. Deaton, "The Structure of Demand", in: C. Cipolla (ed), *Fontana Economic History of Europe*, V/1, pp. 114ff; UN, *The European Housing Problem: A Preliminary Review*, Geneva 1949; UN, *Statistical Yearbook 1960*, pp. 564ff; 1971, 728ff; UN, *Compendium of Housing Statistics*, New York 1974; *Eurostat Social Indicators for the European Community 1960–75*, Luxemburg 1977, pp. 237ff; statistics largely compare only urban life though they do also include rural life. For comparisons of quality of life in European towns they may therefore present a distorted picture of contrasts within Europe.

27. Cf. account of the introduction of state social security in Western European countries (not inc. Spain, Portugal or Greece): Alber, p. 24ff.

28. Cf. for both Germany and Great Britain: Ritter, *Social Welfare*; for Austria: K. Ebert, *Die Anfänge der modernen Sozialpolitik in Österreich*,

Vienna 1975; for Great Britain and Sweden: H. Heclo, *Modern Social Politics in Britain and Sweden. From Relief to Income Maintenance*, New York 1975; for attitudes to German social security among British politicians cf. P. Hennock, "Arbeiterunfallentschädigung und Arbeiterunfallversicherung. Die britische Sozialreform und das Beispiel Bismarcks", in: *Geschichte und Gesellschaft* 11, 1985.

29. Differences become apparent from comparative studies: Alber; Ritter; Heclo; Hennock, "Arbeiterunfallentschädigung"; Rimlinger; Koehler and Zacher, "Sozialversicherung".

30. N.B. in Figures 7 and 9 an average value is calculated for the four types of insurance using a weighting of 1.5 for pensions and health insurance, 1.0 for health and unemployment insurance and 0.5 for accident insurance. Cf. P. Flora and J. Alber, "Modernization, Democratization and the Development of Welfare States in Europe", in: Flora and Heidenheimer (eds), pp. 54ff.

31. Quoted in Ritter, p. 102. Data on British and German pensions: GB, *ibid*, p. 102; Germany: Hentschel p. 26 (average pension); G. Hohorst et al., *Sozialgeschichtliches Arbeitsbuch. Materialien zur Statistik des Kaiserreichs 1870–1914*, Munich 1975, p. 107 (average wage in Germany). This comparison admittedly has its faults because rates of exchange do not necessarily reflect the actual situation in the two countries.

32. Cf. Alber pp. 28ff.

33. H. G. Hockerts, "Die Entwicklung bis zur Gegenwart", in: P. A. Koehler and H. F. Zacher (eds), *Beiträge zur Geschichte und aktuellen Situation der Sozialversicherung*, Berlin 1983, pp. 154ff; H. Heclo, "Toward a New Welfare State?" in: Flora and Heidenheimer (eds), *The Development of Welfare States in Europe and America*, New Brunswick 1981.

34. Alber, pp. 28f, 43ff; K. Teppe, "Zur Sozialpolitik im Dritten Reich am Beispiel der Sozialversicherung", in: *Archiv für Sozialgeschichte* 17, 1977; M. Recker, *Nationalsozialistische Sozialpolitik im zweiten Weltkrieg*, Munich 1985; V. Hentschel, *Geschichte der deutschen Sozialpolitik 1880–1980*, Frankfurt 1983.

35. Cf. lists of insured workers in: Flora and Alber, "Modernization", pp. 74ff. No information there for Spain, Portugal or Greece.

36. Very stimulating general survey of post-war developments in Western Europe: H. G. Hockerts, "Die Entwicklung", in: Koehler and H. F. Zacher (eds), *Beiträge*, pp. 141ff; Heclo, "Toward a New Welfare State?"; G. A. Ritter, *Der Sozialstaat*, Munich 1988; Flora, *Growth to Limits*, vol. 5; growth in numbers of insured workers and social insurance expenditure calculated from: Alber and Flora, pp. 74ff (insured workers); P. Flora, *State, Economy...*, I, pp. 456f (Social security expenditure as a proportion of national product); OECD, *Social*

Expenditure 1960–1990, Paris OECD 1985, p. 21 (overall state expenditure on social insurance).

37. Alber, *Armenhaus*, pp. 28ff, 231ff.
38. Hockerts, p. 154; Heclo, "Welfare State", pp. 391ff. Cf. also H. L. Wilensky, "Leftism, Catholicism and Corporatism: The Role of Political Parties in Recent Welfare State Development" in: Flora and Heidenheimer (eds).
39. See Alber, pp. 28ff, 155ff; Hockerts, 144ff.
40. Calculated from Flora, *State*, I, p. 456. Coefficient of variation for social insurance expenditure (as a proportion of national product) fell from 33% to 18%, for overall social expenditure (also as proportion of national product) from 31% to 19%. These figures must be treated with some caution, however, because they contain a variety of methods of calculation. Cf. also *Eurostat, Social Indicators*, pp. 190f.
41. Definition of women's work in occupational statistics, cf. for countries with very little or very much female labour: P. Schybergen and K. Vettula, "Women's Employment in the Nordic Countries 1870–1940", in: E. Boserup (ed), *Female Labour before, during and after the Industrial Revolution*, 8th International History Congress, Thema B5, Budapest 1982, pp. 52–61; P. M. M. Klep, "Female Labour in the Netherlands and Belgium, 1846–1910", in: ibid., pp. 22–31. Women constituted 39% of all wage earners in Great Britain in 1980, 38% in West Germany, 39% in France and 33% in Italy. ILO, *Yearbook of Labour Statistics 1982*, pp. 17–31; cf. also OECD, *Historical Statistics, 1960–85*, Paris 1987, p. 34; *Eurostat Review 1977–86*, Luxemburg 1988, pp. 105ff.
42. Cf. *Men and Women in Europe*, ed. Commission of the European Community, Brussels 1983; S. Harding, D. Phillips and M. Fogarty, *Contrasting Values in Western Europe. Unity, Diversity and Change*, London 1986, pp. 126ff.
43. Cf. a more detailed study of the female working life: W. Mueller, "Frauenerwerbstätigkeit im Lebenslauf", in: id., A. Willms and J. Handl, *Strukturwandel der Frauenarbeit 1880–1980*, Frankfurt 1983. There are not enough similarly detailed studies for enough other European countries to allow any precise comparisons. Figure 10 is only a rough approximation because it does not actually represent the variations in women's working lives, but female labour in a range of age groups.
44. Cf. Harding, Phillips and Fogarty, pp. 116ff; *Men and Women in Europe*, pp. 11ff (for current attitudes); R. Wall, "The Living Arrangements for the elderly in Contemporary Europe", unpubl. paper 1984, tab. 3, (compares widowhood in Great Britain, France, West Germany, Austria, Sweden, Finland, Iceland, Poland, the GDR, Czechoslovakia); P. Chester (ed), *Divorce in Europe*, Amsterdam 1977.

45. Cf. for infant mortality and birth rates, Table 9 in appendix. For attitudes to children cf. Harding, Phillips and Fogarty, pp. 19ff (aims for upbringing); the Commission of the European Community (ed), *The Europeans and their Children*, Brussels 1979, pp. 42ff (arrangements for child supervision), 51ff (education), 69ff (methods of upbringing, number of children); A. Firard, "Dimension idéale de la famille et tendances de la fécondité: comparaisons internationales", in: *Population* 6, 1976.

46. Historical surveys of various types of European union movements are uncommon. Cf. H. Mommsen, "Arbeiterbewegung", in: *Sowjetsystem und Demokratische Gesellschaft*, I, Freiburg 1966; K. von Beyme, *Gewerkschaften und Arbeiterbeziehungen in kapitalistischen Ländern*, Munich 1977, pp. 19ff (systematic survey without particular historical viewpoint); P. Reynaud, "Synthèse, Unité et Diversité", in: G. Spitaels (ed), *Les conflits sociaux en Europe*, Verviers 1971; J. P. Windmuller and A. Gladstone, *Employers' Associations and Industrial Relations*, Oxford 1983 (situation in the late 1960s); it is often necessary to resort to collections of national union histories: cf. Mielke (ed); J. T. Dunlop and W. Galenson, *Labor in the twentieth century*, New York 1978; H. Ruehle and H.-J. Veen (eds), *Gewerkschaften in den Demokratien Westeuropas*, 2 vols, Paderborn 1983.

47. Cf. C. Tilly and E. Shorter, *Strikes in France, 1830–1968*, Cambridge/Mass. 1974, pp. 306ff; cf. also: F. Boll, "Streikwellen im europäischen Vergleich", in: W. J. Mommsen and H.-G. Husung (eds), *The Development of Trade Unions in Germany and Great Britain 1880–1914*, London 1985; J. E. Cronin, "Labour Insurgency and Class Formation: Comparative Perspectives of the Crisis of 1917–1920 in Europe", in: *Social Science History* 4, 1980; id., "Streiks und gewerkschaftliche Organisationsfortschritte: Grossbritannien und Kontinentaleuropa, 1870–1914", in: Mommsen and Husung; D. Geary, *European Labour Protest 1848–1939*, London 1981; D. Snyder, "Determinants of Industrial Conflict. Historical Models of Strikes in France, Italy and the United States", Ph.D., University of Michigan, Ann Arbor 1974; D. A. Hibbs, "On the Political Economy of Long-run Trends in Strike Activity", in: *British Journal of Political Science* 8, 1978; M. Shalev, "Strikes and the Crisis: Industrial Conflict and Unemployment in the Western Nations", in: *Economic and Industrial Democracy* 4, 1983; W. Korpi and M. Shalev, "Strikes, Power and Politics in the Western Nations, 1900–1976", in: *Political Power and Social Theory* 1, 1980.

48. Cf. E. J. Kirchner, *Trade Unions as a Pressure Group in the European Community*, Westmead 1977, pp. 16ff.

49. *Ibid.*, pp. 22–27.

50. A survey of development of strikes in many Western European

countries appears in: Hibbs, pp. 158ff (working days lost in relation to non-agricultural wage earners); Shalev (for 1960s and 1970s). Cf. also for Switzerland: Arbeitsgruppe für Geschichte jeder Arbeiterbewegung Zurich, *Die schweizerische Arbeiterbewegung*, Zurich 1975, pp. 400ff; for Austria: F. Traxler, *Evolution gewerkschaftlicher Interessenvertretung*, Vienna 1982, p. 267; for West Germany I am indebted to H. Volkmann who will shortly publish corrected long-term accounts of strike development in Germany from 1933 to 1980 (H. Volkmann et al., *Streiks und Aussperrungen in Deutschland, 1936–80*, Ostfildern, probably 1989).

51. An especially stimulating study: S. Pollard, *The Integration of the European Economy since 1815*, London 1981 (exclusively economic integration, does not tackle social integration of Europe).

52. Especially stimulating: B. Lutz, *Der kurze Traum immerwährender Prosperität. Eine Neuinterpretation der industriell-kapitalistischen Entwicklung im Europa des 20. Jahrhunderts*, Frankfurt 1984. Lutz does not examine social integration in Europe, but rather structural change during the boom.

53. Figures 8 and 9 and Table 9 in Appendix. Industrial production and employment runs up to 1980; however, some figures run out earlier: students 1978, proportion of female students 1975, employees covered by state social insurance 1975 and urbanisation as early as 1970. Thus the figures are not available to allow any final statement to be made about the effects of the crisis on social integration. Instead it is possible to use European Community statistics which cover most Western European countries (but not Norway, Finland, Switzerland or Austria) under most headings up to 1981, allowing the effects of the crisis to be traced for nearly another decade. Similarly, these show no disintegrative trends during the period of crisis. Coefficient of variation for proportion of industrial employees: 1974 17%, 1981 12%, 1985 13% (OECD, *Historical Statistics 1960–1985*, Paris 1982, p. 36); industrial production per head: 1970 41%, 1980 36%, 1985 37% (*Eurostat-Review 1977–86*, Luxemburg 1988, pp. 43–45, 94. EC not inc. Ireland and Portugal); students in higher education per head of population: 1974 24%, 1980 25%, 1984 25% (EC only plus Sweden); proportion of female students in higher education: 1973 12%, 1980 10%, 1984 7% (EC only); social security expenditure as percentage of GNP: 1975 13%, 1981 10% (EC only not inc. Greece because of lack of data). Calculated from: *Eurostat Review 1973–1982*, Luxemburg 1984, pp. 103, 116, 122, 134; ibid. *1977–86*, Luxemburg 1988, p. 104.

54. This remains speculative. If new social change in employment structure has recently had a smaller disintegrative effect than in former times, then development of the so-called information sector might be an example (although it is far from undisputed). Certain

social scientists are of the opinion that this is the most important new sector in employment since the origins of industrial employment. The OECD has recently traced the development of this sector from historical data covering six countries since 1950. Variation between European countries in terms of employment in this sector (which included Finland, then a peripheral country, but otherwise only mature industrial societies, France, Great Britain, Austria, Sweden and West Germany) was far smaller in 1950 than their variation in terms of industrial employment at the turn of the century. By 1970 the similarity had become substantial (coefficient of variation for the information sector: 1950 29%, 1960 24%, 1970 15%. Calculated from: OECD, *Information Activities, Electronics and Telecommunications Technologies. Impact in Employment, Growth and Trade*, vol. 1, Paris 1981, p. 125. Coefficient of variation for industrial employment in these countries in 1900: 41%).

Chapter 4: Conclusion (pp. 150–161)

1. This book is a preliminary study for a longer work on twentieth-century European social history.

2. K. Deutsch, "Integration and Arms Control in the European Political Environment: A Summary Report", in: *American Political Science Review* 60, 1960; R. Inglehart and J.-R. Rabier, "La confiance entre les peuples", in: *Revue française de science politique* 1984; Commission of the European Community, *Eurobarometer* 19, 1983, pp. 107ff; J. Stoetzel, *Les valeurs du temps présent*, Paris 1983; S. Harding, D. Phillips and M. Fogarty, *Contrasting Values in Western Europe*, London 1986, ch. 3.

3. Cf. R. Inglehart, "An End to European Integration?", in: *American Political Science Review* 61, 1967; id., "Changing Value Priorities and European Integration", in: *Journal of the Common Market Studies* 10, 1971; Commission of the European Community, *Eurobarometer* 19, 1983, pp. 85ff.

4. For long-term reviews of attitudes to the EC among Western Europeans cf. Inglehart, "Priorities", p. 30 (1952–70); J.-C. Deheneffe, *Die Europäer über sich selbst. Die Meinung der europäischen Öffentlichkeit von 1973 bis 1986*, Luxemburg 1986.

5. Two further aspects of social integration were enumerated in the Introduction, namely exchange relations between European countries outside the usual exchange of goods and capital, and the emergence of organisational interaction other than within the Community framework. There is a dearth of studies on these subjects and developments in these areas cannot therefore be examined in these pages.

Sources for Tables and Figures

Table 1 (p. 16)

European Community countries: *Demographic statistics 1984*, Luxemburg 1984, Table 7 (1970, 1980). Germany: *Statistik des deutschen Reichs*, N.F. Vol 44, p. 127 (all marriages, Prussia, Baden, Bavaria, Württemberg, Hesse, Thüringian states, Oldenburg, Brunswick, Lübeck, Bremen, 1880, calculated on basis of rough age groups); F. Juraschek, *Die Staaten Europas, Statistische Darstellung*, Leipzig 1907, p. 230 (Prussia, Bavaria, Saxony, Württemberg evaluated by population, 1900); *Bevölkerung und Wirtschaft 1872–1972*, Statistisches Bundesamt (ed), Stuttgart 1972, p. 105 (first marriages, 1911 instead of 1910, 1938 instead of 1940). France: *Annuaire statistique* 6, 1883, p. 32 (1880); 23, 1903, p. 42f; ibid 31, 1911, p. 16f (own calculations based on age group-specific marriage figures, first marriage); "Douzième rapport sur la situation démographique de la France", in: *Population* 38, 1983, p. 688 (1930s and 1930 birth cohorts, i.e. 1950s marriage cohorts); INSEE. *Données sociales*, 1981 ed., Paris 1981, p. 22 (1960, 1970). Great Britain: A. H. Halsey, *Social Change in Britain*, Oxford 1978, p. 101 (birth cohorts, 1850, 1870, 1890, 1910, 1930, 1950; first marriage). Italy: "Sviluppo della populazione italiana dal 1861 al 1961", in: *Annali di statistica* 94, vol 17, series VIII, p. 360 (1896–1900, 1906–10, 1916–20, 1926–30, 1936–40, 1946– 50, 1956–60). Finland: *Statistical Yearbook of Finland 1981*, p. 61 (1881–90, 1891–1900, 1901–10, 1911–20, 1921–30, 1931–40, 1941–50, 1951– 60, 1961–70). Norway: *Historisk Statistikk 1978*, Oslo 1978, p. 50 (first marriages 1876–80, 1896–1900, 1906–10, 1916–20, 1926–30, 1936–40, 1946– 50, 1956–60, 1966–70). Netherlands: L. Th. van Leeuwen, *Ontwikkelingsfasen van het gezin*, The Hague 1980, p. 24 (first marriages 1880–89, 1900–09, 1910–19, 1920–29, 1930–39, 1945–49, 1951–55, 1961– 66, 1971–75). Austria: G. Feichtinger and H. Hanslawka, "The Impact of Mortality on the Life Cycle of the Family in Austria", in: *Zeitschrift für Bevölkerungswissenschaft* 3, 1977, p. 62 (first marriages). Ireland: J. Meenan, *The Irish Economy since 1922*, Liverpool 1970, p. 195. United

States (median age at first marriage): *The Statistical History of the United States*, New York 1976, p. 19; *Statistical Abstract of the United States*, 108th Edition, Washington 1987, p. 83 (1970, 1980). Japan: R W Sekiguchi, "Zum Wandel der japanischen Familie seit Beginn des 20. Jahrhunderts", in: P. Borscheid and H. J. Teuteberg (eds), *Ehe, Liebe, Tod*, Münster 1983, p. 103. Australia: Australian Bureau of Statistics, *Demography* 1971, p. 79 (1921–25, 1926–30, 1936–40, 1946–50, 1956–60, 1970). Late marriage in Europe also evident in: *Statistisches Jahrbuch der Schweiz*, vol 73, 1965, p. 67; vol 91, 1983, p. 74 (marriage partners by age group in Switzerland, 1921–1982; *Annuaire Statistique de la Belgique*, vol 102, 1981, p. 84f (Belgium 1890–1981); *Anuario demografico 1961*, p. 21 LXIV (Portugal 1930–1960); *Anuario estadístico España* 1971, p. 60; 1981, p. 57 (Spain 1961–1979). A. Hagami, "Another Fossa magna", in: *Journal of Family History* 12, 1987, p. 61ff (Japan around 1900 and 1920).

Table 2 (pp. 36–37)
K. U. Mayer in: E. Ballerstadt et al., *Soziologischer Almanach*, Frankfurt 1979, p. 308

Table 3 (p. 38)
Selected countries from: H. Kaelble, *Social Mobility in the Nineteenth and Twentieth Centuries*, Leamington Spa 1985, pp. 42ff, 86ff. (United States 1890–1940: proportion of women among B.A. graduates calculated from: *Statistical History of the United States*, New York 1976, p. 386). Table 3 is only a sample of all years contained therein. More countries, dates, other definitions of high schools, precise identification of sources and commentaries are also included. Data for Western Europe are not averages of all countries but indicate all Western European students in relation to all 20- to 24-year-old Western Europeans.

Table 4 (p. 42)
Unfortunately, data for income levels in various comparable income groups are comparatively rare, besides which they are calculated in a confusing number of forms. Only a few comparisons may therefore be drawn. Calculations based on: *The Statistical History of the United States*, New York 1976, p. 292 (families and unrelated individuals United States, 1962, 1969); A. H. Halsey, *Change in British Society*, Oxford 1978, p. 32 (Great Britain 1974/75); H. F. Lydall and J. B. Lansing, "A Comparison of the Distribution of Personal Income in the United States and Britain", in: A. B. Atkinson (ed), *Wealth, Income and Inequality*, Harmondsworth 1973, p. 139 (United States and Great Britain 1954); G. Schmaus, "Personelle Einkommensverteilung im Vergleich

1962/63 und 1969" in: H.-J. Krupp and W. Glatzer (ed), *Umverteilung im Sozialstaat*, Frankfurt 1978, p. 93 (Germany 1962/63 and 1969).

Table 5 (p. 44)

M. Sawyers, *Income Distribution in OECD Countries*. OECD Economic Outlook, Occasional Studies, July 1976, p. 26ff. In addition: H. Suppanz, "Zur personellen Einkommensverteilung in Österreich", in: *Österreichische Zeitschrift für Soziologie* 1978, p. 61 (Austria 1950–70; J. Tinbergen, *Income Distribution*, London 1978 (Germany 1936; The Netherlands 1935, 1946, 1962; Great Britain 1949; Denmark 1939, 1952, 1963); T. Stark, *The Distribution of Income in Eight Countries*, London 1977, p. 32, 105, 135, 147 (Ireland 1973; Sweden 1954, 1963; Canada 1965; Australia 1961–2; Japan 1959); *The Statistical History of the United States*, New York 1976, p. 292 (families and unrelated individuals United States, 1950–76); M. Schnitzer, *Income Distribution*, New York 1974, p. 224, 228 (Japan 1940, 1960).

Table 6 (p. 63)

United States: R. J. Lampmann, *The Share of Top Wealth-Holders in National Wealth 1922–1956*, Princeton 1962, p. 24 (1929, 1933); J. D. Smith and S. D. Franklin, "Concentration of Personal Wealth in the United States, 1922–1969" in: A. B. Atkinson (ed), *Wealth, Income and Inequality*, Oxford 1980, p. 234ff (1953, 1965); S. Lebergott, *The American Economy*, Princeton 1976, p. 242 (United States, 1976); England and Wales: A. B. Atkinson, *The Economics of Inequality*, Oxford 1983, p. 168 (1925, 1936, 1956, 1966, 1972); France: A. Daumard, "Wealth and Affluence in France since the Beginning of the Nineteenth Century", in: W. D. Rubinstein (ed), *Wealth and the Wealthy in the Modern World*, London 1980, p. 115 (1902–13, 1929, 1950); West Germany: H. Kaelble, *Industrialisation and Social Inequality*, Lemmington Spa 1986, p. 52 (Prussia 1911, West Germany 1973); Sweden (1920, 1930, 1951, 1966, 1975):R. Spånt, "Wealth Distribution in Sweden 1920–1983", in: E. N. Wolff (ed), *International Comparison of the Distribution of Household Wealth*, Oxford 1987, p. 60; Switzerland: *Almanach der Schweiz*, Bern 1978, p. 145 (1.1% and 4% of wealth-holders; untaxed wealth, 1969); W. Ernst, *Die Wohlstandsverteilung in der Schweiz*, Diessenhofen 1983, p. 204 (1979); France 1977, Belgium 1969, Denmark 1973, United States 1972, West Germany 1973: D. Strauss-Kahn, "Éléments de comparaison internationale des patrimoines", in: *Le patrimoine national*, *Économie et statistique* no. 144, Paris: INSEE 1983, p. 121.

Table 7 (p. 65)

The table is intended to show the basic geographical movement of the

world's largest cities away from Europe in the direction of Asia and
America. The exact position of cities and agglomerations in the table
is heavily dependent on different geographical boundaries in the col-
lection of data on cities. For this reason there is a range of different
lists ranking the world's largest cities, and these apply to other years
as well as the year 2000.

Calculated from the following sources. 1910: *Statistisches Jahrbuch für
den Deutschen Reich* 54, 1935, p. 14. 1950: *Statistisches Jahrbuch für die Bundesrepublik Deutschland* 1952, p. 17; 1980: *ibid.* 1983 p. 640f. 2000: G.
Chaliand and J.-O. Rageau, *Atlas stratégique*, Paris 1983, p. 190.

Table 8 (p. 85)
Levels of unionisation (i.e. union members expressed as percentage of
all dependent employees) taken from the following sources. United
States, Australia, Canada, Great Britain, Germany, Sweden, Norway
and Denmark: G. S. Bain and R. Price, *Profiles of Union Growth*, Oxford
1980, p. 37, 38, 107, 133f, 142, 151, 158. Austria 1900–80: F. Traxler,
Evolution gewerkschaftlicher Interessenvertretung, Vienna 1982, p. 95, 168,
257. All other figures own calculations based on the following sources.
Union membership: France 1900–50, Italy 1900–20, Netherlands
1900–50, Japan 1921–50: A. M. Ross and P. T. Hartmann, *Changing
Patterns of Industrial Conflict*, New York 1960, p. 200; Italy 1950–76: T.
Treu, "Italy", in: B. C. Roberts, *Towards Industrial Democracy*, London
1979, p. 85; Spain 1900–20, 1980, Portugal 1980, Ireland 1980, Au-
stria 1978, Switzerland 1960–80, Finland 1910–78, Netherlands
1960–80, France 1960–80 (with own estimates), Japan 1950–78: S.
Mielke (ed), *Internationales Gewerkschaftshandbuch*, Opladen 1983; Switzerland: Arbeitsgruppe für Geschichte der Arbeiterbewegung Zurich,
Die schweizerische Arbeiterbewegung, Zurich 1975, p. 396f (1903–50); G.
Unser, "Schweiz", in: Mielke (ed), p. 971 (1960–80). Employees: all
countries except those covered by Bain and Price, 1970 and 1980:
OECD, *Labour Force Statistics* 1970–1981, Paris OECD 1983; also
France and Belgium 1900–60: P. Bairoch, *The Working Population and
its Structure*, Brussels 1968; Italy 1910–60: P. S. Labini, *Saggi sulle classe
sociali*, Rome 1978, Table 1.5; Netherlands: supplied by Henk van
Dijk from personal databank; Switzerland: *Eidgenössische Volks-
zählungen* 1 December 1960, Vol 28, II, Berne 1965, p. 18 (1888–1960);
Spain: W. L. Bernecker, "Wirtschafts- und Sozialgeschichte Spaniens
1914–1975", in: W. Fischer (ed), *Europäische Wirtschafts- und Sozialgeschichte*, Vol 6, 1987; Finland: O. Krantz, "Wirtschafts- und Sozialgeschichte der nordischen Länder 1914–1970" in: W. Fischer (ed),
Europäische Wirtschafts- und Sozialgeschichte, Vol 6, Stuttgart 1985, Table
7; Japan: T. Fukutake, "The Japanese Social Structure", Tokyo,

Tokyo University Press 1982, p. 58, 152. Western Europe: no average value, but all union members in Western Europe as percentage of all dependent employees.

Table 9 (pp. 162–63)
(1) *Per capita* product. P. Bairoch, "Europe's Gross National Product 1800–1975", in: *Journal of European Economic History* 5, 1976, p. 286, 297, 307 (1925 instead of 1920, 1929 instead of 1930, 1938 instead of 1940); OECD, *National accounts*, Vol 1, Main aggregates 1951–1980, Paris 1982, p. 88. *Per capita* industrial production: P. Bairoch, "International Industrialisation Levels 1750–1980", in: *Journal of European Economic History* 11, 1982, p. 294, 302 (1913, 1928, 1938, 1953, 1963, 1973).
(2) Employment. H. Kaelble, "Was Prometheus Most Unbound in Europe?", in: *Journal of European Economic History* 18, 1989 (coefficient of variation for employment in each sector weighted with industrial, service and agricultural employees); P. Bairoch (ed), *The Working Population and its Structure*, Brussels 1968 (income quota and women's work up to 1960); ILO, *Yearbook of Labour Statistics 1975*, Geneva 1976, pp. 36–44 (income quota and women's work 1970); ILO, *Yearbook of Labour Statistics 1982*, Geneva 1983, pp. 27–31 (income quota and women's work 1980).
(3) Family and population. B. R. Mitchell, *European Historical Statistics*, 1750–1975, London 1975, pp. 138–42 (infant mortality up to 1970); *UN Statistical Yearbook* 1981, New York 1982, p. 74 (infant mortality 1980); as far as possible three-year average of quotas around the key year; quota for Great Britain determined by population of Ireland, Scotland, and England/Wales): P. Chester (ed), *Divorce in Europe*, Amsterdam 1977, p. 194 (divorce rate per 1,000 married couples or married women; GB, England/Wales only); *UN Demographic Yearbook 1953*, New York 1953, pp.282–3 (divorce rate Denmark, Portugal 1940 and 1950); *UN Demographic Yearbook 1976*, New York 1977, pp. 486–9 (divorce rate Switzerland, Denmark, Greece, Italy, Portugal 1970); *UN Demographic Yearbook 1970*, New York 1971, pp. 548–63 (number of married women) and *UN Demographic Yearbook 1976*, New York 1977, pp. 640–3 (number of divorces Denmark, Greece, Portugal 1960); Mitchell, *Statistics*, pp. 94–110 (number of births as three-year average around key year, up to 1970—birth rate = number of births per 100 population); *UN Statistical Yearbook 1981*, New York 1982, p. 74 (birth rate 1980); P. Flora, *Quantitative Historical Sociology*, The Hague 1977, p. 40 (average population as ten-year average around key year up to 1970; GB up to 1960 England/Wales and Scotland only); *UN Statistical Yearbook 1972*, New York 1973, p. 72 (Spain 1970); *UN Statistical Yearbook 1970*, New York

1971, p. 122f, (Great Britain, Greece, Portugal 197); *UN Statistical Yearbook 1981*, New York 1982, p. 65 (all countries 1980) average of yearly quotas 1975–80; (1910, 1920, 1940 and especially 1980, negative growth rates included in the calculation, coefficient of variation therefore indicates stronger divergence than was actually present). Age structure: (total population, population up to age 15, population over 65): Mitchell, *Statistics*, pp. 29–34 (up to 1970); *UN Demographic Yearbook 1981*, New York 1982, pp. 257–61 (Finland, Great Britain, Norway, Netherlands 1980); OECD, *Labour Force Statistics 1970–80*, Paris 1983, p. 148ff (all other countries 1980).

(4) Education. H. Kaelble, *Soziale Mobilität und Chancengleichheit im 19. und 20. Jahrhundert. Deutschland im internationalen Vergleich*, Göttingen 1983, p. 200, 222f (as with other areas there is not always information available on all European countries. For 1960 Spain and Greece at least are missing, causing the coefficient of variation to be lower than it would probably have been had these countries been included. 1920–40 universities only; 1950–80 all colleges; 1975 instead of 1980 for female students; 1978 instead of 1980 for the number of students).

(5) Urbanisation. Flora, *Sociology*, pp. 46f (proportion of population in settlements of over 20,000 inhabitants only, since other definitions of towns are not uniformly present in all sets of statistics; Flora's data excludes Spain, Greece, Portugal; cf. Flora, *State, Economy and Society in Western Europe 1815–1975*, II, Stuttgart 1987); *UN Demographic Yearbook 1970*, New York 1971, pp. 497ff (Spain, Greece, Portugal 1950 and 1960).

(6) Welfare state. P. Flora and J. Alber, "Modernisation, Democratisation and the Development of Welfare States in Western Europe", in: P. Flora and H. J. Heidenheimer (eds), *The Development of Welfare States in Europe and America*, New Brunswick 1981, pp. 74, 77 (accident and unemployment insurance); P. Flora et al., *State, Economy and Society in Western Europe 1815–1975*, I, Frankfurt 1983, pp. 460f (old age pensions, health insurance; wage earners covered by the four main areas of social security as a proportion of total workforce from the time when data is available for enough countries); Flora et al., *State*, pp. 456f (social expenditure as proportion of social product; social security and health expenditure as proportion of social product).

(7) Social conflict. Flora, *Sociology*, pp. 74–5 (number of strikers per 100,000 wage earners; either five- or ten-year averages); Table 8 (unions).

Figure 1 (p. 23)
H. Kaelble, "Was Prometheus Most Unbound in Europe?" in: *Journal of European Economic History* 18, 1989, Graph 1.

Figure 2 (p. 47)
T. Stark, *The Distribution of Income in Eight Countries*, London 1977, p. 78f, 130 (Japan, Germany, Series "DIW"); H. Suppanz, "Zur personellen Einkommensverteilung in Österreich", in: *Österreichische Zeitschrift für Soziologie* 1978 (Austria); F. Kraus, "The Historical Development of Income Inequality in Western Europe and the United States", in: P. Flora and A. J. Heidenheimer (eds), *The Development of the Welfare States in Europe and America*, New Brunswick 1981, p. 198ff (Remaining countries. All remaining abbreviations taken from that source). Diagrams contain all available long-term data on higher incomes. At first sight this can be confusing but it shows the scale of error and the caution necessary when drawing conclusions.

Figure 3 (p. 54)
Calculated from the following sources. United States: R. H. Britton after A. Antonovsky, "Social Class, Life Expectancy and Overall Mortality" in: *The Millbank Memorial Fund Quarterly* 45/2, 1967, Part 1, p. 41 (Males 1900, 45–64 years of age, death rate per 1,000, ten American states and Washington D.C.); J. S Whitney after J. Daric, "Mortalité profession et situation sociale" in: *Population* 4, 1949, p. 690 (United States 1930, ten American states, males 15–64 years of age); L. Guralnick, "Socio-economic Differences in Mortality by Cause of Death—United States 1950 and England and Wales 1949–53" in: *International Union for the Scientific Study of Population. International Population Conference*, Ottawa 1963, p. 298 (United States 1950, males 20–64 years of age, professional classes I and V). England: A. H. Halsey, *Trends in British Society since 1900*, London 1972, p. 341 (England and Wales 1949–53, males, 20–64 years of age, professional classes I and V). France: M. Huber after Daric, *op. cit.*, p. 678 (France 1907–08, males, 25–64 years of age, average mortality rate among academic professions i.e. lawyers, doctors, notaries and chemists, and workers in industries with high proportions of unskilled labour such as mining, iron and steel industries, metallurgy, construction and glass manufacture—thus less precisely defined than other rates on the Diagram); G. Desplanques, *La mortalité des adultes suivant le milieu social 1955–1971*, collections des L'INSEE, série D, No. 44, Paris: INSEE 1976, p. 46 (France, males, 35–70 years of age, 1955–71, mortality rate calculated from survival rate). Austria: H. Hansluwka, "Social and Economic Factors in Mortality in Austria" in: *International Union for the Scientific Study of Population. International Population Conference*, Ottawa 1963, p. 335 (Austria, males, 1951–53, 30–64 years of age, calculated as an average of all mortality rates given by Hansluwka, weighted according to average mortality rate of total population).

Figures in this diagram should be regarded with caution because definitions of age and profession vary. Even so, variations between graphs for the United States and Europe seem great enough to rule out statistical error as a cause of apparent variation.

Figure 4 (p. 48)
Calculated from the following sources. United States: P. M. Blau and O. D. Duncan, *The American Occupational Structure*, New York 1967, p. 511 (United States 1962, wives between the ages of 21 and 61, profession of husband and father-in-law). France: *Données sociales*, édition 1981, Paris: INSEE 1981, p. 23, 28f (France 1977, profession of husband and father-in-law). Germany: K. U. Mayer, "Statushierarchie und Heiratsmarkt—Empirische Analysen zur Struktur des Schichtungssystems in der Bundesrepublik und zur Ableitung einer Skala des sozialen Status" in: J. Handl et al., *Klassenlagen und Sozialstruktur*, Frankfurt 1977, p. 175 (West Germany 1971, husband's profession, father-in-law's profession when woman aged 15; wives' age, 41 years maximum). Austria: M. Haller, *Klassenbildung und soziale Schichtung in Österreich*, Frankfurt 1982, p. 397 (Austria 1976, profession of husband and father-in-law, wives between the ages of 16 and 60). Great Britain: K. Hope, "Marriage Markets in the Stratification System" in: K. Hope, *The Analysis of Social Mobility*, Oxford 1972, p. 107 (Aberdeen 1951–61, husband's and wife's profession). Professional categories are not fully comparable. For "professional class", a replacement category "higher officials and white-collar staff" had to be used in the case of West Germany since "professional class" does not exist as a separate category. In Germany and Austria both "higher white-collar staff" and "ordinary white-collar staff and officials" were excluded from the category of "white-collar staff" which included middle and higher grade officials. For America "salaried" and "self-employed profession" were combined to constitute the category "professional class".

Figure 5 (p. 61)
Calculated on basis of: UN, *Growth of the world's urban and rural population 1920–2000. Population Studies* No. 44, New York 1969, p. 27, 31, 98f, 105f; P. Bairoch, *Taille des villes, conditions de vie et développement économique*, Paris 1977, table 4 (worldwide development).

Figure 6 (p. 63)
This diagram expresses population of medium-sized towns, i.e. towns with 20,000 to 100,000 inhabitants as a proportion of all urban dwellers in the country concerned. (Calculated on basis of: UN, *Growth of the world's urban and rural population 1920–2000. Population Studies* No. 44,

New York 1969, p. 98ff).

Figure 7 (pp. 76 and 77)
P. Flora and A. H. Heidenheimer (ed), *The Development of the Welfare States in Europe and America*, New Brunswick 1981, p. 55, 85

Figure 8 (p. 102)
Based on coefficients of variation explained in notes to Table 9. For individual values and sources see also Table 9.

Figure 9 (p. 111)
Based on coefficients of variation explained in notes to Table 9. For individual values and sources see also Table 9.

Figure 10 (p. 132)
Social Indicators for the European Community, 1960–1975, Statistical Office of the European Community, Luxemburg 1977, p. 97

Select Bibliography

*This bibliography lists only comparative works; studies
of individual countries are contained in the Notes.*

1. General Surveys and Reference Works
S. Pollard, *Peaceful Conquest. The Industrialization of Europe 1760–1970*,
Oxford 1981.
S. Pollard, *The Integration of the European Economy since 1815*, London
1981.
W. Fischer (ed.), *Handbuch der europäischen Wirtschafts- und Sozialge-
schichte*, vol. 6, Stuttgart 1987.
F. B. Tipton and R. Aldrich, *An Economic and Social History of Europe in
the 20th Century*, London 1986.
G. Ambrosius and W. H. Hubbard, *Sozial- und Wirtschaftsgeschichte
Europas im 20. Jahrhundert*, Munich 1986.
K. Borchardt and C. Cipolla (eds), *Europäische Wirtschaftsgeschichte*,
vol. 5, Stuttgart 1985.
P. N. Stearns, *Social Upheaval in Europe*, Riverside 1975.
B. Lutz, *Der kurze Traum immerwährender Prosperität. Eine Neuinterpreta-
tion der industriell-kapitalistischen Entwicklung im Europa des 20. Jahr-
hunderts*, Frankfurt 1984.
A. S. Milward, *The Reconstruction of Western Europe 1945–51*, London
1984.
P. Bairoch, "Europe's National Product: 1800–1975", in: *Journal of
European Economic History* 5, 1976.
P. Bairoch, "International Industrialisation Levels from 1750–1980",
in: *Journal of European Economic History* 11, 1982.
S. Rokkan, "Dimensions of State Formation and Nation-Building",
in: C. Tilly (ed.), *The Formation of National States in Europe*,
Princeton 1975.

P. Flora, *State, Economy and Society in Western Europe, 1815–1975*, 2 vols., Frankfurt 1983ff.

B. R. Mitchell, *European Historical Statistics, 1750–1975*, London 1975.

OECD. *Historical Statistics 1960–1984*, Paris 1986.

Eurostat. *Revue 1973–1982*, Luxemburg 1984 (first published in: *Revue 1970–1975*, Luxemburg 1981).

D. Elsner, *Die socialökonomische Lage und ihre Beeinflußung durch die westeuropäischen Integration*, Berlin 1978.

2. History of the European Family

R. Wall et al. (eds), *Family Forms in Historic Europe*, Cambridge 1983.

P. Laslett, *Family Life and Illicit Love in Earlier Generations*, Cambridge 1977.

J. Hajnal, "European Marriage Patterns in Perspective", in: D. V. Glass and D. E. C. Evesley (eds), *Population in History*, London 1965.

M. Mitterauer and R. Sieder, *Vom Patriarchat zur Partnerschaft*, Munich 1980.

P. Chester (ed.), *Divorce in Europe*, Amsterdam 1977.

P. Festy and F. Prioux, "Le divorce en Europe depuis 1950", in: *Population* 30, 1975.

L. Roussel, "Les Ménages d'une personne: l'évolution récente", in: *Population* 38, 1983.

3. History of Employment

H. Kaelble, "Was Prometheus most Unbound in Europe? Labour Force in Europe During the 19th and 20th Centuries", *Journal of European Economic History* 18, 1989.

P. Bairoch et al. (eds), *The Working Population and its Structure*, Brussels 1968.

G. Singelmann, *From Agriculture to Services: the Transformation of Industrial Employment*, Beverley Hills 1978.

OECD, *Labour Force Statistics 1970–1981*, Paris 1983.

W. Fuchs, *The Service Economy*, New York 1968.

W. Molle, *Regional Disparity and Economic Development in the European Community*, London 1980.

H. van Dijk and H. Kaelble (eds), *Employment Structure in 20th Century Europe*, Themenheft der Historischen Sozialwissenschaft (published 1987).

4. Large-Scale Enterprises and Entrepreneurs

J. Kocka and H. Siegrist, "Die hundert größten deutschen Industrieunternehmen im späten 19. und frühen 20. Jahrhundert", in: N. Horn and J. Kocka (eds), *Recht und Entwicklung der Großun-*

ternehmen im 19. und 20. Jahrhundert, Göttingen 1979.
H. van der Wee, *Der gebremste Wohlstand*, Munich 1984.
A. D. Chandler and H. Daems, "The Rise of Managerial Capitalism and its Impact on Investment Strategy in the Western World", in: H. Daems and H. van der Wee (eds), *The Rise of Managerial Capitalism*, Louvain 1974.
A. D. Chandler, *The Visible Hand, The Managerial Revolution in American Business*, Cambridge/Mass. 1977.
A. D. Chandler, "Managers, Families, and Financiers", in: K. Kobayashi and H. Morikawa (eds), *Development of Managerial Enterprise*, Tokyo 1986.
J. Kocka, "Großunternehmen und der Aufstieg des Manager-Kapitalismus im späten 19. und frühen 20. Jahrhundert: Deutschland im internationalen Vergleich", in: *Historische Zeitschrift* 232, 1981.
V. Berghahn, "Montanunion u. Wettbewerb", in: H. Berding (ed.), *Wirtschaftliche und politische Integration in Europa im 19. und 20. Jahrhundert*, Göttingen 1984.

5. Social Mobility and Education
H. Kaelble, *Social Mobility in the 19th and 20th Centuries*, Leamington Spa 1985.
S. M. Lipset and R. Bendix, *Social Mobility in Industrial Society*, Berkeley 1967.
S. M. Miller, "Comparative Social Mobility", in: *Current Sociology* 3, 1960.
K. U. Mayer, "Class Formation and Social Reproduction—Current Comparative Research on Social Mobility", in: R. F. Geyer (ed.), *Cross-National and Cross-Cultural Comparative Research in the Social Sciences*, Oxford 1979.
D. B. Grusky and R. M. Hauser, "Comparative Social Mobility Revisited: Models of Convergence and Divergence in 16 Countries", in: *American Sociological Review* 49, 1984.
K. U. Mayer, "Berufsstruktur u. Mobilitätsprozess: Problem des internationalen Vergleichs objektiver Indikatoren zwischen England/Wales und der Bundesrepublik Deutschland", in: H.-J. Hoffmann-Novotny (ed.), *Soziale Indikatoren im internationalen Vergleich*, Frankfurt 1980.
R. Erikson et al., "Intergenerational Class Mobility in Three Western European Societies: England, France and Sweden", in: *British Journal of Sociology* 30, 1979.
R. Erikson et al., "Intergenerational Class Mobility and the Convergence Thesis: England, France and Sweden", in: ibid., 34,

1983.

W. König, *Berufliche Mobilität in Frankreich u. der Bundesrepublik. Eine Untersuchung der Auswirkungen länderspezifischer Bildungs- und Arbeitsmarktstrukturen auf die berufliche Karrieremobilität von Männern zwischen 1956 und 1970*, VASMA Arbeitspapier Nr. 34, Mannheim 1983.

B. Lutz, "Bildungssystem und Beschäftigungsstruktur in Deutschland und Frankreich. Zum Einfluß des Bildungssystems auf die Gliederung betrieblicher Arbeitskräftestrukturen", in: H. G. Mendius et al., *Betrieb, Arbeitsmarkt, Qualifikation*, Frankfurt 1976.

F. K. Ringer, *Education and Society in Modern Europe*, Bloomington 1979.

A. J. Heidenheimer, "Education and Social Security Entitlements in Europe and America", in: P. Flora and A. J. Heidenheimer (eds.), *The Development of the Welfare States in Europe and America*, New Brunswick 1981.

K. H. Jarausch (ed.), *Transformation of Higher Learning 1860–1930*, Stuttgart 1983.

R. Premfors, *The Politics of Higher Education in a Comparative Perspective, France, Sweden, United Kingdom*, Stockholm 1980.

R. L. Geiger, "The Changing Demand for Higher Education in the Seventies: Adaption within Three National Systems", in: *Higher Education* 9, 1980.

R. Schneider, "Die Bildungsentwicklung in den westeuropäischen Staaten, 1870–1979", in: *Zeitschrift für Soziologie* 10, 1982.

6. Social Inequality

K. F. Lydall and J. B. Lansing, "A Comparison of the Distribution of Income and Wealth in the United States and Great Britain", in: A. B. Atkinson (ed.), *Wealth, Income and Inequality*, Harmondsworth 1979.

H. van der Wee, *Der gebremste Wohlstand. Wiederaufbau, Wachstum und Strukturwandel der Weltwirtschaft seit 1945*, Munich 1984.

Royal Commission on the Distribution of Income and Wealth. "The International Comparison of Income Distributions", in: A. E. Atkinson (ed.), *Wealth, Income and Inequality*, Oxford 1980

T. Stark, *The Distribution of Income in Eight Countries*, London 1977.

E. Smolensky et al., "Postfisc Income Inequality: A Comparison of the United States and West Germany", in: J. R. Moroney (ed.), *Income Inequality*, Lexington/Mass. 1979.

M. Sawyers, *Income Distribution of OECD Countries*. (OECD Economic Outlook, Occasional Papers). July 1976.

M. Schnitzer, *Income Distribution. A Comparative Study of the United States, Sweden, West Germany, East Germany, the United Kingdom, and Japan*,

New York 1974.

F. Kraus, "The Historical Development of Income Inequality in Western Europe and the United States", in: P. Flora and A. J. Heidenheimer (eds), *The Development of Welfare States in Europe and America*, New Brunswick 1981.

J. Tinbergen, *Einkommensverteilung. Auf dem Weg zur neuen Einkommensgerechtigkeit*, Wiesbaden 1978.

W. D. Rubinstein (ed.), *Wealth and the Wealthy in the Modern World*, London 1980.

A. Babeau and D. Straus-Kahn, *La richesse des français*, Paris 1977.

L. Guralnick, "Socio-economic Differences in Mortality by Cause of Death: United States, 1950, and England and Wales, 1949–53", in: *International Population Conference*, Ottawa 1963.

A. Antonovsky, "Social Class, Life Expectancy and Overall Mortality", in: *Millbank Memorial Fund Quarterly* 41/2–1, April 1967.

J. Kocka, *Angestellte zwischen Faschismus und Demokratie. Zur politischen Sozialgeschichte der Angestellten: USA 1890–1940 im internationalen Vergleich*, Göttingen 1977.

J. Kocka (ed.), *Angestellte im europäischen Vergleich*, Göttingen 1981.

H. Kaelble, *Industrialisation and Social Inequality*, Leamington Spa 1986.

Y. S. Brenner, H. Kaelble and M. Thomas (eds), *Income Distribution in Historical Perspective* (in preparation).

7. Urbanization and Urban Development

P. Bairoch, "Population urbaine et taille des villes en Europe de 1600 à 1970", in: *Revue d'historie économique et sociale* 54. 1976.

P. Bairoch, *De Jéricho à Mexico*, Paris 1985.

UN. *Growth of the World's Urban and Rural Population, 1920–2000*, Population Studies 44, New York 1969.

B. J. L. Berry and Q. Gillard, *The Changing Shape of Metropolitan America. Commuting Patterns, Urban Fields, and Decentralisation Processes, 1960–1970*, Cambridge/Mass. 1977.

A. Lees, *Cities Perceived. Urban Society in European and American Thought, 1820–1940*, Manchester 1985.

P. Hall, *Growth Centers in the European Urban Systems*, London 1980.

P. Hall, *Urban and Regional Planning*, Harmondsworth 1974.

P. Cheshire and D. Hay, *The Development of the European Urban System, 1971–81*, unpublished paper 1984.

Die Regionen Europas, edited by the Commission of the European Community, Luxemburg 1981.

C. J. Adams, "Urban Planning", in: A. J. Heidenheimer et al., *Comparative Public Policy*, London 1983 2.

A. Sutcliffe, *Towards the Planned City. Germany, Britain, the United States and France 1780–1914*, Oxford 1981.

A. Weber, *The Growth of Cities in the 19th Century*, Ithaca 1963

8. Development of the Welfare State

P. Flora and A. J. Heidenheimer (eds), *The Development of the Welfare States in Europe and America*, New Brunswick 1981.

G. A. Ritter, *Sozialversicherungen in Deutschland und England. Entstehung und Grundzüge im Vergleich*, Munich 1983.

G. A. Ritter, "Entstehung und Entwicklung des Socialstaats in Vergleichender Perspektive", in: *Historische Zeitschrift* 234, 1986.

W. Fischer, *Armut in der Geschichte*, Göttingen 1982.

P. Hennock, "Arbeiterunfallentschädigung und Arbeiterunfallversicherung. Die britische Sozialreform und das Beispiel Bismarcks", in: *Geschichte und Gesellschaft* 11, 1985.

V. Hentschel, *Geschichte der deutschen Sozialpolitik 1880–1980*, Frankfurt 1983.

J. Alber, *Vom Armenhaus zum Wohlfahrtsstaat*, Frankfurt 1982.

P. Flora, "Krisenbewältigung oder Krisenerzeugung? Der Wohlfahrtsstaat aus europäischer Perspektive", in: J. Matthes (ed.), *Sozialer Wandel in Westeuropa*, Frankfurt 1979.

H. G. Hockerts, "Die Entwicklung vom Zweiten Weltkrieg bis zur Gegenwart", in: P. A. Kohler und H. F. Zacher (eds), *Beiträge zur Geschichte und zur aktuellen Situation der Sozialversicherung*, Berlin 1983.

P. A. Kohler and H. F. Zacher (eds), *Ein Jahrhundert Sozialversicherung in der Bundesrepublik Deutschland, Frankreich, Großbritannien, Österreich und der Schweiz*, Berlin 1981.

W. J. Mommsen (ed.), *The Emergence of the Welfare State in Britain and Germany*, London 1981.

G. V. Rimlinger, *Welfare Policy and Industrialization in Europe, America, and Russia*, New York 1971.

H. Heclo, *Modern Social Politics in Britain and Sweden*, New Haven 1974.

9. Industrial Relations

E. Shorter and C. Tilly, *Strikes in France, 1830–1968*, Cambridge 1974.

E. M. Kassalow, *Trade Unions and Industrial Relations: An International Comparison*, New York 1969.

A. M. Ross and P. T. Hartmann, *Changing Patterns of Industrial Conflict*, New York 1960.

P. Lösche, "Vereinigte Staaten von Amerika", in: S. Mielke (ed.), *Internationales Gewerkschaftshandbuch*, Opladen 1983.

K. v. Beyme, *Gewerkschaften und Arbeitsbeziehungen in kapitalistischen Ländern*, Munich 1977.

P. Rehnaud, "Synthèse. Unité et diversité", in: G. Spitaels (ed.), *Les conflits sociaux en Europe*, Verviers 1971.

W. J. Mommsen and H.-G. Husung (eds), *Die Entwicklung der Gewerkschaften in Deutschland und Großbritannien 1880–1914*, Stuttgart 1984.

J. E. Cronin, "Labour Insurgency and Class Formation: Comparative Perspectives of the Crisis of 1917–1920 in Europe", in: *Social Science History* 4, 1980

D. Snyder, *Determinants of Industrial Conflict. Historical Models of Strikes in France, Italy, and the United States*, Ph.D. Diss. University of Michigan, Ann Arbor 1974.

D. A. Hibbs, "On the Political Economy of Long-Run Trends in Strike Activity", in: *British Journal of Political Science* 8, 1978.

M. Shalev, "Strikes and the Crisis: Industrial Conflict and Unemployment in the Western Nations", in: *Economic and Industrial Democracy* 4, 1983.

W. Korpi and M. Shalev, "Strikes, Power and Politics in the Western Nations, 1900-1976", in: *Political Power and Social Theory* 1, 1980.

E. J. Kirchner, *Trade Unions as a Pressure Group in the European Community*, Westmead 1977.

S. M. Lipset, *The First New Nation*, New York 1967.

M. Mommsen, "Arbeiterbewegung", in: *Sowjetsystem und demokratische Gesellschaft*, vol. 1, 1966.

D. Geary, *European Labour Protest 1848–1939*, London 1981.

P. N. Stearns, *Lives of Labour, Work in Maturing Industrial Society*, London 1975.

K. Tenfelde (ed.), *Arbeiter und Arbeiterbewegung im Vergleich. Berichte zur internationalen historischen Forschung*, Munich 1986.

H. Kaelble, *The Dissolution of a European Strike Pattern? Disparities and Convergences in 20th-Century European Industrial Relations*, unpubl. paper 1986.

Index